Joyce's
Book
of
Memory

JOYCE'S BOOK OF MEMORY

The Mnemotechnic of *Ulysses*

John S. Rickard

DUKE UNIVERSITY PRESS

Durham and London 1999

© 1998 Duke University Press
All rights reserved
Printed in the United States of America on acid-free paper ∞
Typeset in Trump Mediaeval by Tseng Information Systems, Inc.
Library of Congress Cataloging-in-Publication Data appear
on the last printed page of this book.

For Martha

Contents

Acknowledgments   ix

Introduction   1

1 Personal Memory and the Construction of the Self   15

2 The Past as Obstruction   45

3 Memory, Destiny, and the Limits of the Self   87

4 Joyce's Mnemotechnic: Textual Memory in *Ulysses*   118

5 Intertextual Memory   167

Conclusion   181

Appendix   199

Notes   203

Bibliography   223

Index   233

Acknowledgments

The most daunting part of finishing this project is the necessity of acknowledging and thanking all of those persons who have helped me learn, write, and grow over the many years in which I have worked on this project. Without the kind and thoughtful teaching and mentoring of Weldon Thornton I would never have written about *Ulysses* in the manner that I have, and I am forever indebted to the examples he set me as a scholar and teacher. George Lensing, Jerry Mills, William Harmon, Louis Rubin, Linda Kaufmann, Logan Browning, Dick Ruppel, and Gunilla Theander were just a few of the colleagues and teachers who helped me improve upon my work while I was in Chapel Hill.

I owe various debts of gratitude to a number of scholars of Joyce in particular, or Irish literature in general, including Michael Patrick Gillespie, Cheryl Herr, R. B. Kershner, Susan Shaw Sailer, Fritz Senn, John Bishop, Jos Knippen, Meg Harper, Patrick McCarthy, Morris Beja, Marlena Corcoran, Adam Piette, Vincent Deane, Lucy McDiarmid, Rand Brandes, Kevin Dettmar, Wolfgang Wicht, Bob Janusko, and Peter Rudnytsky, among many others who have discussed my work with me and helped me reach a better understanding of Joyce. Of course, the usual disclaimer applies, and none of these individuals should be held responsible for my follies or foibles. A week-long workshop on "Joyce's Multiple Memories" at the Zürich James Joyce Foundation in 1994 proved to be a memorable experience and a valuable contribution to my work. I also thank the staff of the Harry Ransom Humanities Research Center in Austin, Texas, where I was allowed access to Joyce's Trieste library, a rich and exciting archive that I hope to visit again.

My colleagues and students at Bucknell University have also been instrumental in helping me complete my work. In particular, Karl Patten read the manuscript repeatedly and carefully, and Harold Schweizer collaborated with me in my study of narrative theory. Mark Padilla helped me with my shaky Greek and Latin skills, Pauline and Dave Fletcher helped me with literature and evolution, and my colleagues in the English Department have given me invaluable support and guidance. I could not have successfully completed my work, either, without the help of a number of research assistants, including Tom Stone, Steve Baliko, Bill Kupinse, Simon Corby, and Sarah Farrant. Many of the undergraduate and graduate students who studied Joyce with me at Clemson University and at Bucknell have given me invaluable insights into my work as well.

I am also grateful to Reynolds Smith, my editor at Duke University Press, who has waited the return of my manuscript at times with the patience of Penelope, helping me weave and unweave it day by day; his insightful and tactful comments have made this a stronger book. Bob Mirandon and Pam Morrison also provided wonderful editorial assistance.

Finally, this book is dedicated to my wife, Martha Holland. She and my sons, Stephen and James, have tolerated years of distraction as I worked on this project and yet have endured all with good humor and love. They, with my parents and sisters, make all things worthwhile.

Joyce's
Book
of
Memory

Introduction

We must be content, therefore, with having clearly recognized the obscurity.
—Sigmund Freud

Mnemosyne—the goddess of memory—and her sister Lesmosyne, who presides over forgetting, once occupied high places in Western cosmology. Appropriately, Mnemosyne was in Greek legend the mother of the muses, the source from which all human culture—art, history, science—springs. Without memory, the imaginative reshaping or re-membering of experience would be impossible, for which reason Giambattista Vico wrote in his discussion of "Poetic Wisdom," that imagination "is nothing but the springing up again of reminiscences, and ingenuity or invention is nothing but the working over of what is remembered. . . . With reason, then, did the theological poets call Memory the mother of the Muses; that is, of the arts of humanity" (264).

James Joyce, echoing Vico, once told Frank Budgen that "imagination was memory" (Budgen, *Myselves* 187), and a remarkable number of those who have written their own reminiscences of Joyce describe his "marvelous" or "prodigious" memory. Budgen once told Clive Hart that Joyce "prized memory above all other human faculties" (Hart, *Structure* 53), and Sylvia Beach recalled that Joyce had consciously developed his own powers of memory, once keeping himself amused while recovering from painful eye surgery by memorizing "The Lady of the Lake." Joyce, she explained, had practiced such "memory exercises" since his "early youth," which "accounted for a memory that retained everything he had ever heard. Everything stuck in it, he said" (71). Joyce's friend Jacques Mercanton claimed: "Joyce's company forced me to train my memory: he expected people to recall things precisely, and in detail" (206). Joyce spent his life recalling, reimagining, and revising his memories of Dublin. "The daughters of memory," Richard Ellmann says, "received regular employment from Joyce. . . . He was never a creator *ex nihilo;* he recomposed what he remembered, and he remembered most of what he had seen or had heard other people remember" (*JJII* 364–65).[1]

The importance of memory in Joyce's work, however, extends far beyond his own mnemonic powers and his obsession with reworking and renaming his own past, for his writings, more than those of most writers of prose, depend on elaborate repetitions, reworkings, and distortions of their own materials. "The hallucinations in *Ulysses*," Joyce told Mercanton, "are made up out of elements from the past, which the reader will recognize if he has read the book five, ten, or twenty times" (207). His writing is famous as well for recollecting and reworking the other texts, other languages, and other traditions that he encountered and remembered in his travels throughout Europe.

Furthermore, Joyce's texts demonstrate a deep interest in the nature and workings of memory itself. Much of Joyce's writing involves itself in a reflection on the nature and extent of our access to the past—personal and collective—and the effects the past has on the present and future. His fascination with memory amounts to a philosophical and psychological obsession that profoundly influences not only the content but the form of his work. The various forms of memory—psychological, philosophical, and textual—provide a valuable context for a full investigation of Joyce's work, and many critics, especially in recent years, have taken up issues related to memory in his texts.[2]

This book will examine some of the ways that memory functions within Joyce's writing—especially the text of *Ulysses*—and also the ways in which Joyce's writing functions within memory, by which I mean the ways that *Ulysses* reflects and responds to different "versions" or modes of memory within the traditions of Western metaphysics and psychology. I will not concern myself to any significant degree with Joyce's biography or the relation of his own personal memories to his writing, but rather I will look at some of the ways in which Joyce's historical position—as determined partly by his general education, his reading, and his comments about his own writing—supplied him with various and conflicting notions of what memory is and how it works. I will expose the traces of these philosophical and psychological models of mind in some of Joyce's writings prior to *Finnegans Wake,* and I will outline some ways in which these ideas work themselves into the plot and textual operations of *Ulysses,* making use of intellectual history, genetic criticism, and narratology to elucidate the ways in which these conflicting philosophies of mind and incompatible theories of human development are put into play against each other in the text.

I choose to focus most of my attention on *Ulysses* because it is so often seen as a book "in-between"—in between Joyce's early and late work, in between symbolism and realism, in between modernism and postmodernism—displaying many of the tensions inherent in the intellectual culture of what we now call the modernist period. Much of the power and appeal of *Ulysses* derives from the liminal or conflicted status of this text caught between traditional and modern (or even postmodern) philosophical positions, between modernist nostalgia and postmodernist play, between order and disruption.[3] *Ulysses* can be read as a philosophically hybrid text in a number of ways: Patrick O'Donnell has conceived of *Ulysses* as "a liminal text" and Joyce as "a liminal author who stands between the 'symbolic' and the 'semiotic,' the 'paternal' and the 'maternal,' even as his writing approaches the limits of these polarities" (64). Udaya Kumar has described *Ulysses* as "a complex transitional text, where widely heterogeneous and even contradictory impulses are at work" (4), and Patrick McGee has argued for Joyce's "special place in the history of postmodern thought," seeing him "as a symbolic bridge between the modern and the postmodern" (2).[4] In much the same way, I see Joyce's text as torn, split, or caught between different and competing modes of memory, modes that at times can be associated with modernism or postmodernism.

I hope to show specifically how *Ulysses* functions as a site of struggle or tension between competing philosophical and psychological conceptions of the nature of human subjectivity and the role of memory within that subjectivity or selfhood. *Ulysses*—shaped both by the dominant philosophical and psychological discourses of its own time and by older models of mind or self—enacts or works through the struggle between these often incompatible models rather than presenting one version or model of subjectivity. In valorizing *Ulysses* as a modernist or postmodernist text, many contemporary readers read back onto Joyce an anachronistic postmodernism that comfortably fits our own often unstable and transitional stories or models of subjectivity. Our postmodernist or poststructuralist assumptions about the instability and constructedness of subjectivity were certainly part of the epistemological crisis of the early part of our century, and we can see—as Joyce would have seen—these assumptions reflected in much of the avant-garde culture of the period. At the same time, Joyce was profoundly interested in and affected by models of mind that we apparently can no longer take seriously. How many contemporary Westerners, for example, would be willing to concede the possibility of a human being's inheriting knowledge derived from his ancestors' or even his parents' experiences? How many of us, with our epistemological perspective now rooted in empiricist or poststructuralist (un)certainties, accept any notion of innate ideas, or of racial memory? Our contemporary notions regarding the formation of subjectivity—in the humanities, at least—reflexively privilege either personal experience or the power of linguistic and ideological systems over questions of "nature" or inheritance, questions that were still very much alive during the years when Joyce composed *Ulysses*.

More than any of Joyce's other works, *Ulysses* reflects this conflict concerning the nature of the self and of memory within Western thought. We can read *Dubliners* and *A Portrait of the Artist as a Young Man* as works that limit or restrict the power of memory by representing the mind of the individual subject circumscribed by personal memory, limited to the data of the *tabula inscripta*. *Finnegans Wake*, on the other hand, loosens the limits of consciousness so radically that the individual subject dissolves into a sea of human language, time, and memory. *Ulysses* represents a transition between these extremes of subjectivity and universality, a halfway point where the boundaries of the mind and self are still there to be dissolved.[5] As Patrick O'Donnell states it, *Ulysses* "puts the subject on trial—a narrative trial that is conceivably 'over' in the writing of *Finnegans Wake*" (203, n. 2); this "narrative trial" of the subject in *Ulysses* is conducted partly in the conflicts and contradictions between various philosophical and psychological paradigms of subjectivity implied by or incorporated into the text. *Ulysses* contains the conscious and unconscious assumptions and conflicts about mind and memory encountered by a modern Irish writer well-read in a number of traditions, including Classical and Renaissance writings on memory, the prevailing models of mind and memory inherent in his own Irish Catholic culture, and contemporary intellectual currents popular in Europe and the United States.

Umberto Eco and Cheryl Herr have developed readings of *Ulysses* as a liminal or transitional text that are particularly useful in articulating my sense of the book as a site of historical struggle or tension. Eco provides a compelling view of *Ulysses* as a composite, transitional, or hybrid text in his *Aesthetics of Chaosmos: The Middle Ages of James Joyce*. In it, he sees Joyce's art as a complex, shifting, and uneasy marriage of modern and medieval paradigms or systems. Eco's assumption is that works of art can be read as "epistemological metaphors" (vii), and that *Ulysses* is "the node where the Middle Ages and the avant-garde meet" (xi), displaying a creative tension between the medieval systems of order that dominated Joyce's education and a growing modern sense of disruption, disorder, and decay. Eco neatly captures this fundamental tension in *Ulysses* in the Wakean term "chaosmos,"⁶ a conflation of the orderly connotations of the medieval *cosmos* and the modernist awareness of chaos. Eco's sense of *Ulysses* as an illustration of "the dialectical movement of various opposite and complementary poetics" (1-2) is central to my own reading of the novel as an unresolved set of oppositions, or, as Eco puts it: "a continuous polarity between Chaos and Cosmos, between disorder and order, liberty and rules, between the nostalgia of Middle Ages and the attempts to envisage a new order. Our analysis of the poetics of James Joyce will be the analysis of a moment of transition in contemporary culture" (2-3). For Eco, *Ulysses* "succeeds in being revelatory because the contradictions of its poetics are those of our culture" (56).

In her essay, "Art and Life, Nature and Culture, *Ulysses*," Cheryl Herr has developed another method of analyzing the tensions or contradictions in *Ulysses* by arguing that the text enacts a struggle between opposing terms—art/life and nature/culture—and that this struggle situates the novel "on the borderline between art and life" (19). Adapting Fredric Jameson's concept of the "political unconscious" to the cultural discourses of *Ulysses* (which necessarily remain reflections of political and economic realities), Herr examines some of the ways in which Joyce's novel oscillates between ostensibly internal discourses, which Herr claims represent traditional notions of the self and of "nature" (for example, the stream-of-consciousness representations in *Ulysses*), and external organizing patterns such as the schemas, which she argues represent culture and art over nature.⁷ Herr articulates the ways in which the text calls attention to what we might consider to be "natural," while at the same time "this schematic book directs us toward a concept of culture, toward the domain of art. Life and art, nature and culture—on these grand dichotomies *Ulysses* is constructed, and to the exploration of these oppositions as such the fiction is dedicated" (22-23). In this interplay between "assertion and challenge," Herr finds "the force of the narrative for a surprisingly diverse community of readers" (23).

Herr provides a useful framework for my discussion of memory in *Ulysses* in her explanation of a repressed, even absent, "nature" in *Ulysses* so weakened in status that it is relegated to the "cultural unconscious" (20). Although Arthur Power claimed that Joyce once argued that "the modern theme is the subterranean forces, those hidden tides which govern everything and run humanity counter to the apparent flood: those poisonous subtleties which envelop the soul, the ascending fumes of sex" (quoted in Herr 22), Herr contends that these once-powerful premodern constructions of what is "natural" or instinctive or vital are present in *Ulysses* only as repressed elements in the cultural unconscious, part of a "complex nostalgia" for holistic discourses that the novel indulges in but ultimately rejects. Although my reading of *Ulysses* views these holistic discourses in the text as more conspicuous and more influential than Herr does, she provides me with another useful way to discuss the collision of different models of mind and memory in *Ulysses*. As I will argue, within the text of the novel we can observe a tension between randomness and meaning as the bases of human experience and culture, between wandering and destiny, chance and entelechy, as the underlying metaphors for human life. *Ulysses* enacts an argument between conflicting paradigms of order and disorder, an argument reflected, as we will see, in the text itself and even in Joyce's processes of composition. Herr notes that the words "culture" and "entelechy" share the same Indo-European root (*kwel*; Herr 36), but in *Ulysses* they stand in for two incommensurable views of human experience. This book will focus primarily on the contents of what Herr would call the cultural unconscious—on those very elements that she believes are repressed and dispersed to the point of being "unrepresented" or "inaccessible" in the text (33, 34)—arguing that they do in fact exert a powerful, dynamic pressure on Joyce's writing that is unresolved at the end of the book. Herr notes that "the measure of the narrative's affirmation of this discourse's potency is the constant stream of coincidence that textures the fiction and tempts us always to discern within difference the presence of consubstantiality, connection, and communication" (34). My investigation of memory in *Ulysses* will demonstrate that these intimations of or desires for purpose, connection, and coherence in life are locked into an unresolvable tension with conflicting discourses which imply that randomness and incoherence may in fact be the ultimate grounds of human experience. One example of this sort of contradiction in *Ulysses* is the tension between different models of evolution that seems to have influenced not only Joyce's views on the nature of memory, but even his processes of composition—his construction of a "textual memory" in *Ulysses*.

To sum up, *Ulysses* enacts, in my reading, a dialogue or dialectic between, on the one hand, the instability and fragmentation of culture represented in the overwhelming detail of the text, in the variation and dissolution of the narrative styles, and in the various schematic frameworks that Joyce provided to accompany the text,[8] and, on the other hand, the continuing presence in the novel of a drive or desire for closure, "cure," and some sort of deep connection to areas of consciousness beyond those normally considered accessible in modernist and postmodernist epistemologies. Memory is at the core of many of these repressed or obscured discourses of desire and holism in *Ulysses*, and it provides the connective tissue for most of the traditional and more contemporary models of subjectivity that we find woven into *Ulysses*. The importance of these varied attempts to read *Ulysses* as a book struggling to negotiate a zone of conflict between order and disorder is their overt or implied insistence that the discourses of purpose and coherence within the novel are essential to our understanding of it and cannot be dismissed. Our most influential contemporary notions of subjectivity, based on assumptions about the indeterminacy of language and the constitution of the subject within and through language, may blind us to the older epistemological models embedded in Joyce's novel. The dominant paradigm for subjectivity in our contemporary intellectual culture is fundamentally empiricist, in that it conceives of subjectivity as a product—even if irrational and fragmented—of the various ideologies, social and economic pressures, and other discursive forces or grids that provide the available subject positions within a given culture. Contemporary theories of the subject in the humanities and social sciences stress culture and experience over nature and inheritance to the point that many of us consider any question of innate ideas, inherited knowledge, or other pre-experiential data absurd. Despite the apparent antipathy between poststructuralism and empiricism, then, both are philosophically modernist in conceiving of the human subject as—in Locke's terms—"white paper, void of all characters" (*Essay* 2.8), paper that can only be inscribed by one form or another of individual experience. Many theories of mind that were still taken seriously in Joyce's lifetime have been pushed into our own "cultural unconscious" by the increasingly skeptical nature of late-twentieth-century philosophy. Our dominant contemporary theories of subjectivity, then, may obstruct our reading of Joyce if we unconsciously consider our view of the subject as a given and are embarrassed and put off by older, more essential models of subjectivity. We may be tempted to deemphasize the "cosmos" in the Joycean chaosmos in order to claim Joyce as "our own" by reading out those premodern elements of his writing that conflict with our desire to find in these texts "Joyce our contemporary," the first postmodernist. Like Herr and Eco, I want to argue that the conflict between incommensurable paradigms—between the premodern and the modern, between the essential and the existential, between nature and culture—infuses Joyce's texts with much of their power for twentieth-century readers.

Joyce's own historical position as a subject ensured that he would write *Ulysses* amid a number of now almost forgotten debates concerning the nature of memory, chance, habit, and the self. Joyce's Jesuit education introduced him to models of mind and memory shaped by Plato,

Augustine, Aquinas, and even the rituals of the Roman Catholic mass. His hereticophilia led him to writers such as Giordano Bruno, in whose work investigations into memory and the occult were central. Joyce's reading also led him to controversial thinkers such as Samuel Butler, who waged war against the exponents of Darwinism in the name of another theory of evolution based on memory, a theory stemming from the evolutionary views of the French naturalist Jean Baptiste de Lamarck, espoused to various degrees by Henri Bergson, William James, the members of the Theosophical Society, Sigmund Freud, and other writers that Joyce encountered.

My attempt to situate Joyce historically in terms of subjectivity and memory fits in with a renewed interest in historicist approaches to studying Joyce's texts.[9] While I focus primarily on intellectual contexts for Joyce's positions on memory and subjectivity, the various positions articulated here form a vital part of the cultural quilt that Joyce stitched together out of his education, reading, theatergoing, and other pursuits. Some of these intellectual positions—such as those held by the Theosophists—are themselves marginal; spiritualism and its attendant philosophical rationale provide, in fact, a borderland between intellectual history and popular culture.

Much of this study concerns itself with texts that may have provided the substance for Joyce's evolving understanding of mind and the working of memory. Although at times I explore sources and influences, I want to move beyond the implications of influence (the implication of conscious agency and authorial control) and into the area covered by contemporary investigations of intertextuality,[10] with their assumption that the agency of one text upon another operates often in an unconscious, polyvocal, ambivalent, and even confused manner. The texts that helped to construct Joyce's notions of memory and mind operated along with the "climate of opinion" of Joyce's time and the assumptions that he inherited from his Jesuit education to create a confusing variety of choices or struggles between often conflicting theories concerning the nature of the self and the role of memory in shaping and delineating the self rather than a coherent, controlled position from which Joyce could masterfully construct a single, stable model of mind in *Ulysses*. Thus, this study also concerns itself with Joyce's memory, by which I mean the ways in which his mind must have held in tension ideas of self and mind that were in fact contradictory, a memory that worked unconsciously as well as consciously to construct texts that remember, repeat, and work through these conflicting epistemologies. In *Ulysses*, then, some of the most powerful modern intellectual paradigms (Freudian or Darwinian, for instance) collide with older systems (theological or Lamarckian, for example) to stimulate a textual practice that consciously and unconsciously reproduces these tensions in what John Paul Riquelme has called a textual "representation of mind" (xv) or "mimesis of consciousness" (151). Joyce's memories of other texts and older philosophical systems, then, haunt the text, like the outlines of theoretical limits left behind that nonetheless inhabit and inform the perspectives gained by later reading and study. These intellectual negativities remain, much as Roman Catholicism does in the mind of the apostate Stephen in the final chapters of *A Portrait*, to engage with newer theoretical frameworks in the body of the text, to produce "symptoms" available for analysis by the reader who seeks to unravel the nature of mentation implied by complex texts such as *A Portrait of the Artist as a Young Man*, *Ulysses*, and *Finnegans Wake*.

In *Remembering: A Phenomenological Study*, Edward S. Casey has introduced a useful distinction between what he sees as the two dominant approaches to the study of memory: passivist and activist models. Casey argues that since Plato and Aristotle "secularized" memory as simply "an instrument of dialectical inquiry" and a twice-removed reflection of imperfect reflections of perfect forms, Mnemosyne has gradually lost her stature in the West. Once the Mother of the Muses, the inspiration of poets, a virtually omniscient deity, she has become mechanical: a mirror that reflects the quotidian occurrences filling the *tabulae* of the human mind from birth, or even a computer—a machine that stores and retrieves data. As Casey puts it: "Where once Mnemosyne was a venerated Goddess, we have turned over responsibility for remembering to the cult of the computers, which serve as our modern mnemonic idols" (2). Casey argues that because "we tend to regard [the past] as something merely 'fixed' and 'dead,'" we can view the occurrences of the past as simply collectible and retrievable data (4). Mnemosyne has fallen from her throne, and in her place rules Lesmosyne, for as Casey points out, our major modern theoreticians of memory—Nietzsche, Freud, Martin Heidegger, and Hermann Ebbinghaus—approach memory "through the counterphenomenon of *forgetting*" (7).

Casey labels as passivists those for whom "remembering is reduced to a passive process of registering and storing incoming impressions." For Casey, passivism is the paradigm for the empiricist model of memory that has become "the predominant, and typically the 'official' (i.e., the most respected and respectable), view of memory" (15). Tracing this passivist view of memory from its roots in the Aristotelian tradition through Spinoza, Hume, Kant, Ebbinghaus, and others, Casey identifies its central characteristic as the tendency to reduce all mnemonic functions to simple replication and retrieval and to deny or ignore what he calls the "transcendent aspects of memory" by insisting on "the intimate link between memory and the *personal* past" (14). Perhaps the earliest example of this view of memory as nothing more than "imprinting" is Plato's metaphor of memory as a wax tablet in the *Theatetus* (197d–99b). In Casey's view, empiricist models in contemporary psychology and artificial intelligence studies tend to replicate this passivist view of the brain as a machine or sophisticated computer.

The other approach to memory, according to Casey, is activism, which views memory as at once a more unreliable and more powerful function of the mind. For the activist, according to Casey, "memory involves the creative transformation of experience rather than its internalized reduplication in images or traces construed as copies" (15). Activist views of memory have often tended to develop on the margins of Western philosophy and psychology. Casey traces the activist tradition after Plato through the hermetic, magical "art of memory" practiced by such Renaissance philosophers as Giordano Bruno, Tommaso Campanella, and Raymond Lull to modern writers such as William James, Edward Husserl, Bergson, Pierre Janet, and Jean Piaget. Perhaps the best paradigm for the activist view is provided by the metaphor of the "search," accompanied by the assumption that this search through the past is rarely a straightforward process of retrieval, but rather a creative or active search back through language and experience guided by imagination and as dependent on the contexts of the present as on the past.

Activist memory is always problematic, for many activist writers on memory doubt the availability of any final truth at the end of their search. Memory is for them a sifting back through language that cannot get beyond language to any transcendent truth or solid epistemological ground. Many of Freud's later writings can be classed within this activist tradition, for he came to feel that "the weak spot in the security of our mental life [is] the untrustworthiness of our memory" (10:243).[11] On reflection, Freud found that in his case studies of neurotic patients such as the Wolf Man, what he had once seen as "primal scenes" reconstructed from the actual earliest memories of his patients were actually constructions rather than literal reconstructions. Freud came to see that what mattered was whether this construction of the past—this story of neurosis—proved to be an effective version of the past for the purposes of psychoanalysis.[12] Thus, the activist tradition sees memory as an intersection between actual experience and interpretation, imagination, and repression.[13]

Memory in *Ulysses*, then, operates in a contested zone constructed by modern philosophical and psychological discourses as well as by older epistemological models, and thus, predictably, it contains elements of both the passivist and the activist visions of memory. In reading *Ulysses* as the site of a dialectic between various ontological and epistemological modes and models, differing stories of the self and the workings of memory, we come upon a central question of the nature of past experience and our relationship to it. Does memory mummify or "mumorise" the past (*FW* 180.29)—that is, store it away in an unchanging and unchangeable form that can be "dug up" years later—or is memory a form of "mummery" (*FW* 310.23 and 535.30) masked, hidden, changeable, and subject to interpretation? Do we always rewrite the past to some extent when we remember? Is our access to the past limited to our personal experience, as the passivist tradition would have it, or are we capable of "remembering" much more, drawing memories from the minds of others, even those who are dead, as some activist writers would argue?

A focus on memory in *Ulysses* leads us ineluctably beyond a simple description of the various cultural and historical "memories" present in the text and into questions of narrative. By examining the ways in which *Ulysses* incorporates memory and works through the tensions implied above, we can see how the novel stages the clash of conflicting paradigms and how, in its incorporation of activist models of memory, *Ulysses* creates a "textual unconscious,"[14] or textual memory,[15] that preserves and deploys the "natural" or vitalist elements that Herr believes have been suppressed by the modernist emphasis on the dominance of culture and art in *Ulysses*. The cultural unconscious, then, is a form of memory—authorial and intertextual—that structures the narrative, providing resistance to forces of fragmentation by constructing a nostalgic textual memory that mimics older models of mind.

Memory can have a dual role in narrative, serving both as an agent of desire—building and moving the plot forward—and as an agent of delay. In *Reading for the Plot*, Peter Brooks examines Freudian psychoanalysis as a form of narrative in order to develop a model for reading fiction based not on formalized structure, but on the "psychic dynamics" of the text, the dynamics of desire. Brooks focuses on the tension between textual forces that move the reader and the plot toward the resolution of desire and forces that delay or defer the reader's or character's arrival at or attainment of that goal. According to Brooks, plot itself involves a tension between forces that work to defer, dissolve, or defeat desire and those that work to further and resolve it. Brooks uses Freud's concept of a tension between *eros* and *thanatos* as his model for the workings of plot. For Brooks, the traditional plot—for example, a Grimm fairy tale—"works through the problem of desire gone wrong and brings it to its cure" (9). The novel traditionally "desires," like Odysseus, to end in a "place" of homeostasis, resolution, and fulfilled desire—a textual Ithaca. The novelist's business becomes the deferral of that desire, the creation of a textual "odyssey" that the characters and readers must travel before they can reach their goal. While the classic novels of the nineteenth century often deliver a textual Ithaca—a neatly woven extinction of narrative desire through the final marriage, deliverance, or death of the protagonist—modernist and postmodernist texts more often complicate and even frustrate this quest, denying the availability of such a textual quietus, yet insisting in some way on the motive energy of desire. "We are thus," Brooks claims, "always trying to work back through time to that transcendent home, knowing, of course, that we cannot" (111).

Following Brooks, we can conceive of two basic types or forms of narrative memory—a voluntary, hermeneutic memory that presses back into the past in a conscious attempt to decipher and "cure" the problems of the past, and an involuntary, unconscious, or proleptic memory in which forces outside the character or subject deploy memory in order to break through the impasse of the present moment and move the character dynamically into the future. While voluntary or hermeneutic memory depends on a conscious investigation of, and intervention in, the past as the key to the future, proleptic or dynamic memory is a force that propels the present inevitably toward the future.[16]

It is this second, proleptic form of memory, I will argue, that functions as a powerful subterranean force in *Ulysses*. Gérard Genette has best defined the use of prolepsis for narratology in *Narrative Discourse: An Essay in Method*, where he defines prolepsis as "any narrative maneuver that consists of narrating or evoking in advance an event that will take place later" (40). Proleptic memory involves those textual reoccurrences that imply a dynamic movement forward in plot through recollection on the part either of readers or characters, suggesting an eventual narrative resolution or at least a movement "forward" toward the resolution of narrative desire. The proleptic operation of memory preserves and repeats elements of the past in a textual memory that anticipates the future and carries a sense of the plot driving forward toward its own resolution, an anticipation of completion brought about by the power of the past moving unconsciously and inexorably toward the future. Proleptic memory is involuntary, spontaneous, and dynamic in its suggestion of a vital, unconscious, future-oriented function of memory; it resembles the function of the cultural unconscious outlined by Herr, which preserves "a cultural master-narrative (no doubt specific to the social formation in and through which the work was written) of human connection with primal instinct and authentic wholeness" (34). We will see that this proleptic textual memory mimics or echoes the assumptions embedded in various non-Darwinian evolutionary theories that Joyce was familiar with, theories that implied an unconscious, structured, teleological memory operating within evolution. Therefore, while Herr suggests that the cultural unconscious of *Ulysses* retains "a nature that is in fact absent from the work" (30), in my reading this dynamic force of memory is very much an active force in the text.

If, as Brooks claims, "Desire is always there at the start of the narrative," what desires announce themselves in need of fulfillment in *Ulysses*? And to what extent does the proleptic force of memory work toward their fulfillment? Certainly, these questions are connected to the issue of closure in modernist writing, to the modernist unwillingness or inability to fulfill reader expectations and desires by providing the kind of tidy, satisfying endings typical of more traditional realist novels. Historically, much critical and readerly consternation over *Ulysses* has resulted in attempts to "close" the novel, to speculate on "how it ends." Do Stephen and Bloom come to "atonement," as many critics would like to think, and as many others have denied? Do Stephen, Bloom, and Molly come to make up a "family" (usually described nebulously as a mystical or spiritual union)? Does *Ulysses* struggle toward an affirmative, unified, transcendent closing, or is it rather a book of play and indeterminacy or even paralysis and savage irony that finally frustrates and mocks any desire for resolution? What role does memory play in bringing about or frustrating any such resolutions?

The best place to begin any examination of James Joyce's *Ulysses* may be with the metaphor of the *Odyssey*. At the simplest level, encouraged by Joyce's schemas and letters, we may read the *Odyssey* as a parallel for Leopold Bloom's wanderings through the novel and through the day of June 16, 1904. Others have described *Ulysses* as an "odyssey of style," referring to the changing narrative voices of the novel, or an "odyssey" for the reader.[17] While acknowledging the interest and usefulness of these approaches, I propose instead to read *Ulysses* as an "odyssey" of memory or an "odyssey" through memory, a novel in which characters and readers struggle to come to terms with the past in order to move toward the resolution of the desire for closure—for Ithaca. Just as Ulysses seeks to return to his wife, his son, and his kingdom—to put all right again—so many readers of *Ulysses* seek, at least on one level of reading, possible resolutions of the problems or situations of Joyce's fictional characters.¹⁸ Just as the *Odyssey* tantalizes its listeners or readers by delaying the resolution of the plot, weaving and unweaving Odysseus' movements toward Ithaca through his successes and reversals, so *Ulysses* involves the reader in a narrative odyssey through the lives of Joyce's characters and the frustrating cityscape of Dublin. These characters and their often paralyzing environment present the reader with many problems in the past and the ways by which the past is accessed and interpreted through memory.

The Homeric parallel has certainly added to the bafflement of Joyce's readers, providing an intertextual memory of gratified desire "behind" the plot of *Ulysses*. Generations of readers have now debated the question of whether this parallel plot is an ironic, mocking memory of a heroic past world that emphasizes the emptiness of modern life, or whether it provides a source of enrichment, a promise of wholeness and atonement to come, a hidden resource "beneath" the text that somehow contributes to the book's unity and hopefulness. Or is it somehow both?

My examination of *Ulysses* through the lens of memory outlines the fundamental connections between memory and subjectivity in the book and looks at the ways in which memory has constructed the individual lives of Leopold and Molly Bloom and Stephen Dedalus as the reader finds them there. I explore the action of voluntary, hermeneutic strategies of memory as Joyce presents them in the text, and I try to show that some types of memory—habit and nostalgia, for example—delay and defer the final atonement or fulfillment that the reader desires, while other versions of memory—metapersonal and dynamic—hint at the involuntary modes of memory at work in the margins or under the surface of the text that promise to deliver the characters from their tangled pasts. The examination of these involuntary, metapersonal modes of memory, operating in the form of shared and universal memories, and the operations of Joyce's own textual memory, through which the text itself seems to mimic the operation of a human mind by developing a textual and intertextual memory accessible to both characters' and readers' minds, constitutes the core of my book. At the conclusion, I return to the issues of closure and nostalgia raised in this introduction to see where the odyssey of memory in *Ulysses* has led us.

1   Personal Memory and the Construction of the Self

The traits featuring the chiaroscuro coalesce, their contrarieties
eliminated, into one stable somebody—*FW* 107

From his earliest writings through *Finnegans Wake*, the nature of personal identity is a central question in Joyce's work. As a *künstlerroman*, Joyce's *A Portrait* focuses on a young artist's attempts to "find himself," in terms of vocation, of course, but also, literally, in terms of his establishing a coherent sense of self. *Ulysses* also confronts its characters with the most fundamental questions about the nature of identity, about our ability or inability to consider the changing collections of events, sensations, and thoughts that make up the histories of our bodies and minds as stable, unified selves.

No discussion of the role of memory in *Ulysses* can begin without our questioning the nature of subjectivity in Joyce's novel and the role of memory in constructing or deconstructing identity. Joyce's writing has been valorized by traditional humanist critics for its reification of consciousness through the stream-of-consciousness technique, for its creation of a modern everyman in Leopold Bloom, ennobled by his connection with the mythic Odysseus, and so on. On the other hand, Joyce's writing is held up by poststructuralist readers as an exemplary site for what Hélène Cixous calls "discrediting the subject" ("Ruse" 15) or Maud Ellmann dubs "disremembering" the subject.

In *The Modernist Self in Twentieth-Century English Literature*, Dennis Brown sees Joyce as one of a number of modernist writers whose works break down traditional notions of unified subjectivity. Literary modernism, Brown argues, "was a movement that radically probed the nature of selfhood and problematized the means whereby 'self' could be expressed." In a now-conventional formulation, Brown describes modernist writing as a sort of objective correlative for "the general diffusion of social alienation, the rise of the psychoanalytic movement, the disorientation brought about by the shock of the Great War and the increasing experimentation of almost all the contemporary artistic movements." Social, cultural, and political challenges to traditional notions of coherence and autonomy led to a new sense of the self developing in the work of Joyce, Woolf, Pound, Eliot and others, "a selfhood which is pluralist, heterogeneous and discontinuous" (1).[1] Joyce, of course, was directly affected by the dislocations of World War I, and while living in Zurich and Paris during the years that *Ulysses* was being composed, he certainly encountered the artistic avant-garde of the time.[2]

Much attention in recent years has focused on the social and cultural construction of subjectivity in Joyce, notably Brandon Kershner's investigations into Joyce's use of popular literature in *Joyce, Bakhtin, and Popular Literature: Chronicles of Disorder* and Cheryl Herr's examination of the place of Irish popular culture in Joyce's art. Herr articulates her view of the nature of subjectivity in Joyce's work in *Joyce's Anatomy of Culture*, where she argues that generally in Joyce's texts the subject is constructed, or *subjected*, "from birth to adulthood through the pressure of familial, educational, religious, and political institutions" (25). Joyce's fiction, for Herr, presents the literary character as "a coded ideological construct" (158) or "a collection of institutional attitudes and practices" (80). Despite the inevitable tension of these "various codes, ideologies, and censoring mechanisms" within the fictional subject, however, "the triumph is that warring ideologies *are* internalized and continue forever in their uneasy juxtaposition within the 'text' of the individual persona" (25; original emphasis).

Our contemporary sense of an unresolvable tension within the subject, our sense that the modern subject is both multiple and historically conditioned, is echoed in the questioning of subjectivity that takes place throughout Joyce's writing, from the fractured psychology and language of "The Sisters" to the fluid personalities of *Finnegans Wake*. This consciousness of the dissolution or multiplicity of subjectivity may stem generally—as Brown implies—from the conditions of modernity, or more specifically from Joyce's own awareness of his status as a split subject constructed by the opposed discourses of, for example, Roman Catholicism and modern skepticism, the British Empire and Irish nationalism, and so on. Joyce, then, like Stephen Dedalus, was the subject or "servant of two masters" (*U*1.638). In internalizing these warring discourses, Joyce's texts explore a series of positions on identity, so that Joyce's works in many ways anticipate Paul Smith's description of subjectivity as a series of overlapping subject-positions which may or may not be present to consciousness at any given moment, but which in any case constitute a person's *history*. And a person's lived history cannot be abstracted as subjectivity pure and simple, but must be conceived as a colligation of multifarious and multiform subject-positions. (32; original emphasis)

In *Discerning the Subject*, Smith examines the ways in which recent theories of subjectivity attempt to "*dis-cern(e)* the subject/individual" (5). Smith plays with the word *discern*, finding within it two obsolete verbs: *to cern* and *to cerne*. The former means " 'to accept an inheritance or a patrimony,' " and Smith connects this with the traditional Western philosophical tendency to construe the subject "as the unified and coherent bearer of consciousness." The second term—*to cerne*—meaning " 'to encircle' or 'to enclose,' indicates the way in which theoretical discourse limits the definition of the human agent in order to be able to call him/her the 'subject' " (xxx). These two activities—connecting the self or the subject with a traditional heritage and limiting the concept of the self so that it can be mastered or contained—are the philosophical strategies that Smith seeks to *dis-cern(e)*, to loosen or release, in order "to argue that the human agent *exceeds* the 'subject' as it is constructed in and by much poststructuralist theory as well as by those discourses against which poststructuralist theory claims to pose itself" (Smith xxx).

This terminology of cerning and discerning the subject can be brought to bear on Joyce's texts in an attempt to articulate the tension between modernist and postmodernist subjectivities that Dennis Brown, Judith Ryan, Cheryl Herr, Maud Ellmann, and others find there and older models of the self or the subject that inhabit the cultural unconscious of a transitional text like *Ulysses*. Brown argues that "the Modernist discourse of selfhood is haunted by the ghost of some lost self which was once coherent and self-sufficient" (2), and *Ulysses* is haunted as well by discourses of wholeness, purposiveness, and presence that may inhabit the margins of the text—the cultural unconscious—and yet still exert a shaping influence on the plot, the characters, and the textual operations of the novel. Judith Ryan argues:

> With regard to the self, Joyce's *Ulysses* proposes and explores a series of different conceptions: the self that exists as "ideas and sensations," the self that finds its continuity in memory, the self that moves towards a predetermined goal ("entelechy"), the transforming self of metempsychosis, the self of "hypnotic suggestion and somnambu-

lism" . . . , the self of the author that projects itself as a literary character (as in Shakespeare's *Hamlet*), the self that is passed down from father to son, the self that exists only by virtue of a name (the mysterious "McIntosh" of Paddy Dignam's funeral), the self divided into its component senses ("Miss voice of Kennedy" and "Miss gaze of Kennedy" . . .). All these are playfully suggested in the course of the novel. Joyce makes it clear that he has been following the debates about the self but that he is not fully prepared to settle for any one "solution." The ground of Joyce's novel is constantly shifting, and even its most ambitious mythic structures, the fundamental patterns that hold it together, are subject at one moment or another to ironic distancing and internal self-parody. (149)

We encounter the urgency of establishing a sense of identity on the first page of *A Portrait*, when the infant Stephen, hearing his father read a story about "Baby Tuckoo," thinks,

> He was baby tuckoo. The moocow came down the road where Betty Byrne lived: She sold lemon platt.
> *O, the wild rose blossoms*
> *On the little green place.*
> He sang that song. That was his song.
> *O, the green wothe botheth.* (P 7)

As Hugh Kenner and others have shown, the infant artist begins at once to form—or to *cern(e)*, in Paul Smith's terms—a self out of his sensations (every sense is involved in these early perceptions), using the artist's power to appropriate sense data to "rewrite" the details of experience. As Kenner points out in "The *Portrait* in Perspective," "By changing the red rose to a green and dislocating the spelling, he makes the song his own" (34).[3] By acting upon experience, by making it "his own," Stephen begins at once to distinguish himself from the world.

The reader follows Stephen's attempts to define himself throughout *A Portrait* as he experiments with the roles of sensualist, of religious devotee, and so on, finally settling on the persona of the artist as the most appropriate. However, despite Stephen's attempts to *cern(e)* a self, to construct a stable sense of himself and his place in the world in response to the roles, personae, or "voices" that he encounters in the world,[4] the reader sees rather a *series* of selves, a sequence of attempts to secure himself in one or another orientation—social, sexual, religious, artistic—and we have no reason to believe that Stephen's stridently self-confident position as a self-proclaimed artist at the end of *A Portrait* is as permanent, stable, or functional as Stephen seems to believe it is. In his early essay "A Portrait of the Artist," written in 1904, Joyce describes the young boy who serves as an early model for the Stephen of *Stephen Hero* and *A Portrait* as subject to "continued shocks, which drove him from breathless flights of zeal shamefully inwards" (*P* 258).[5] Joyce intimates that these repeated shocks bring about a "crisis" of personality or identity and that in response "the enigma of a manner was put up at all corners to protect the crisis" (*P* 258). Strangely, the wording here suggests that "the enigma of a manner," which we can take as the representation of a unified subjectivity to oneself and the world, does not protect the artist *from* the crisis, but rather protects the crisis itself, implying perhaps that the best the subject can hope to achieve is a cordoning off or repression—a *cerning*, in Paul Smith's terms—of the crisis of identity. This crisis of identity is central to *A Portrait of the Artist as a Young Man* and *Ulysses*, and, despite the reader's suspicion that "the enigma of a manner" may simply cover rather than solve a crisis of identity, Stephen seems to feel by the end of the novel that he has "found" himself as an artist. By constructing and investing himself in a personal mythology of the artist as priestlike and powerful, Stephen temporarily finds solid ground in a seemingly stable, seemingly permanent identity. He views himself as both formed and transformed by his choice of vocation, as he indicates in conversation with Cranly, when he dissociates himself from the religion of his youth by claiming "I was someone else then. . . . I was not myself as I am now, as I had to become" (*P* 240). We may suspect, however (as Stephen apparently does not at the end of *A Portrait*), that Stephen's problems in constructing a self cannot be solved through a simple choice of vocation. Joyce's novel constantly and ironically undercuts Stephen's exhilaration and sense of certainty, even in the last lines of the book, where Stephen unwittingly identifies himself with Icarus rather than with Daedalus as he prepares to "fly" into exile.

While *A Portrait* may seem superficially to validate the strong sense of self-presence and sureness of identity that Stephen feels at the end of the book, in *Ulysses* anxieties about the solidity of personal identity, about the possibility of positing and believing in a stable "self" that underlies time and change, are more insistent and tenacious. In *A Portrait*, the phrase *Tempora mutantur nos et mutamur in illis* (*P* 94) leaves no impression on Stephen except perhaps as another proof of the tediousness of his father's Cork friends (one of whom quizzes him with this line to test his Latin), but by the "Scylla and Charybdis" episode of *Ulysses* the notion that "Times change and we change with them" has become a recurrent problem that Stephen must once again set to rest.

By June 16, 1904, of course, Stephen has been forced to realize that he has not become the soaring Daedalian artist which he thought he would become at the end of *A Portrait;* he is, in fact, Icarus, who soared too high and fell: "Fabulous artificer. The hawklike man. You flew. Whereto? Newhaven-Dieppe, steerage passenger. Paris and back. Lapwing. Icarus. *Pater, ait.* Seabedabbled, fallen, weltering. Lapwing you are. Lapwing be" (U9.952-54).

The Stephen Dedalus of *Ulysses* takes up the issue of *Tempora mutantur nos et mutamur in illis* with obsessive interest, realizing now that he who can say "I was someone else then" cannot necessarily lay any certain claim to a constancy of self in the present or the future. The motif of the "other me" runs throughout the early chapters of *Ulysses,* occurring not only to Stephen but also to Leopold Bloom, who thinks, as he reminisces on his past life with Molly: "I was happier then. Or was that I? Or am I now I?" (U8.608).

This motif in *Ulysses* calls the nature of personal identity into question, so that we may be led to agree with Maud Ellmann's conclusion regarding *A Portrait* that identity is "a scar without an author, without an origin, and at last, without even a name. And this identity is a wound that constantly reopens" (191). For Ellmann, identity is a "process" of reopening and rehealing the scar of identity, a process of *brisure*—of "cleaving" and "joining"—that "belongs not only to the subject but to the text itself, which both suffers and enacts the mutilation by which identity reconstitutes itself. . . . Once named and maimed, the subject, rather than a plenitude, erupts henceforth as punctuation, as a gap or wound that rips the fabric of the text at irregular intervals" (192).

Ellmann recalls a phrase of Davin's from *A Portrait* when she labels this process of *brisure* in the novel "Disremembering Dedalus." We must also remember, however, to avoid the temptation to view Joyce's writing as ultimately or only disrupted and fragmentary; we must insist on maintaining the uneasy balance implied in terms such as Eco's "chaosmos" between centrifugal and centripetal forces. The formation of identity in *A Portrait* and *Ulysses,* then, occurs within a tension between the "disremembering" or dissolution of the self and the re-membering that seeks continually to shore up the fragments of experience into a coherent and purposive narrative. In much the same way, it has been argued by Karen Lawrence and others, the text itself constructs a normative style, or "Rock of Ithaca," or "initial style," in the first six chapters, which is then dissolved and reassembled in later episodes.[6] Remembering is one tool that the Joycean subject uses to pull things together, to "protect the crisis" of identity, attempting to create a narrative of wholeness or integrity. In *Ulysses*, memory is the central thread of the cultural and textual unconscious, one that intertwines with teleological notions of destiny and entelechy to become a proleptic, dynamic force struggling to connect past and future into a coherent narrative of the self. Thus, Herr finds within the cultural unconscious of *Ulysses* "the summoning up of an unknown sphere of inevitability and instinct, which appears to counter the recurrently asserted constructedness of all conditioning forces and the reflexively self-contained quality of *Ulysses*" ("Art" 28). In Joyce's transitional text we find both a modern awareness of the instability of personal identity *and* a nostalgic longing for unified and purposive experience; indeed, the forces of fragmentation and disruption at work in the novel do much to stimulate a reaction in the text that taps into the cultural unconscious to provide a holistic response, a suturing of these gaps in unity and identity.

This conflict between centrifugal and centripetal currents—between a textual "conscious" or surface that foregrounds the dissolution of self in linguistic and stylistic experimentation and a textual or cultural unconscious that preserves the desire for wholeness—is represented in the conflict between various models of mind and memory that supply the paradigms which Joyce uses to construct the "mimesis of consciousness" that John Paul Riquelme has found in *Ulysses*. In *Ulysses* we hear the echoes of the many philosophies or models of mind that Joyce encountered in his eclectic reading, in his conversations with friends and acquaintances, or, more generally, in the cultural assumptions that constructed his own position as a writer. These models of memory form a central part of the cultural unconscious, in Herr's terms, that exists in tension with what Maud Ellmann calls the "disremembering" tendencies in *Ulysses*.

Empiricist philosophy has traditionally viewed memory as the primary guarantor of personal identity, and yet one can argue that in doing so, it also weakened traditional notions of a unified self based on a transcendent self or soul. From this point of view, the "self" seems to be simply a collection of events and sensations, a procession of present instants; each individual personality is defined by the aggregation of his or her experiences, and each new experience therefore alters that personality. The importance of "instants" is emphasized throughout *A Portrait*, and, except for the case of the epiphanic moment, instants seem to constitute a threatening notion. Father Arnall, for example, tells the boys on retreat that "one single instant was enough for the trial of a man's soul" (*P* 113), and a few pages later Stephen thinks of Lucifer's "sin of pride, the sinful thought conceived in an instant" that ironically comes later to symbolize his own rejection of the Church: "*non serviam: I will not serve*" (*P* 117).

The notion of the self as a collection of instants is typical of the empiricist model of mind articulated by John Locke, who argues in *An Essay Concerning Human Understanding* that the human mind contains no "innate ideas" and that the "vast store" of ideas a person comes to possess all derive from "experience," which Locke divides into "sensation" and "reflection" (42). Following Descartes, Locke argues that consciousness alone constitutes our sense of self, and that personal identity can only be a creation of memory uniting successive states of consciousness and not the result of the continuity of physical substance (189–90). Approaching personal identity as a forensic issue, that is, as an "object of reward and punishment," Locke attempts to demonstrate that we hold people responsible for their actions according to our consciousness of their continuity as "thinking things," and not simply as the same body as that which committed the action in question (194–95). For Locke, memory unites discrete experiences—sensations and reflections—into a unified "self" or person, "and as far as this consciousness can be extended backwards to any past action or thought, so far reaches the identity of that person; it is the same self now it was then, and it is by the same self with this present one that now reflects on it, that that action was done" (188).

David Hume[7] argued that we experience only a succession of "passions and sensations" or "impressions," and that there is no stable entity that remains "identical" or "same" behind or throughout these impressions. In *A Treatise of Human Nature*, Hume claims that human beings "are nothing but a bundle or collection of different perceptions, which succeed each other with an inconceivable rapidity, and are in a perpetual flux and movement" (252). Hume does not, however, deny the *perception* of self; although it is "a fiction" (254), we think of ourselves as continuous entities by mistaking *relation* for identity, and we do this through memory. Hume does not deny, then, that some sort of relation exists between our present self and our past selves, but he sees this relation as more akin to a "republic or commonwealth, in which the several members are united by the reciprocal ties of government and subordination" than to a self or soul that remains continuous under change. Our perception of personal identity is dependent upon memory, for since it is "memory alone" that "acquaints us with the continuance and extent of this succession of perceptions, 'tis to be consider'd, upon that account chiefly, as the source of personal identity" (261).

For Edward Casey, Hume is a "passivist," since he argues that "the chief exercise of the memory is not to preserve the simple ideas, but their order and position" (Hume 9). If, Casey claims, "memory is constrained to depict past events in the precise order in which they occurred, it is thereby compelled to mimic them, to offer an image or copy that is related to them by isomorphic representation of position or form. . . . in the agile hands of Hume, memory has become a copying machine, a mere replicator of experience" (17).

Stephen Dedalus considers the problem of stability under flux again and again in *Ulysses* and most often ends by asserting the continuity of the self. Reflecting on his days at Clongowes in the "Telemachus" episode, Stephen thinks, "I am another now and yet the same" (*U*1.311–12). Just as Locke determines memory to be the forensic basis for personal responsibility, Stephen decides that memory gives sameness or continuity to experience and forms the "I" that travels through the changing worlds of space and time. Stephen facetiously applies this forensic notion of identity to himself in the "Scylla and Charybdis" episode when he tries to reason himself out of a debt owed to George Russell, who wrote under the pseudonym AE:

> . . . You owe it.
> Wait. Five months. Molecules all change. I am other I now. Other I got pound.
> Buzz. Buzz.
> But I, entelechy, form of forms, am I by memory because under everchanging forms.
> I that sinned and prayed and fasted.
> A child that Conmee saved from pandies.
> I, I and I. I.
> A. E. I. O. U. (*U*9.203–13)

Here Stephen acknowledges his debt to AE by acknowledging the essential unity of his "self." His memories of sinning, praying, and fasting recall once again the most intense moments of his youth and enable him to assert through memory a fundamental link between the young boy at Clongowes and the young man of *Ulysses*. But the nature of identity that Stephen describes in the passage above goes beyond Locke and Hume, for he finds identity and sameness not only "by memory," but in the "entelechy," the eternal and unchanging Aristotelian "form of forms" or soul that underlies experience. Richard Ellmann recognizes the difference between Stephen's views on identity and Hume's in *Ulysses on the Liffey*, where he argues:

> Hume was the master of those who do not know. Hume is not prepared to assert, as Stephen is, that the soul is the form of forms, and instead declares that questions about the soul's essence, such as its degree of materiality, are unintelligible. Although he agrees with Aristotle, and Stephen, that memory is a source of personal identity, he insists that "all the nice and subtle questions concerning personal identity can never possibly be decided, and are to be regarded rather as grammatical than as philosophical difficulties." Against Stephen's theory of persons and things having each its signature, Hume refuses to concede uninterrupted identity. (95)

Significantly, it is Buck Mulligan, not Stephen or Bloom, who alludes to the empiricist model of memory very early in the novel when he claims "I can't remember anything. I remember only ideas and sensations" (U1.192–3).[8]

One powerful counterpoint to this sort of empiricist skepticism must have come in the form of Joyce's Jesuit teachers' notions of the self and personal identity. Many of these traditional, antiempiricist ideas about the nature of the self and memory are formulated in great detail in *Psychology*, a book written by the Rev. Michael Maher, S.J., and marked and annotated in Joyce's hand.[9] As a young man, Joyce apparently spent much time studying Father Maher's learned and aggressive arguments for a modern Catholic psychology, which were formulated primarily, it seems, to combat the growing power of empiricist and evolutionist theories about the nature of the mind.[10] Father Maher addresses the adherents of what he calls at different points empiricism or materialism or skepticism—including Locke and Hume—while carefully reminding "the young Catholic reader that the fact of my frequently citing or referring to certain writers does not in any way imply a general recommendation of their works as likely to assist in the attainment of truth" (ix). In Maher's book, Joyce encountered explications and refutations of many of the leading intellectual theories of the late nineteenth century, as well as detailed discussions of Plato, Aquinas, and, above all, Aristotle.

Maher's chapter on "Memory" is a dry and rather mechanical survey of various theories for the workings of memory and "mental association," but it becomes more interesting when his arguments turn to memory in relation to personal identity and, especially, to the Aristotelian concept of entelechy. Locke and Hume are two of Maher's antagonists, and in his responses to associationism and empiricism, Maher constructs arguments that closely resemble those that Stephen puts forward in defense of his own identity in *Ulysses*. Indeed, Maher's arguments may well have served as sources for some of the philosophical musing on identity in *Ulysses*. For example, Stephen's assertion, "I, entelechy, form of forms, am I by memory because under everchanging forms," is echoed in Maher's discussion of Aristotle's notion of entelechy and its correspondence to Scholastic definitions of the soul. Echoing Aristotle's definition of the soul as the "form of forms" in *De Anima* (3:432a; see Gifford and Seidman 32) Maher asserts:

> The true doctrine is the Peripatetic theory. This explanation was formulated by Aristotle, and later on adopted by St. Thomas and all the leading Scholastic philosophers. The soul is described by these writers as the *substantial form* of the body. The living being is conceived as the resultant of two factors,—the one active and determining, the other passive and determinable. The first is called the *Form*, the second the *Matter* of the being. (515–16; original emphasis)

Stephen's logic in the "Scylla and Charybdis" episode resembles Maher's conclusion:

> Through memory we are aware of our own abiding personal identity. We know with the most absolute certainty that we are the same persons who yesterday, last week, fifty years ago, had some very vivid experience. But this would be impossible were the mind constituted of successive states, or were the material substance the substantial principle in which these states inhere. The constituent elements of the latter, it is a generally admitted physiological fact, are completely changed in a comparatively short time. . . . It is only an indivisible principle, persisting unchanged amid transitory states, that is able to afford an adequate basis for the faculty of remembrance. (447)

Attacking "Locke's definition of a Person as *a self-conscious substance*," Maher rejects the notion that a history of self-consciousness alone can guarantee personal identity; rather, he suggests, identity "has its basis in the persistence of the same indivisible soul throughout the life of each individual." Thus, he continues, "memory and self-consciousness *reveal*, but they do not *constitute* personal identity" (343; original emphasis). Similarly, he argues against Hume's assertion that the self is a fiction by stating:

> If the mind were but a succession of transient states, then judgment, reasoning, self-conscious reflexion, and rational memory would be absolutely impossible; but this is not the case; therefore the mind is not merely such a series. Judgment requires the indivisible unity

of the agent which compares the terms; reasoning cannot take place unless the premises successively apprehended are combined by one and the same simple energy; lastly, self-conscious reflexion and rational memory evidently imply the persistence of an abiding subject which can juxtapose the past with the present. (345)

Maher's assertion of a basis for stable identity over time resembles other theories of personal identity that we will see Joyce weaving into the cultural unconscious of *Ulysses* in that it depends on the idea of some sort of purposive or directed "substance" or force that underlies change and accident: "since an infinite series of accidents inhering in each other is an absurdity, we must come at last to a something which exists *per se*. Substance, then, is conceived as a subsisting something that abides the same amid the change of its accidents" (348). Identity or "the true mind" is for Maher "the subject plus its states, or the subject present in its states" (347).

Joyce may well have referred back to his copy of Maher's *Psychology* as he thought through many of the passages on memory, identity, soul, and entelechy in *Ulysses*. In a later chapter on "The Union of Soul and Body," Joyce took care to mark a number of passages in which Maher summarized his belief in a soul or vital principle. When Maher remarked that "*a substantial form* is accordingly defined as *a determining principle which by its union with the subject that it actuates constitutes a complete substance of a determinate species*" (518; italics in original), Joyce underlined the words "substantial form," "determining principle," and "substance of a determinate species." Similarly, Joyce made a marginal mark next to another passage in which Maher argued:

> It is on the permanence of the substantial form that the identity of the individual depends. The material constituents of the living body are nearly all changed, as we have before stated, in the course of a few years, yet we affirm that the man of sixty is identical with the boy of six: the soul has persisted unchanged. It is this same simple informing principle which reduces the different parts and organs of the body to the unity of a single being. Neither a bale of cotton nor a bucket of water forms *one being*; each is but a mere aggregate of parts.[11] Even a watch or a steam-ship—although the parts are unified by its end or purpose—wants the unity of being which is exhibited in man, in the brute, and in the plant. (519)

Maher clearly considered Darwin particularly dangerous, and in his textbook he expends considerable energy in denouncing Darwin and other evolutionists as "the Atheistic Materialistic school" who believe that "all things in the world, the human eye as well as the instincts of the bee, are ultimately the result not of a designing Mind, but of the fortuitous collisions of blind material forces" (540). Maher goes so far as to claim that "there is no theory, however wild, that has ever been broached on the subject—not even that of the ante-natal existence of the soul conjured up by the poetic fancy of Plato—which is more utterly beyond the possibility of scientific proof than the new doctrine" (285). Countering Darwin and echoing Aristotle, but also stemming from some of the leading counter-Darwinian evolutionary theories of his own time, Maher argues: "We are justified . . . in assuming a new internal energy, a directing force which determines and governs the stream of activities described as the phenomena of life. This force is what is meant by the so-called '*vegetative soul*' or '*vital principle*'" (508; original emphasis). Thus, Maher unites the Catholic idea of the soul with the Aristotelian notions of the "substantial form" and the "vital principle," which insist that

> there must be in each living being, and therefore *a fortiori* in man, a vegetative soul, or vital principle, to which is due the natural unity of activity comprising the phenomena of his life. . . . But such a principle must be the substantial form of the living human being. For, since *actio sequitur esse*—since every *action* of an agent flows from the *being* of that agent—the principle which is the root of the natural activity of a substance must be the determinant of its being and nature. (518)

Significantly, Joyce emphasized the lines from "from the being of that agent" through to the end of this passage with a mark in the margin of the text.

So, when Stephen questions the nature of his debt to AE in the passage from "Scylla and Charybdis" discussed above, he reacts to his own skepticism about what Maher calls the "physiological fact" that the elements of our bodies are constantly in flux ("Molecules all change. I am other I now") by establishing an identity based *both* on the memory of successive states ("I by memory because under everchanging forms") and on the Aristotelian theory favored by Father Maher—that is, the existence of an "informing principle," or "dominating force" (520) that Maher equates with the soul or entelechy ("I, entelechy, form of forms"). Joyce's reading in Maher's *Psychology* textbook provides a clear example of the ways in which his training in traditional Catholic philosophy influenced his ideas about memory and identity, creating a cultural unconscious in his writing that operated in a chaosmic tension with the more materialist prevailing discourses of the late nineteenth and early twentieth centuries.

Most significant for the connection between Maher's *Psychology* and Stephen's arguments for the unity of the soul in *Ulysses* is Maher's Aristotelian conclusion to the subject of "The Union of Soul and Body," where he explicitly brings up the term "entelechy":

> Our present chapter ought to have rendered intelligible and justified Aristotle's celebrated definition: "The soul is the first entelechy of a natural organized body potentially having life," or "the first entelechy of a natural body capable of life." By *entelechy* is meant in the Peripatetic philosophy an actualizing or determining principle, as opposed to a recipient or determinable subject—*form* as contrasted with *matter.* (523; italics in original)

In this muscular theory of identity, the soul dominates all else to create unified identity in a *"suppositum* or *hypostasis"* that unites soul and body in much the same way that the body of Christ could incarnate the human and the divine simultaneously (521). Entelechy, the word that Stephen Dedalus uses to identify the soul—that which, "by memory," provides continuity "under everchanging forms"—provides a convenient and appropriate way of discussing much that belongs to what I have called, following Cheryl Herr, the cultural unconscious of *Ulysses.* Originally developed by Aristotle in *De Anima,*[12] *De Generatione Animalium,* and *Metaphysica,* the term *entelechy* has come to have a number of meanings relevant to the interplay of desire and memory in *Ulysses:*

> (1) Aristotle used the word to denote the actualization of what is potential or possible in an organism;
> (2) As noted above, it has become identified in Roman Catholic theology with the soul;
> (3) Based on the previous meanings and on its etymology (ἐντελέχεια, derived from the Greek τέλος, fulfillment or consummation), entelechy has come to signify a vital, motive, teleological, and unconscious force that drives ineluctably toward some form of completion, wholeness, or closure.

All of these meanings are contained in the correspondence between entelechy and personal identity—the soul or unifying principle unconsciously informs and develops or actualizes the inherent potentialities of a human being. This notion of entelechy, as we will see, was used by other antiempiricist writers of the early twentieth century—especially

Henri Bergson—to indicate a vital, unconscious, teleological force, and it will serve us as well, in the end, as a useful narratological term for Joyce's development of plot in *Ulysses*. The tension between the skepticism and indeterminacy of Hume's theory of identity and the holism and purposiveness of the Aristotelian model of the soul as entelechic force is echoed significantly in the now largely forgotten but once fierce debate concerning the roles of chance and purpose in biological evolution. This debate, which I will return to in later chapters, attracted some of the most influential writers of Joyce's time (including Samuel Butler, George Bernard Shaw, William James, and Henri Bergson). Entelechy, then, is not simply Stephen's way of facing his debts but is an important way of thinking about many of the centripetal, holistic elements of *Ulysses* that work to provide the essential tension with the book's postmodernist and fragmentary tendencies.

Maher's book, of course, is not the only influence on the cultural unconscious of *Ulysses*. Joyce's characters and writings often enunciate notions similar to those current in the philosophy of Henri Bergson—arguably the most influential Continental philosopher of the early twentieth century—of life as a "stream," of the "flow" of experience, and of the immediacy, vitality, and power of the past. Joyce's Trieste library included two of Bergson's books and one critical text on Bergson (Gillespie, *Trieste* 46–47 and 221); in a note to *Exiles*, Joyce labeled Bergson a "Celtic philosopher," who, like Hume and Berkeley, was "inclined towards incertitude or scepticism" (*E* 125). Bergson wrote on many topics, including dreams and laughter, that might seem relevant to a study of Joyce, but here I wish primarily to concern myself with his consideration of memory, its relation to what he called creative evolution, and his use of a concept of vital force similar to the third definition of entelechy outlined above.[13] In his formulation of a fluid sense of identity that rejected both the skeptical assumptions of empiricist philosophy *and* the traditional need for a stable, unchanging core identity, Bergson provided a middle ground, a way of seeing the self as both discrete and in flux. Bergson's difficult and poetic style emphasized the inadequacy of our philosophical language for describing the actual experience of reality. Thus, as Joseph Solomon explains, Bergson could conceive of the self as a "continuously changing whole" equivalent to "what common sense calls the Soul, Spirit, or Mind, and philosophers the 'Ego,'" and at the same time warn against the tendency "to suppose that it is some sort of permanent substantial reality on which the various states of consciousness are beaded, as on a string" (36).¹⁴ Access to Bergson's ideas provided Joyce with a way to see the self as both holistic and transitional, as Stephen does in "Scylla and Charybdis."

The earliest version of *A Portrait of the Artist as a Young Man*, an essay written in 1904, begins on a Bergsonian note:

> The features of infancy are not commonly reproduced in the adolescent portrait for, so capricious we are, that we cannot or will not conceive the past in any other than its iron, memorial aspect. Yet the past assuredly implies a fluid succession of presents, the development of an entity of which our actual present is a phase only. Our world, again, recognises its acquaintance chiefly by the characters of beard and inches and is, for the most part, estranged from those of its members who seek through some art, by some process of the mind as yet untabulated, *to liberate from the personalised lumps of matter that which is their individuating rhythm*, the first or formal relation of their parts. But for such as these a portrait is not an identificative paper but rather the curve of an emotion. (*P* 257–58; emphasis added)

In the "Lotus-Eaters" episode of *Ulysses*, Bloom considers the instability of the weather in relation to the constant flux of life: "Won't last. Always passing, the stream of life, which in the stream of life we trace is dearer thaaan them all" (*U*5.563–64). Fritz Senn points out that Bloom's meditations allude to a ballad entitled "In Happy Moments Day by Day," which goes:

> Some thoughts none other can replace,
> Remembrance will recall;
> Which in the flight of years we trace,
> Is dearer than them all.

As Senn notes, "The 'flight of years' has given way to 'the stream of life,'" for Joyce "presented memory as a flux or aptly 'stream of consciousness'" ("Classical" 33). Again, in the "Lestrygonians" episode, Leopold Bloom contemplates the River Liffey and thinks "It's always flowing in a stream, never the same, which in the stream of life we trace. Because life is a stream" (*U*8.93–95). Fritz Senn hears in this "an echo from Greek thinkers, mainly Heraclitus, who is reported to have said that you cannot enter the same river twice, that everything flows" ("Classical" 32); we can hear echoes of William James and Bergson in these passages as well.¹⁵ Arguing that "consciousness cannot go through the same state twice," Bergson claims: "Our personality, which is being built up each instant with its accumulated experience, changes without ceasing. By changing, it prevents any state, although superficially identical with another, from ever repeating it in its very depth" (*Creative Evolution* 8).

This accretion of experience creates (in the most active sense) personality in Bergson's philosophy. For "What are we," Bergson asks,

> in fact, what is our *character*, if not the condensation of the history that we have lived from our birth—nay, even before our birth, since we bring with us prenatal dispositions? Doubtless we think with only a small part of our past, but it is with our entire past, including the original bent of our soul, that we desire, will and act. (*Creative Evolution* 7–8; original emphasis)

Thus, while the River Liffey remains the River Liffey from day to day, it also changes from moment to moment; in the same way, Stephen Dedalus can claim to remain Stephen Dedalus even though "molecules all change" (*U*9.205). Yet buried within or beneath the flux of personality lie "prenatal dispositions" and "the original bent of our soul," notions of identity closer to Plato and Aristotle than to Locke and Hume.

Much of the thrust of Bergson's writing was the exposition of the fundamental error he felt we make in conceiving of time as a form of space. While this spatial view of time may be indispensable for us in obtaining our quotidian, practical needs, for Bergson it obscures the true nature of time as an unfolding, active process. Bergson viewed memory as an "antidote" or counter to the Lockean spatialized notion of life as a "line" of instants, a succession of "personalized lumps of matter" (*P* 258). Memory allows the past to persist into the present, to remain active and influential, rather than "stored" and passive, and it provides us with an intuition, a feeling of "duration" (Bergson's term for time as we truly experience it, rather than as we are trained to think of it). Joyce owned a copy of *L'évolution créatrice* (Gillespie, *Trieste* 46), in which Bergson explains:

> Duration is the continuous progress of the past which gnaws into the future and which swells as it advances. And as the past grows without ceasing, so also there is no limit to its preservation. Memory, as we have tried to prove, is not a faculty of putting away recollections in a drawer, or of inscribing them in a register. . . . In reality, the past is preserved by itself, automatically. In its entirety, probably, it follows us at every instant; all that we have felt, thought and willed from our earliest infancy is there, leaning over the present which is about to join it, pressing against the portals of consciousness that would fain leave it outside. (7)

While Bergson admitted that our conscious minds have both the practical need and the ability to "drive back into the unconscious almost the whole of this past," he believed that our present selves and our future are intimately related to the whole of our personal histories, which, whether we realize it or not, we are always "dragging behind us unawares" (7). According to Bergson, our past pushes us into our future as "our personality shoots, grows and ripens without ceasing" (8), so that each of us, as Lenehan says about Moses in *Ulysses*, has "a great future behind him" (*U*7.875).

The passivist or empiricist, then, conceives of the personal past as a "repository" of images that we store and carry with us as we move along the "timeline" of our lives, almost as if it were a sack full of photographs or records we could reach into when we needed to remember something. Bergson's activism, on the other hand, conceives of the past as an active, overflowing collection of experiences that motivates and presses upon the present. The passivist idea of time and memory is diachronous in that it views identity as an individual sequence of moments of time, while, in contrast, the Bergsonian notion is synchronous: past, present, and future are interpenetrating and interrelated; the past will not "stay put." While the discrete instants of linear, passivist time are photographic and static, Bergson and Joyce conceive of moments when consciousness is opened up to a truer, more powerful perception of time and its nature. Thus, "instants" are central to Bergson's philosophy as they are to Stephen Dedalus in *A Portrait of the Artist as a Young Man*, but for Bergson they are not like pearls strung one after another on the thread of identity, but rather they are opportunities for the intuitive perception of duration, individual and unique portals for realizing the true nature of time, not unlike Joyce's moments of epiphany.

Stephen Dedalus gives John Eglinton a rather contorted explanation of this Bergsonian interrelatedness of time past, time present, and time future in the library episode of *Ulysses*, in the process of explaining how Shakespeare used his own past as the stuff of his art:

> And as the mole on my right breast is where it was when I was born, though all my body has been woven of new stuff time after time, so through the ghost of the unquiet father the image of the living son looks forth. In the intense instant of imagination, when the mind, Shelley says, is a fading coal, that which I was is that which I am and that which in possibility I may come to be. So in the future, the sister of the past, I may see myself as I sit here now but by reflection from that which then I shall be. (*U*9.378–85)

Similarly, Bloom says in the "Circe" episode: "But tomorrow is a new day will be. Past was is today. What now is will then tomorrow as now was be past yester" (*U*15.2409–10).

This Bergsonian sense of the interrelatedness of past, present, and future depends upon the existence of an unconscious force within the psyche or self, whether we see it in Joyce's terms as an "individuating rhythm" (*P* 258) or in Bergson's phrase, "the original bent of our soul" (*Creative Evolution* 8). Both of these phrases imply the existence of an entelechic force within the self, a force that provides each individual thing with its "nature" and drives it to fulfill that nature. Bergson's notion of the élan vital, the motive force in what he called "creative evolution," was an influential idea in Joyce's time that bears some similarity to definitions of the entelechy that Joyce was familiar with (in *Finnegans Wake*, for example, we read of "Promptings by Elanio Vitale" [*FW* 221.22]).[16] Bergson's notion of the élan vital is difficult because he wanted to stake out a position between determinism and indeterminacy as well as a position, as I will demonstrate later, between two competing theories of evolution, one (neo-Lamarckism) holistic and the other (Darwinism) dependent on random accidents of mutation. Bergson defined the élan vital as a motive force within all forms of life that moves them "forward" toward greater complexity and yet is not teleological in any mechanical or deterministic fashion. Thus, he could write: "the rôle of life is to insert some *indetermination* into matter. Indeterminate, *i.e.* unforeseeable, are the forms it creates in the course of its evolution. More and more indeterminate also, more and more free, is the activity to which these forms serve as the vehicle" (*Creative Evolution* 139–40; original emphasis).

Bergson struggled against what he saw as mechanistic tendencies in Western thought, against our habit of seeing the world and time as mechanical and measurable, a tendency that in Bergson's eyes lay behind modern science. Bergson allowed that this mechanistic way of proceeding works in transforming the physical world, but he cautioned that it also obscures other, more vital aspects of our life in the world. In *Creative Evolution*, Bergson rejects Darwinism—specifically natural selection—as too mechanistic, too materialistic. Employing a favorite example of counter-Darwinian evolutionists, Bergson asks how a complex organ such as the eye could evolve so similarly in species that have been widely separated for aeons, if not for some sort of internal guiding principle. Bergson's response emphasizes desire or effort within what Bergson called the unconscious, orthogenetic vital spirit in organisms. Creative evolution is brought about by "a cause of a psychological nature," Bergson writes, "an effort of far greater depth than the individual effort, far more independent of circumstances, an effort common to most representatives of the same species, inherent in the germs they bear rather than in their substance alone, an effort thereby assured of being passed on to their descendants" (*Creative Evolution* 97).

Bergson firmly rejected what he called Finalism, however—the sense that this evolutionary drive was oriented toward any definite or fixed goal:

> It would be futile to try to assign to life an end, in the human sense of the word. To speak of an end is to think of a pre-existing model which has only to be realized. It is to suppose, therefore, that all is given, and that the future can be read in the present. . . . Of course, when once the road has been travelled, we can glance over it, mark its direction, note this in psychological terms and speak as if there had been pursuit of an end. Thus shall we speak ourselves" (*Creative Evolution* 58–59).

Thus, while the élan vital within each organism drives it to fulfill itself, to move toward some telos or perfection, that goal is not predetermined in any mechanical sense, but is always being created. Evolution for Bergson is vital, unconscious, and creative, but not fully teleological. Joyce catches some of the sense of Bergson's élan vital in his statement in his 1904 "A Portrait of the Artist" essay that he wishes *"to liberate from the personalised lumps of matter that which is their individuating rhythm,* the first or formal relation of their parts. But for such as these a portrait is not an identificative paper but rather the curve of an emotion" (*P* 258).

Given this assumption that, at least during the time in which he wrote *A Portrait of the Artist as a Young Man* and *Ulysses*, memory is for Joyce the binder of personality and identity—the landscape of the self—how does memory work for and on the characters in *Ulysses*? Can we use memory consciously to advance our desires? Are our memories fully accessible to us? Can memory block us in our lives, preventing the attainment of desirable ends and goals? And can we be at all sure that what we remember is what actually occurred? As the plot of *Ulysses* begins to unfold, the reader comes to realize that both Stephen Dedalus and Leopold Bloom have reached impasses in their lives, mental blocks that result to a large degree from disruptions or problems in their memories; both are in danger of falling into the inactivity, the paralysis, that constitutes the principal danger of Dublin life in Joyce's writings. In a Bergsonian sense, the past is very much with them and very much a prologue to what will come, for it presses against their thoughts and imposes on their lives constantly throughout the day. They have not left the past behind, and, try as they might to repress and forget these disruptions of memory, they cannot.

What are these troubling memories, these snags or traumas in the past that threaten to paralyze Stephen and Bloom? Like Plato's *pharmakon*, memory is both a poison and, potentially, a cure for Joyce's characters.[17] Stephen and Bloom both must deal with a complex set of memories buried in the pasts that Joyce has constructed for them, and by examining the personal histories that Joyce has constructed for his characters, we can begin to understand the ways in which memory and repression work unconsciously in the text of his novel. Both Stephen and Bloom return obsessively during the day to a number of upsetting events and problems in their pasts—Bloom's father's suicide and Stephen's pandybatting at Clongowes, for example—but certain particular memories remain especially powerful for each character, in that these repressed and painful memories have collected around them other memories and problems. In some ways, these traumatic memories would seem to function in a fashion similar to Freud's "primal scenes," although rarely in Joyce's work do we get the sense that most of a character's problems can be traced back to one event alone, as often seems to be the case in Freud's case studies (there is no need to claim that either the Christmas dinner or the pandybatting constitutes a Freudian "primal scene" for Stephen Dedalus in *A Portrait*, for example, though both scenes remain potent and active in his memory).

The issue of Freud and Joyce is complex and delicate, having been argued, exaggerated, and dismissed by various critics. Unfortunately, the question of whether we can identify any direct, conscious influence has too often clouded a fruitful discussion of the important similarities and differences that characterize the works of these two seminal twentieth-century writers. Clearly, Joyce knew of Freud's work—his Trieste library contained copies (in German) of *The Psychopathology of Everyday Life* and *A Childhood Memory of Leonardo da Vinci* (Gillespie, *Trieste* 101–2). Numerous accounts by friends and acquaintances detail Joyce's discussions of Freud's ideas; apparently in public Joyce dismissed psychoanalysis more often than not.[18] More important, however, Freud's theories were —to use W. H. Auden's famous phrase—part of the "climate of opinion" during the period in which Joyce wrote *Ulysses*; as participants in a wider modern European culture, Joyce and Freud appear to have shared some of the same assumptions concerning the workings of the mind and memory. By viewing Joyce side-by-side with Freud as a product of a similar cultural climate, we can examine Freud's thought carefully and provisionally to articulate and develop insights into Joyce's writing, using Freud's writings as a useful gloss, counterpoint, or parallel to Joyce's, without needing to assert any deliberate, direct connection between the two.[19]

In *Ulysses*, then, we find nodes of pain and guilt that trouble Stephen and Bloom, memories that, unlike Freud's primal scenes, were formed not in infancy or early childhood, but later in life—in the death of Stephen's mother and the death of Bloom's son, for example. The death of Stephen's mother (and his role in contributing to her death) has become for him an obsessive block to any action, any change or movement "forward" in life. Stephen, who has struggled to escape the paralysis of Dublin life, is nonetheless paralyzed by this unresolved source of fear and guilt in his memory. As readers we sense that none of his desires—for artistic recognition, for instance, or for an end to his isolation from others, especially women—can be satisfied without the removal of this mnemic abcess. Yet the death of May Goulding Dedalus has become the center of a complex of problems and anxieties associated with, but not directly related to, her death. Similarly, Leopold Bloom has avoided coming to terms with the death of his infant son, Rudy, almost eleven years before June 16, 1904, an event that has, over time, become enmeshed with other concerns—particularly, the suicide of Bloom's father and the issue of patrilinear descent, Bloom's guilt and sexual dysfunction as a result of his perceived culpability in his son's death, and more.

Over the course of time and through the workings of memory, these painful past events have collected around themselves associated feelings of guilt, remorse, and fear, and in doing so these feelings have become deeper, more tangled, and more problematic than may have been warranted by the original events. These sorts of traumatic memories, then, are more akin to tapestries than to photographs of the past, for they are woven from many different strands in each character's memory. We can view many or most of Stephen's and Bloom's problems as symptoms, according to Freud's sense of symptoms as "residues—'precipitates' they might be called—of emotional experiences. To these experiences, therefore, we later gave the name of 'psychical traumas,' while the particular nature of the symptoms was explained by their relation to the traumatic scenes which were their cause." "What left the symptom behind," Freud continues, "was not always a single experience. On the contrary, the result was usually brought about by the convergence of several traumas, and often by the repetition of a great number of similar ones" (11:14).

Because of their troubling memories, Bloom and Stephen find themselves cut off from the present as well. Stephen has limped back from the Continent, no longer the "hawklike man" he thought himself to be, but rather Icarus dampened by his fall. He has returned from the exile that he so boldly chose to the labyrinth of Dublin, not in triumph but in confusion, not to recognition and acclaim, but rather to the terror of his mother's death from cancer. He has produced nothing of note and shows no sign of direction in his life or art. Memories of his mother "beset his brooding brain" (U1.265-66). Stephen's refusal to pray by her deathbed when she asked him to has produced a sense of guilt that has fused with his defiant attempts to reject the Catholic faith. Thus, when Stephen thinks of his mother as "Ghoul! Chewer of corpses!" (U1.278), he conflates his image of her dead body with his memory of her as a partaker of the Eucharist.

May Goulding Dedalus's death carries connotations in *Ulysses* that are linked through an intertextual memory to earlier events in Stephen's life outlined in *A Portrait*, for in the "Telemachus" episode Stephen unconsciously connects his mother's death to a motif associated with the revulsion that he experienced after being pushed into a ditch full of stagnant water as a young boy at Clongowes. Often throughout *A Portrait of the Artist as a Young Man*, Stephen feels revulsion and fear at the sight or thought of anything resembling the "cold slimy water" (P 10) of the ditch, as when he sees the "foul green puddles and clots of liquid dung" in a cow yard (P 63) or imagines the scene of an incestuous love affair later in the book: "A game of swans flew there and the water and the shore beneath were fouled with their greenwhite slime" (P 228). In *Ulysses*, Stephen links these images—green, stagnant liquid associated with fear and illness—with his mother's death: "The ring of bay and skyline held a dull green mass of liquid. A bowl of white china had stood beside her deathbed holding the green sluggish bile which she had torn up from her rotting liver by fits of loud groaning vomiting" (U1.107-10). Stephen unconsciously supplements his memory of this already disturbing event with additional feelings of guilt and fear from his past, and *Ulysses*, at its inception, demonstrates to the reader that the text itself is subtly dependent on the intertextual recollection of an earlier novel, a memory of Stephen's "experiences" as they occurred in another text.

Although he hopes that he can come to "no more turn aside and brood," Stephen's mind is drawn compulsively back to his mother's death. Mulligan's crude taunting ("The aunt thinks you killed your mother" and "You crossed her last wish in death"—U1.88 and 1.212) cuts through the cold, impersonal persona—"the enigma of a manner"—that Stephen has "put up at all corners to protect the crisis" (P 258) created by his mother's death and leaves "gaping wounds . . . in his heart" (U1.216-

17). By night he dreams of "Her glazing eyes, staring out of death, to shake and bend my soul. On me alone. . . . Her eyes on me to strike me down" (U1.273-76). His obsession has brought him to the point where he seems to have no memory of his mother uncomplicated by guilt and remorse. She has become for him the agent of "the lord of things as they are whom the most Roman of catholics call *dio boia*, hangman god" (U9.1048-49), a ghost who seeks revenge, not only for what Stephen sees as his contribution to her own death, but also for his apostasy. Every word that Stephen hears related to death, motherhood, or guilt calls up a tortured memory of May Goulding Dedalus, "a ghostwoman with ashes on her breath" (U3.46-47), and these troubled memories are often mixed with his present sense of failure and the punishing Catholicism he has tried to leave behind.

Bloom's deepest problems on June 16, 1904, can be traced almost eleven years into the past to the death of his son, Rudy, on January 9, 1894 (U17.2281). Rudy's death is certainly not the only problem in Bloom's past, but it forms a nexus for many of his doubts and anxieties about his identity as a Jew, as a son and father, and, most obviously, as a husband. Bloom thinks often of his desire for a son—"Something to hand on. . . . My son. Me in his eyes" (U6.74-76)—and we learn in the "Cyclops" episode of Bloom's great anticipation of his son's birth eleven years earlier:

> —Yes, says J.J., and every male that's born they think it may be their Messiah. And every Jew is in a tall state of excitement, I believe, till he knows if he's a father or a mother.
> —Expecting every moment will be his next, says Lenehan.
> —O, by God, says Ned, you should have seen Bloom before that son of his that died was born. I met him one day in the south city markets buying a tin of Neave's food six weeks before the wife was delivered. (U12.1646-51)

The Citizen takes these reflections as an opportunity to question Bloom's manhood ("Do you call that a man?"), while Joe Hynes responds ambiguously, "I wonder did he ever put it out of sight" (U12.1655). While Hynes's comment may simply be a lewd allegation of Bloom's impotence, we may also see this remark as a textual repetition of earlier comments about memory and forgetting. Although Bloom has tried to convince himself earlier in the day that to die is to "Begin to be forgotten. Out of sight, out of mind" (U6.872), the reader of *Ulysses* may consider Simon Dedalus's opinion on the presence of the dead more accurate: "Though lost to sight, Mr Dedalus said, to memory dear" (U6.457).

While Stephen's memory of his mother's death produces violent and terrible images in his mind, Rudy's death affects Bloom more subtly, especially regarding his relationship with Molly Bloom. Bloom, like Stephen, has come to blame himself for the death of a loved one, but Bloom's guilt takes on a sexual tone rather than a religious one. Rudy was born on December 29, 1893, and lived for just eleven days. The novel hints that Rudy was a deformed infant, for Molly Bloom thinks, in "Penelope," "what was the good in going into mourning for what was neither one thing nor the other the first cry was enough for me" (U18.1307–9). As Bloom remembers it, the midwife also "knew from the first poor little Rudy wouldn't live. Well, God is good, sir. She knew at once" (U4.418–20). Bloom blames himself not only for Rudy's death, but for his weakness and deformity as well, and this sense of guilt has far-reaching effects. In the "Hades" episode, Bloom sees a child's coffin on a coach heading for Glasnevin Cemetery, and he imagines the corpse inside: "A dwarf's face, mauve and wrinkled like little Rudy's was. Dwarf's body, weak as putty, in a whitelined deal box. . . . Our. Little. Beggar. Baby. Meant nothing. Mistake of nature. If it's healthy it's from the mother. If not from the man. Better luck next time" (U6.326–30).[20] Bloom's attempt to pass this troublesome memory off as meaningless is, as we will see, typical of him. The actual impact of Rudy's death becomes clearer, however, when we come to realize that no "next time" occurred for Bloom and Molly.

Bloom's sexual dysfunction is imaged in the topsy-turvy nature of his household economy, in which he cooks for his wife and tacitly clears the way for her meeting later in the day with Blazes Boylan. According to the terms of Joyce's Dublin, Bloom is unmanned by these arrangements in that he consistently rejects a traditional, active male sexuality. We see him instead as a voyeur who obtains what sexual satisfaction he can from writing and receiving obscene letters from women he does not know and from masturbating. He fears, at least subconsciously, that he is impotent—a fear best expressed in the frequent variations of the phrase "get it up" and "keep it up," which Bloom invariably relates to Molly's affair with Boylan and his own sexual ineffectiveness. Particularly haunting is the little rhyme that Bloom remembers after reading a letter he has received from Martha Clifford:

O, Mairy lost the pin of her drawers.
She didn't know what to do
To keep it up.
To keep it up. (U5.281–84)

Bloom responds logically and grammatically to his memory of the song—
"It? Them" (U5.285)—but "it" is more appropriate as a representation
of Bloom's anxieties and thus more logical as a parapraxis than Bloom
realizes. This motif takes on a life of its own within the novel's textual
memory, resurfacing throughout the text until the "Circe" episode, when
Bloom finally hears (or thinks he hears) "two sluts of the Coombe" sing,

> O, Leopold lost the pin of his drawers
> He didn't know what to do,
> To keep it up,
> To keep it up. (U15.3444–47)

The sexual anxieties stemming from Rudy's death have driven
Bloom into distanced, onanistic relationships with women, as we see
in his dealings with Martha Clifford (whom he never sees) and Gerty
MacDowell (whom he sees, but never speaks to or touches). When he
thinks of women as sexual objects or partners, Bloom tends to do so only
in stereotyped, romanticized images drawn from pornographic novels.
He imagines women such as Gerty and Martha as oversexed temptresses;
indeed, he would rather imagine them than encounter them in the flesh.
Bloom's imaginings tend to go to extremes, however, for he thinks of
women as pure, virginal, and nunlike as often as he thinks of them as
lascivious and whorish.[21] Ironically but appropriately, Bloom's flirtation
and masturbation with Gerty (a virgin whom Bloom imagines to be a
"Hot little devil" [U13.776]) occurs in the shadow of the Chapel of Mary,
Star of the Sea, on Sandymount Strand.

The image of woman as archetypal virgin is as fundamentally destructive and sterile in *Ulysses* as it was for Stephen in *A Portrait*,
for it reinforces Bloom's disinclination to act sexually. The problematic, threatening quality of the virgin figure for Bloom is revealed in his
memories of a nun he met when he once tried to collect on an account
at Tranquilla Convent, for while he thinks of her as "a nice nun . . .
really sweet face" (U8.144), he also remembers that "It was a nun they
say invented barbed wire" (U8.154). Bloom's idealization of the feminine
is most clearly symbolized by the picture of the Nymph he has placed
above his and Molly's bed and by the statues of "Shapely goddesses"
(U8.920) that he seeks out in the National Museum.

Bloom's fear of impotence and his retreat to a fantasy world of virgins and whores has poisoned his marriage over the past eleven years
and contributed to Molly's desire to take a lover. In the "Ithaca" episode,
we learn, in the peculiarly clinical language of that chapter, that husband and wife last had "complete carnal intercourse, with ejaculation

of semen within the natural female organ" on November 27, 1893, after which "there remained a period of 10 years, 5 months and 18 days during which carnal intercourse had been incomplete, without ejaculation of semen within the natural female organ" (U17.2278-84). Thus, Bloom is hampered not only by the actual memory of his son's death, but also by the insecurities and anxieties that this memory has produced in him over time.

Stephen and Bloom both find themselves in mourning on June 16, 1904, and their sartorial similarity demonstrates more obviously than anything else the similarity of their situations. Mourning is, after all, a ritualized, public form of memory, a way that we demonstrate our grief and, we hope, help ourselves to work through and beyond it. We learn quickly in the first episode of *Ulysses* that Stephen wears only black in strict observance of the mourning ritual for his mother, the anniversary of whose burial will be June 26, 1904 (U17.951-53). As Mulligan puts it, articulating the guilt that he helps to keep alive in Stephen's heart, Stephen "kills his mother but he can't wear grey trousers" (U1.122).[22] Coincidentally, but appropriately, Bloom also wears black in *Ulysses* (4.79). Bloom has put on mourning clothes to attend Paddy Dignam's funeral, but his suit ties him to Stephen symbolically, for both characters have been unable to cease mourning their dead loved ones.

Sigmund Freud's writings on mourning as a type of memory echo the kinds of psychic processes that cause and maintain this situation in *Ulysses*. In his essay "Mourning and Melancholia," Freud views mourning as a "normal" process, "a reaction to the real loss of a loved object" (14:250). For Freud, mourning is a regenerative or healing ritual in which the bereaved person learns to "detach the libido" once invested in a loved one who is now absent. The mourner goes through a period of detachment from the outside world—that which is not associated with the loved one—but learns to adjust to loss over time, until "the work of mourning is completed" and "the ego becomes free and uninhibited again" (14:245).

Freud notes, however, that mourning does not always work itself out so clearly and simply—that sometimes, in fact, it fails to work out at all. According to Freud, normal mourning can become "blocked" and lead to a paralyzing and stagnant melancholy, a refusal or inability to complete the process of detachment from the lost object, especially in

> those cases in which the patients have not reacted to a psychical trauma because the nature of the trauma excluded a reaction, as in the case of the apparently irreparable loss of a loved person or be-

cause social circumstances made a reaction impossible or because it was a question of things which the patient wished to forget, and therefore intentionally repressed from his conscious thought and inhibited and suppressed. (2:9-10)

In Freud's general scheme of repression and psychic health, affective material that would normally be discharged through the process of mourning is retained and repressed in the melancholic patient. A mnemic abscess develops in the psyche of the mourner, partly because the melancholic mourner does not "see clearly what it is that has been lost" (14:245) and partly because mourning in these cases is complicated by an inability to mourn.

Freud's ideas on mourning help to elucidate the characters' situations in *Ulysses*, for neither Stephen nor Bloom, for a number of reasons, has been able to come fully to terms with the deaths in their pasts. For both men, in Freud's terms, "traumatic experiences in connection with the [lost] object may have activated other repressed material" (14:257). The death of May Dedalus is connected in Stephen's mind with his continued rejection of Catholicism, which in turn is necessarily accompanied by earlier unpleasant memories. Stephen's deep-rooted conflict with authority has thus become interwoven with his feelings about his mother's death. Bloom has not fully mourned Rudy either, partly because Rudy's death has "activated other repressed material," namely, doubts about his own sexuality and virility. This repressed material festers in the memory and poisons the psyche. Or, as Freud puts it, "The complex of melancholia behaves like an open wound drawing to itself cathectic energies . . . from all directions" (14:253).

It is no coincidence, then, that the most important subtext or literary analogue to *Ulysses* after the *Odyssey* is *Hamlet*. While many observers focus on *Hamlet* because it echoes the theme of paternity in *Ulysses*, the play also exemplifies the problem of mourning, for *Hamlet* is not only a play about revenge for the death of a father, but is also, as Jacques Lacan claims, "a tragedy of the underworld," a play concerned with "insufficient mourning" (39). Hamlet is angry even before he understands that his father has been murdered, for while he insists on wearing his "inky cloak" (1.2.77), his mother and Claudius have dishonored his father's memory by their "o'erhasty" marriage (2.2.57). *Hamlet* is a play about memory, specifically about remembering the dead. Although Hamlet asks himself, "Heaven and earth,/Must I remember?" (1.2.142-43), the ghost enjoins him to "Remember me" (1.5.92). Hamlet responds:

> ... Remember thee!
> Ay, thou poor ghost, whiles memory holds a seat
> In this distracted globe. Remember thee!
> Yea, from the table of my memory
> I'll wipe away all trivial fond records,
> All saws of books, all forms, all pressures past
> That youth and observation copied there,
> And thy commandment all alone shall live
> Within the book and volume of my brain,
> Unmix'd with baser matter. (1.5.96–105)

The presence of *Hamlet* in *Ulysses* adumbrates the theme of a repressed affect or ambivalence that blocks mourning. The play poses not only the question of how Hamlet will avenge his father's murder, but of how he will properly resolve his mourning and brooding on his father's ghost, all the while attempting to keep his father's memory from mixing "with baser matter." Lacan claims that "from one end of *Hamlet* to the other, all anyone talks about is mourning" (39), and acts of mourning are indeed central to the play. As Lacan notes, "in all the instances of mourning in *Hamlet*, one element is always present: the rites have been cut short and performed in secret" (40).

Like Hamlet, Stephen and Bloom are obsessed and paralyzed by their unresolved feelings surrounding the deaths of loved relatives. Like Shakespeare's hero, Stephen and Bloom must decide to act in order to reconcile themselves with the past, and yet they are unable to do that which will put to rest the ghosts of the past. A passage from one of Freud's early lectures—"The Mechanism of Hysterical Phenomena"—may best articulate the process we as readers come to expect in *Hamlet* and *Ulysses*:

> The fading of a memory or the losing of its affect depends on various factors. The most important of these is *whether there has been an energetic reaction to the event that provokes an affect*. By "reaction" we here understand the whole class of voluntary and involuntary reflexes—from tears to acts of revenge—in which, as experience shows us, the affects are discharged. If this reaction takes place to a sufficient amount a large part of the affect disappears as a result.... If the reaction is suppressed, the affect remains attached to the memory. (2:8; original emphasis)

Stephen and Bloom, like Hamlet, must find appropriate ways to end their mourning, to "no more turn aside and brood," in order to rid themselves of the problems these traumatic memories have created in their lives. Like Ulysses, they must journey to Hades to confront the dead, but, again like Ulysses, they may require a visit to the enchantress Circe before they can find what they seek and resume their journey home.

2   The Past as Obstruction

'That corpse you planted last year in your garden,
Has it begun to sprout? Will it bloom this year?
Or has the sudden frost disturbed its bed?
Oh keep the Dog far hence, that's friend to men,
Or with his nails he'll dig it up again!'
—T. S. Eliot, *The Waste Land*

"our hysterical patients suffer from reminiscences."
—Freud, "Five Lectures on Psycho-Analysis"

Responding to Mr. Deasy's thumbnail history of the Jews in the "Nestor" episode of *Ulysses*, Stephen answers enigmatically: "'History . . . is a nightmare from which I am trying to awake'" (*U*2.377). Although Stephen may be simply and diplomatically evading the anti-Semitism of Mr. Deasy's version of history, this statement, like many which Stephen and Bloom make during the "day" that is *Ulysses*, takes on added, unconscious connotations. Stephen and Bloom need to confront and somehow come to terms with the disturbing collections of guilt, fear, and doubt that have come to dominate their histories of themselves, but how does one awaken from one's own history, from one's own self?

If we adopt a Lockean or passivist model of mind, we might expect that each person, each character, could simply retrace their paths back into the past—along the "line" of sequential, discrete sensations or experiences that make up the self—to sort out the confusion that has occurred, to re-collect or re-member what happened. We find in *Ulysses*, however, that recollection is not always a simple or reliable process. To revert to our Odyssean metaphor, if Locke is correct, the return to Ithaca—the return through memory to a definite locus of well-being and stability—should be a straightforward retracing of experience, a recollection of instants and images from the mental storehouse that constitutes our memory of the past. However, for Joyce the past is a much more complex landscape, largely unmappable and uncertain. Though Bloom and Stephen need somehow to confront the past, to find and, if possible, untangle the anxieties and doubts knotted around the traumatic deaths of May Goulding Dedalus and Rudy Bloom, they, like Odysseus, may have difficulty returning the way they came and may require more than their own cunning to reach their goal, if they are to reach it at all.

From a Bergsonian perspective, the fundamental difference between the voyage of Ulysses and the individual's attempts to retrieve, order, and interpret the past is that Ulysses' return, or *nostos*, occurs in space: the paths taken may be uncharted, yet the destination is fixed. Ulysses knows Ithaca is there. On the other hand, the voluntary, hermeneutic attempt to recollect and decipher the past is a journey back through *time*. Though we proceed moment-by-moment through time and experience in a seemingly straightforward manner, if we attempt to go back into the past "the way we came" in order to retrieve an exact replica of an experience or to reestablish a wholeness or sense of integrity that we feel we have left behind, we may find ourselves, like Ulysses, delayed, detoured, and sometimes deceived. Like Ulysses' sailors, we may be tempted to eat the lotus and rest secure in false images of peace and well-being. What seems clear to the reader of *Ulysses*, however, is that the conscious, voluntary use of memory is insufficient to rescue and revive the past. Or, as the narrator of the "Oxen of the Sun" episode puts it, "as no man knows the ubicity of his tumulus nor to what processes we shall thereby be ushered nor whether to Tophet or to Edenville in the like way is all hidden when we would backward see from what region of remoteness the whatness of our whoness hath fetched his whenceness" (U14.396–400).

As we will see, in Joyce's writings from "The Sisters" to *Ulysses* the assumptions behind a passivist or hermeneutic view of memory—that the past is a storehouse of images readily available to the probing mind and that the proper untangling and understanding of the past can lead to a simple resolution—are undercut and thwarted by the obscurity of the past and the blocking powers of repression, habit, and nostalgia. The search for lost time seems destined to fail in Joyce's Dublin, but the past remains nonetheless very much alive.

In the climactic "Circe" episode of *Ulysses*, Leopold Bloom encounters the apparition of his grandfather, Lipoti Virag, who advises him, "Exercise your mnemotechnic. *La causa è santa.* Tara. Tara. (*aside*) He will surely remember" (U15.2383–86). We will find that exercising mnemotechnic in *Ulysses*—using memory to reenter and repair the past—is no simple task, and that Virag's advice is much more complex than it first appears. The deliberate, voluntary search through the past for the sources of trauma constitutes one part of the "odyssey" of memory in *Ulysses*. I will call this feature "hermeneutic memory": the characters' abilities to discover, unravel, interpret, and clarify the traumas in the pasts of Stephen Dedalus and Leopold Bloom that paralyze them in the present of June 16, 1904. Hermeneutic memory in *Ulysses* is an attempt to search back through the past, or, more accurately, through *memories* of the past to unravel the puzzle that is the present, to attempt to return to some state of psychic wholeness or health symbolically analogous to the reinstatement of Odysseus at the end of the *Odyssey*.

This search for present "cure" and future "health" through the landscape of the past should sound familiar to us, for it is essentially the project of psychoanalysis: the search for psychic equilibrium or wholeness that can occur only by confronting and deciphering moments of original trauma, or primal scenes. Just as the mythic Ulysses set out from Troy presumably expecting to journey home as quickly and directly as possible only to find himself everywhere blocked and delayed, so we post-Freudians find the search for a psychic "Ithaca" a tricky and often frustrating path, full of blockages and delays, to the extent that some psychoanalysts have dispensed with the idea of the "cure"—the psychoanalytic Ithaca—altogether. In *Ulysses*, then, Joyce constructs a set of problems that his characters must work through, and yet their conscious attempts to do so seem inadequate. The text of the novel itself, however, develops and provides an *unconscious* textual memory or textual unconscious, suggesting in its workings the same sorts of unconscious, teleological drives we have earlier identified with entelechy. This textual entelechy relies upon elements of the cultural unconscious of *Ulysses* to suggest and work toward the resolution of these paralyzing memories. In this sense, Joyce's text operates in a fashion similar, in some ways, to the operation of Freud's notion of the unconscious—using memory and repetition as a way to work through painful problems—yet Joyce's mnemotechnic requires no involvement on the part of any conscious agent in the text corresponding to Freud's psychotherapist (unless we think of either the author or the reader as this agent), depending instead on a textual force or instinct that works constantly to recollect and repeat repressed elements from the characters' pasts.

The Freudian psychoanalytic paradigm of memory is probably the most familiar and complete modern model for the understanding of memory, and it clearly formed part of the climate of opinion during Joyce's lifetime as well as our own. Yet, if we observe the changes that occurred in Freud's notions of our ability to discover the past, we can begin to see some of the problems associated with this reliance on hermeneutic memory. A brief investigation of the development of Freud's thinking on memory and repression will provide a lexicon and paradigm for exploring the workings of memory within the textual unconscious of *Ulysses*. No one has done more to problematize and articulate the connections between narrative and psyche than Joyce's Viennese contemporary, and Freud's thoughts on narrative provide a useful framework for discussing memory, narrative, and models of mind in *Ulysses*.

Freud begins his 1914 essay, "Remembering, Repeating and Working-Through," with a history of "the far-reaching changes which psychoanalytic technique has undergone since its first beginnings" (14:147). He relates the complications encountered by the psychoanalytic movement in its attempts to discover and control the causes of psychic illness brought about by repressed memories in order to cure neuroses and allow people to get on with their lives. Freud outlines three phases of this history, beginning with "Breuer's catharsis," which "consisted in bringing directly into focus the moment at which the symptom was formed. . . . Remembering and abreacting, with the help of the hypnotic state, were what was at that time aimed at." In the second phase, "when hypnosis had been given up, the task became one of discovering from the patient's free associations what he failed to remember," still with the intent of finding the "situations which had given rise to the formation of the symptom," but with less confidence in effecting an abreaction and more emphasis on "the expenditure of work which the patient had to make" in overcoming his or her resistance to the therapy. "Finally," Freud says, "there evolved the consistent technique used today, in which the analyst gives up the attempt to bring a particular moment or problem into focus." The analyst's role now becomes "studying whatever is present for the time being on the surface of the patient's mind" and "recognizing the resistances which appear there, and making them conscious to the patient." Freud ends rather complacently: "From this there results a new sort of division of labour: the doctor uncovers the resistances which are unknown to the patient; when these have been got the better of, the patient often relates the forgotten situations and connections *without any difficulty*" (14:147; emphasis added). Though Freud ends his history on a note of confidence, as if it reflects a progressive evolution toward more effective techniques and more certain cures, the reader may see instead a progressive loss of confidence in discovering the actual, indentifiable roots of neuroses and in effecting a definite, dramatic abreaction or cure. The final "without any difficulty" seems too easily achieved, given this progressive lessening of expectations.

From its inception, Freudian psychoanalysis included the assumption that the patient alone cannot rediscover the traumas of the past, that the analyst's aid and expertise are required for full knowledge or recollection of past traumas. Various psychoanalytic processes—hypnosis, association, etc.—were also needed to break through the psychic defense mechanisms of repression and resistance. In his 1896 essay "The Aetiology of Hysteria," Freud outlined a seemingly straightforward paradigm, beginning with

> Josef Breuer's momentous discovery: *the symptoms of hysteria . . . are determined by certain experiences of the patient's which have operated in a traumatic fashion and which are being reproduced in his psychical life in the form of mnemic symbols.* What we have to do is to apply Breuer's method—or one which is essentially the same—so as to lead the patient's attention back from his symptom to the scene in which and through which that symptom arose; and, having thus located the scene, we remove the symptom by bringing about, during the reproduction of the traumatic scene, a subsequent correction of the psychical course of events which took place at the time. (3:192–93 original emphasis)

At the time that Freud wrote "Remembering, Repeating and Working-Through," he still seemed confident that such psychic defenses could be dissolved—"the patient often relates the forgotten situations and connections without any difficulty"—but the process of lessening confidence outlined above continued, and Freud began more and more to abandon the notion of finding "the forgotten situations" themselves and to focus instead on narrative as a way of explaining the past. As Freud constructed his case histories of the Rat Man, the Wolf Man, and others during the same period that Joyce was writing *Ulysses*, he began to admit the unverifiability of the "primal scenes" he had constructed for his patients, the early, forgotten traumatic scenes in which their neuroses originated.

In *Primal Scenes: Literature, Philosophy, Psychoanalysis*, Ned Lukacher claims that the failure of analyst and patient to arrive at a point of true recollection makes the Wolf Man case "at the most fundamental level a paradigm of the fate of analysis" (29). "In the case history of the Rat-Man," Lukacher notes,

> Freud writes that the narrative construction through which an individual creates its identity involves "a complicated process of remodelling analogous in every way to the process by which a nation

constructs legends about its early history." Freud's effort as an analyst is to construct the subtext behind these legends and, in so doing, to bring the patient to recollect these originary scenes. But by the time he gives such constructions the name "primal scenes" (*Urszenen*), in the Wolf-Man case history (1918), he is forced to admit that they cannot be reproduced as recollection. (19)

Freud's version of psychoanalysis thus moves from a model of hermeneutic confidence (the past, the primal scene, may be hidden but is nonetheless *there* to be found and cured) to a narrative model (whether we know what really happened or not, by transforming our *story* of the past we can correct or ameliorate our present state). Freud ended his case history of the Wolf Man ("From the History of an Infantile Neurosis") with a chapter entitled "Recapitulations and Problems," which he begins by conceding that "I do not know if the reader of this report . . . will have succeeded in forming a clear picture of the origin and development of the patient's illness. I fear that, on the contrary, this will not have been the case" (17:104). He goes on to plead as a mitigating circumstance the difficulty of delving into the early history of a child's mind, concluding, "We must be content, therefore, with having clearly recognized the obscurity" (17:104–5). By 1937, in "Constructions in Analysis," Freud had come to admit that the task of the analyst is "to make out what has been forgotten from the traces which it has left behind or, more correctly, to *construct* it" (23:258–59; original emphasis). According to Peter Brooks:

> Freud writes further that the path starting from the analyst's construction ought to lead to the patient's recollection but does not always succeed in doing so. Instead of recollection of the repressed, the analysis may produce in the analysand something else: "an assured conviction of the truth of the construction which achieves the same therapeutic result as a recaptured memory." (Brooks 322; Freud 23:266)

As Lukacher points out, this transition from scientific hermeneutic to narrative hermeneutic "reveals the utopian nature of the psychoanalytic project," since "Freud insists that analysis must be conducted on this ontologically undecidable ground, and that the therapeutic results thus obtained are entirely valid" (19–20).

Freud, then, seems to have concluded that the past is "writable," or at least as writable as it is readable. Constructing a viable, healthy narrative of the past thus becomes a goal of the later Freud's researches into the personal past. In other words, if the patient is able, with the help of the analyst, to construct and believe the proper story about his or her past, the patient will presumably be able to go on to complete the story, to control the rest of their life history more fully and happily.

Of course, the point is not that what happened is no longer there, or that we can never reliably retrieve important information or determine, to some extent, whether a past occurrence was fact or fiction. While we can have access to some of the past at will (especially that which is useful or that which is habitually imprinted; for example, a telephone number), much of the past—especially complex, difficult, or deeply affective experiences—is available only through interpretation; by attempting to bring it "to light," we inevitably change it, since its contexts—many of which we can no longer be aware of—are no longer present. As Freud says in "The Aetiology of Hysteria" of the complexity of chains of association that lead back into memory,

> we must not fail to lay special emphasis on one conclusion to which analytic work along these chains of memory has unexpectedly led. We have learned that *no hysterical symptom can arise from a real experience alone, but that in every case the memory of earlier experiences awakened in association to it plays a part in causing the symptom.* . . . there exists a chain of operative memories which stretches far back behind the first traumatic scene. . . . (3:97; original emphasis)

For Freud, then—especially after 1918 and the Wolf Man case report—memory is a form of *reading* the past rather than a reliable retrieval of data. Freud's views on memory can be said to move from an early passivist model to a later, activist paradigm.

The Freudian model of hermeneutic memory serves us well as a model for what the narrative desire or goal of *Ulysses* might be and as a warning of how difficult it may be to reach that goal. If we expect that by the end of the novel Stephen and Bloom will have worked together to remember, repeat, and work through the problems in their past lives that block them in the present, if we expect that they will arrive at an Ithaca of psychic health and equilibrium, we will find, as Freud did, that the process of untangling the past, of curing the present by curing the past, is more difficult than it first seems.

Even in Joyce's earliest prose the past is a complex and subtle text that can be read only with difficulty and rarely with any certainty. Nowhere in Joyce's writings is the difficulty of accurately and correctly assessing the past more evident than in the first story of *Dubliners*, "The Sisters." The narrator remembers his reactions to the death of his closest childhood friend, an aged priest, paralyzed and strangely "gnomic" (in the sense of being puzzling and incomplete, like the geometrical *gnomon* that fascinates the boy). The boy struggles to understand the priest's nature and the nature of their relationship, but he is finally unable to find his way out of the labyrinth of memory. His own memories and fantasies, the disturbing hints that he hears about the priest, the old women's story of the broken chalice—none of these adds up to a coherent picture or a clear construction of the past that might prove useful to the boy, but rather they form a riddle, a puzzle, at most the tangled elements of a story that still begs for narrative reconstruction. The epistemological confusion the reader finds in the story is inscribed in the inscrutable title, which simultaneously begs for and frustrates interpretation.[1]

The difficulty the boy in "The Sisters" has in understanding his immediate past, in constructing a viable narrative to explain his troubling memories of the priest, provides a clear introduction—in the first story that Joyce published—of the "tenebrosity of the interior" (*U*14.380) that is memory in Joyce's works. As Joseph Buttigieg writes, "It is hard to imagine how any careful reader of Joyce could possibly entertain the idea that what is past and gone is fixed" (30). Understanding and controlling the past is no simple matter for Joyce's characters, or, to be more exact, when one's relationship with the past becomes simple or simplistic, one is both misguided and in grave danger.

The tenebrosity of memory that we find in Joyce's works is supplemented or complicated by other factors—patterns of behavior and ways of seeing the past that make voluntary, hermeneutic memory even more difficult. Although both Stephen and Bloom are paralyzed in the present by memories of the past, neither seems willing to take matters in hand and to face the specters that plague him. Once again, Freud's writings provide the most pervasive or influential contemporary attempt to explain the mechanisms of psychic repression and resistance, explanations that Joyce certainly would have been familiar with, perhaps through his reading of Freud's *The Psychopathology of Everyday Life*, published in 1917 (Gillespie, *Trieste* 101).

Freud used the term repression to label the initial tendency to force "pathogenic experiences . . . out of consciousness" (11:24), while he employed resistance to describe all subsequent efforts to suppress the emergence of recollections and associations related to these experiences. The Freudian unconscious preserves repressed memories and continues to manifest and repeat repressed material through the workings (or misworkings) of memory in everyday life. In *The Psychopathology of Everyday Life*, Freud explains the phenomenon of parapraxes—incidental, unconscious misrememberings in which either words or phrases related to unpleasant subconscious content unexpectedly take the place of innocent words (the Freudian slip) or, vice versa, in which one fails to remember words and phrases associated with unpleasantness:

> Here for the first time, in this reason for objecting to remembering a name, we come across a principle which will later on reveal its enormous importance for the causation of neurotic symptoms: the memory's disinclination to remembering anything which is connected with feelings of unpleasure and the reproduction of which would renew the unpleasure. This intention to avoid unpleasure arising from a recollection or from other psychical acts, this psychical flight from unpleasure, may be recognized as the ultimate operative motive not only for the forgetting of names but for many other parapraxes, such as omissions, errors, and so on. (15:74–75)

Joyce clearly makes use of parapraxis in *Ulysses* to show how the characters avoid unpleasant memories. Bloom's inability to remember the name "Penrose" in the "Lestrygonians" episode seems to reflect a psychic process similar to what Freud describes here. Thinking of happier days with Molly before Rudy was born, Bloom pauses and wonders, "What was the name of that priestylooking chap was always squinting in when he passed? Weak eyes, woman. . . . Pen something. Pendennis? My memory is getting. Pen . . . ? Of course it's years ago. Noise of the trams probably" (U8.176–9). Although Bloom remembers later in the episode when he sees a blind man with a "Bloodless pious face like a fellow going in to be a priest" and thinks, "Penrose! That was that chap's name" (U8.1112–14), there may be a reason for his initial amnesia. Penrose comes up four more times in the course of the novel: once when the apparition of Lipoti Virag says of Zoe's mention of a disguised priest at the brothel, "Fall of man. . . . Penrose" (U15.2545–48); once in a list of phantasmagorical pursuers as Bloom follows Stephen (U15.4357); once as one in a "series" of lovers that Bloom imagines Molly has had (U17.2133); and, finally, in Molly Bloom's recollection of the voyeur Penrose, who "nearly caught me washing through the window" (U18.572–73). Bloom may have difficulty consciously remembering Penrose because, in Bloom's imagination, Penrose represents a sexual threat. Penrose may threaten in another way as well, however. Just as M'Coy's earlier seemingly innocent question, "Who's getting it up?" (U5.153)—referring to the concert that Boylan and Molly are arranging in Belfast—becomes a motif that reawakens Bloom's anxieties about Molly and about his sexual potency later in the novel, it may be that the name "Penrose" calls up associations of "Penis rose"—that is, the idea of erection—for Bloom. Suggestively, Bloom's parapraxis for Penrose is Pendennis, the name of a character in William Makepeace Thackeray's *The History of Pendennis*, who, as Don Gifford and Robert J. Seidman note, "nearly ruins himself in imprudent love affairs before he gets straightened out" (161–62). Joyce here neatly mixes contrasting images of sexual potency (Penrose, a possible suitor of Molly's) and impotency (Pendennis, "weak eyes, woman") through the agency of Bloom's "defective mnemotechnic" (U17.766). Bloom's attempt to remember a seemingly insignificant detail reveals more about Bloom than he himself is aware of and demonstrates the way that repressed material persists in the unconscious and insists on forcing itself into consciousness.

Bloom is prone to avoid all his problems, including unpleasant memories of the past. When Bloom becomes upset remembering his father's suicide in the "Lotus-Eaters" episode, he quickly decides, "No use thinking of it anymore. Nosebag time" (U5.211). "Nosebag time" is one of the quick turns that characterize the stream of consciousness technique Joyce employs, but it also characterizes Bloom's habitual shifting away from unpleasant thoughts. As usual, however, a shift in thought can tell us something about Bloom's motives, about emotions he himself may not realize. "Nosebag time," for example, is a reference to the dilapidated nags that Bloom sees eating their oats in the street, yet it also ironically links him with the horses, for in his avoidance of unpleasantness he resembles them: "Damn all they know or care about anything with their long noses stuck in nosebags. Too full for words. . . . Gelded too: a stump of black guttapercha wagging limp between their haunches. Might be happy all the same that way" (U5.215–19). Like the horses, with their noses "stuck" in their feedbags, Bloom is stuck in mental patterns that prevent him from confronting problems he needs to face. This passage—appropriately from the "Lotus-Eaters" episode—reveals not only Bloom's habitual avoidance of disturbing problems, but, more specifically, his recurrent desire to somehow opt out of sexuality, to find instead the deadly stasis or paralysis of the lotus eater; accordingly, his contemplation of castration borders on admiration.

Oppressive, frightening thoughts of the past (of Rudy, of Bloom's father) and of the present (Milly's sexuality and Molly's impending meeting with Blazes Boylan) press themselves forward relentlessly into Bloom's consciousness throughout the day. Bloom tries to escape them, but the problems of the past and the present follow him inevitably. The "Lestrygonians" episode provides apt examples of the ways through which Bloom tries and fails to escape from these troubling thoughts, which, like the cannibal Lestrygonians of the *Odyssey*, threaten to eat up our Ulysses with anxiety. The theme of escape runs through this episode; Odysseus' cunning enables him to escape the Lestrygonians, while Bloom "escapes" an encounter with Blazes Boylan at the end of the episode. For the most part, Bloom manages to evade and escape his anxious thoughts and memories in this episode, yet we must remember that Homer's Odysseus escapes from the Lestrygonians only to sail directly to the isle of Circe and further trials. For Bloom, escape becomes escapism, and, like Odysseus, our Ulysses must eventually face his Circe.

Stephen's reaction to his memories is a mixture of brooding, despair, and repression. Early in the day, as he teaches a class of young boys in Dalkey, he begins thinking of riddles—first, Christ's answer to the Pharisees ("To Caesar what is Caesar's, to God what is God's"—*U*2.86), and then a riddle about writing:

> *Riddle me, riddle me, randy ro.*
> *My father gave me seeds to sow.* (*U*2.88–89)

As Weldon Thornton points out in his *Allusions in "Ulysses,"* "Stephen simply suppresses the final lines of this riddle, as he suppresses parts of other things he alludes to . . . . Probably he does so here because the riddle and its solution remind him of his failure to justify himself as an author" (30). The suppression that Thornton speaks of here is a characteristic of Stephen's way of thinking; although he obsessively returns to thoughts of his past—especially of his mother—he compulsively avoids and represses thoughts, words, and images that surface to remind him of that which is unpleasant in the past.[2] As in "The Sisters," we get the sense that these riddles and puzzles serve not to clarify but to confuse or obscure; they function as linguistic gnomons in which the missing element has been deliberately suppressed. Stephen follows these two riddles with a third. Asked by his students for a "ghoststory," he responds with a riddle that goes nowhere:

> *The cock crew*
> *The sky was blue:*
> *The bells in heaven*
> *Were striking eleven.*
> *'Tis time for this poor soul*
> *To go to heaven.* (*U*2.102–7)

The answer traditionally given for this nonsense riddle is, "The fox burying his mother under a holly tree" (Thornton 30), yet when Stephen, "his throat itching," answers it for his puzzled students, he changes it to "The fox burying his grandmother under a hollybush" (U2.115), narrowly deflecting the memory of his mother's death embedded in the riddle. Although the past may seem an unanswerable riddle to Stephen, we will see that this seemingly meaningless puzzle becomes in *Ulysses* "a riddling sentence to be woven and woven" (U2.87) throughout the text, for bits and pieces of it pop into his mind throughout the day, gathering associations of guilt and building up symbolic potency until the words of this riddle become intricately involved in evoking the cataclysmic visions of the "Circe" episode. Thus, while Stephen's riddle seems nonsensical and can be read as a "symptom" of the insolubility of his emotional state regarding his mother's death,[3] it comes to have much more meaning than he can realize consciously. Similarly, where the conscious process of hermeneutic investigation fails to find an answer to the riddles of experience and the riddles of the past, the answer may come of its own accord.

Stephen's attempts to avoid and repress thoughts of the dead are futile, for as Bloom says later of Paddy Dignam, "Going to crop up all day, I foresee.... Turn up like a bad penny"\(U8.215–16). Images of burial and exhumation abound in *Ulysses*, surfacing frequently in the thoughts of both Stephen and Bloom, serving well as metaphors for the repression of unpleasant or disturbing memories and for the inevitable way that these memories return over and over again to consciousness. Again, Freud provides an interesting contemporary supplement to Joyce in his development of similar metaphors for the workings of repression. For example, Freud took great interest in the excavation of Pompeii and found in archaeological excavation a metaphor for the psychoanalytic recovery of the past: "There is, in fact, no better analogy for repression, by which something in the mind is at once made inaccessible and preserved, than burial of the sort to which Pompeii fell a victim and from which it could emerge once more through the work of spades" (9:40). It is especially interesting that Freud emphasizes the special preservation that burial allows. He repeated this point, again with reference to Pompeii, in the Rat Man case, describing how he explained matters to his patient:

> I then made some short observations upon *the psychological differences between the conscious and the unconscious,* and upon the fact that everything conscious was subject to a process of wearing-away, while what was unconscious was relatively unchangeable; and I illustrated my remarks by pointing to the antiques standing about in my room. They were, in fact, I said, only objects found in a tomb, and their burial had been their preservation: the destruction of Pom-

peii was only beginning now that it had been dug up. (10:176; original emphasis)

In the "Hades" episode, Bloom worries about Paddy Dignam's corpse falling out of its coffin with its mouth open: "Much better to close up all the orifices. Yes, also. With wax. The sphincter loose. Seal up all" (U6.425-26). Later, thinking of the normal privacy of the coffin, he unintentionally and unconsciously "buries" his and Stephen's central repressed problems when he thinks: "Only a mother and deadborn child ever buried in the one coffin" (U6.819-20).

Stephen's dead mother and Bloom's dead child are buried in memory, shoved "underground" into the unconscious and sealed up—or so Bloom and Stephen would like to think. As Freud observed, however, that which is buried may simply be better preserved. In *Ulysses*, it seems that what goes down must come up, and what is sealed up and forced under will fester until it erupts into consciousness again, like the drowned man Stephen thinks about in the "Proteus" episode, who rises "saltwhite from the undertow" (U3.472-73), refusing to stay in "his green grave" (U3.481). Similarly, in the "Wandering Rocks" episode, Stephen considers "leprous and winedark" jewels "Born all in the dark wormy earth, cold specks of fire, evil, lights shining in the darkness.... Muddy swinesnouts, hands, root and root, gripe and wrest them" (U10.804-7). Stephen thinks of himself as one who wishes to "wrest old images from the burial earth" (U10.815), referring presumably to his desire to be an artist, but his phrase has as much relevance to his own personal, psychological needs as it does to his artistic vocation. In *Ulysses*, that which is repressed, valuable, dark, powerful, or evil will find its way back into men's hands and minds again.

Ulysses is full of fossorial animals—animals that bury or dig up the dead—and animals that gnaw the dead, again reminding us (and Bloom and Stephen) that the dead will not stay peacefully at rest—"Out of sight, out of mind"—as Bloom hopes in "Hades" (U6.872). In "Proteus," for example, Stephen watches a dog digging in the sand and is reminded of the fox of his riddle: "His hindpaws then scattered the sand: then his forepaws dabbled and delved. Something he buried there, his grandmother. He rooted in the sand, dabbling, delving and stopped to listen to the air, scraped up the sand again with a fury of his claws, soon ceasing, a pard, a panther, got in spousebreach, vulturing the dead" (U3.359-64). Similarly, in the "Hades" episode, Bloom thinks of coffins "All gnawed through" (U6.816) and of necrophiliacs "scraping up the earth at night with a lantern ... to get at fresh buried females .... Give you the creeps after a bit. I will appear to you after death. You will see my ghost after death. My ghost will haunt you after death. There is another world after death named hell" (U6.998–1002).

Appropriately, a number of these images of exhumation involve Paddy Dignam, who is buried in the "Hades" episode but reappears in one form or another in Bloom's thoughts throughout the day. At the end of "Hades," Bloom sees "An obese grey rat" (U6.973) who "would make short work of a fellow" (U6.980), and he thinks "Got wind of Dignam" (U6.993). Bloom remembers the "old grey rat tearing to get in" to Dignam's grave (U7.83) on at least three occasions after he first sees him in the graveyard,[4] but for all his activity, the rat cannot consume Dignam fast enough to keep him from reappearing to Bloom in the "Circe" episode, where a beagle trailing Bloom reveals himself as Dignam, who "has gnawed all. He exhales a putrid carcasefed breath. . . . Half of one ear, all the nose and both thumbs are ghouleaten" (U15.1204–8). When Dignam leaves Bloom and "worms down through a coalhole," we see "an obese grandfather rat on fungus turtle paws" toddling after him (U15.1255–57).

Though Bloom and Stephen return obsessively to the idea that the dead decay, dissolve, and fade away, the dead refuse to do so and remain—"ghouleaten"—to embody the memories that keep them alive in the minds of the living, as W. B. Yeats implies in "Under Ben Bulben,"

> Though grave-diggers' toil is long,
> Sharp their spades, their muscles strong,
> They but thrust their buried men
> Back in the human mind again. (325)

In Joyce's writings, this persistence of the dead—as in the powerful memory that Gretta Conroy has of Michael Furey in "The Dead"—is most often a form of what Stephen calls "Agenbite of inwit: remorse of conscience" (U9.809–10), an appropriate phrase for the gnawing-back of memory blocked by repression and resistance, the "again-biting" into the past that characterizes the psyche agonized by memories.

References to ghosts and other apparitions of the dead return us to a consideration of the relationship between *Hamlet* and *Ulysses*. Like Stephen and Bloom, young Hamlet has visions of the dead; despite his doubt and uncertainty, he cannot repress or avoid his father's command to remember and to revenge, for the ghost's visitations drive him on. Similarly, Bloom and Stephen cannot fully avoid and repress the past, for the spirits that plague them have their own mnemic authority and will not rest until mourning is complete, until the guilt and fear clustered around the memories of their deaths have been dissipated or dispelled.

The "Scylla and Charybdis" episode of *Ulysses* is more obsessed than any other with *Hamlet*, and thus, when we listen to Stephen's clever arguments for the continuity of personal identity ("the mole on my right breast is where it was when I was born") despite physical change ("molecules shuttled to and fro"), we may hear echoes of Shakespeare's play, for in *Hamlet* the word "mole" takes on a complex multivalence. Ironically, though "mole" is part of "molecule," the two represent opposing extremes of reality, for while Stephen's molecules change, his mole does not. For Prince Hamlet, however, a mole can be an undesirably constant presence, a flaw that determines the limits of one's life:

> So, oft it chances in particular men,
> That for some vicious mole of nature in them,
> As in their birth—wherein they are not guilty,
> Since nature cannot choose his origin—
> By the o'ergrowth of some complexion,
> Oft breaking down the pales and forts of reason,
> Or by some habit that too much o'er-leavens
> The form of plausive manners, that these men,
> Carrying, I say, the stamp of one defect,
> Being nature's livery, or fortune's star,
> Their virtues else, be they as pure as grace,
> As infinite as man may undergo,
> Shall in the general censure take corruption
> From that particular fault. (1.4.23–36)

Hamlet speaks these words immediately before the first apparition of his father's ghost. After he has spoken with his father's spirit and received his admonition to "Remember me" (1.5.92), Hamlet finds a new use for the word, for as his father's spirit speaks to him from under the stage on its way back to purgatory, he replies "Well said, old mole! Canst work i' th' earth so fast?" (1.5.163). The irony of Hamlet's use of "mole" as a description of the Ghost burrowing its way back to purgatory (and back into memory) is that his obsession with the Ghost's injunction has become his "mole," the character trait that will determine all others for him for the remainder of the play.

It is very appropriate, therefore, that Stephen should refer to his "mole" in the midst of his discussing *Hamlet*. For Stephen, as for Hamlet, the memory of the unfinished business of mourning, the ghostly embodiment of guilt, can become a mole that burrows into the subconscious and lives on in torment there, an unchanging mark of unresolved loss. This center of anxiety and remorse becomes in its turn a mole, or flaw, that dominates the rest of the personality. Thus, we can read Stephen's proud use of the mole on his chest as proof of constancy as an unintended irony, for in *Ulysses* we see that this "mole" is less a positive source of identity than a center of pain around which he revolves. In this light, his description of the ghost's obsession with the past takes on a meaning for Shakespeare, Stephen, and Bloom as well: "That is why the speech (his lean unlovely English) is always turned elsewhere, backward.... He goes back, weary of the creation he has piled up to hide him from himself, an old dog licking an old sore" (U9.471–76).

Repression, resistance, and mourning have thus become habitual for Stephen and Bloom, blocking access to the past and preventing any confrontation with the problems that the two must deal with if they are to go on with their lives. In his extempore discussion of *Hamlet*, Stephen says "Dane or Dubliner, sorrow for the dead is the only husband from whom they refuse to be divorced" (U9.1036–38), a claim that applies to Stephen and Bloom as much as it does to Hamlet. Habitual mourning becomes melancholia, and habitual avoidance of problems leads to their metastasis, until, like cancers, they begin to eat away at the present and the future.

Habit is a major problem for Joyce's characters, from *Dubliners* through *Ulysses*, a force that prevents a proper orientation toward both the past and the present. There are many habits in Joyce's Dublin: Gerty MacDowell's father, like many other Dubliners, has "the drink habit" (U13.291), for example, and the ironic relation between the habits worn by Catholic clergy and the religious and ritualistic habits of the faithful would not have been lost on Joyce. Habit becomes in Joyce's works the true *dio boia*, the "hangman god" and "lord of things as they are" (U9.1048–49), for habit is the great enemy of change and the great enforcer of stagnation and paralysis.

As an automatic response to a present situation or stimulus based on past experience, habit is a form of unconscious memory. Bergson considered "habit-memory"—which he also called "motor-memory" and "acquired memory"—one of the two kinds of memory, "of which the one *imagines* and the other (i.e., habit) *repeats*" (*Matter* 93); imaginative memory he labeled pure memory or spontaneous memory. Habits, Bergson writes, "do not represent the past, they merely act it" (*Matter* 92). Habit for Bergson is a product of evolution (this may be what he means by calling it "acquired memory"), a faculty that allows us to function in the body in the world by filtering out and storing—in the form of automatic, mechanical responses—what is useful and applicable to our everyday life. What does not seem immediately useful to the conscious mind is stored in all its intensity deeper in the mind, while that which is assimilated to habit loses its uniqueness and intensity. Bergson claims that "almost the whole of our past is hidden from us because it is inhibited by the necessities of present action" (*Matter* 199). Thus, while what Bergson calls "true memory" or "spontaneous memory" is potentially much more powerful and "faithful" than habitual memory, it is always "fugitive" (e.g., *Matter* 102 and 129).

Habit is essential but dangerous for Bergson, for if it develops unchecked, it can overrule and bind one's conduct: "Our freedom, in the very movements by which it is affirmed, creates the growing habits that will stifle it if it fails to renew itself by a constant effort: it is dogged by automatism" (*Creative Evolution* 141). A. E. Pilkington summarizes Bergson's views on the subject in *Bergson and His Influence*:

> In the *Essai* Bergson describes how the mind often fails to make the total response to a situation which is the guarantee of its freedom. Economy of effort leads the individual to become for much of the time an "automate conscient," who responds mechanically to impressions and sensations, and who abdicates his freedom of action simply because for much of the time a useful saving of effort can thus be made.... In Bergson's thought, the role of habit is unambiguous. It stands opposed to the self as free creative activity and represents a perpetual threat to its autonomy; the automatic is always ready to encroach upon the living and immediately to occupy any ground lost by it.... it becomes an imperative to retain as great a degree of consciousness and freedom of action as possible, and to yield as little ground as possible to the surreptitious advent of merely habitual modes of behaviour. (164–65)

To better understand the operation of memory in Joyce's texts, it is useful to explore the writing of another influential contemporary—Marcel Proust—for *A la recherche du temps perdu*, like Bergson's writings and Freud's, formed part of the "climate of opinion" in which *Ulysses* was written. The valorization of powerful, unconscious, involuntary, or spontaneous memories over conscious or voluntary memory by both Bergson and Proust may well constitute a strong current in the cultural unconscious of Joyce's *Ulysses*, for the distinction between these two forms of memory is certainly implied in Joyce's prose as well. Although most of Proust's major work came later than the works of Bergson and Freud discussed in this chapter, Joyce certainly knew of Proust, had met him, and could easily have perused *Du côté de chez Swann* (*Swann's Way*), published in 1913, by the time that he finished *Ulysses* (the second volume, *A l'ombre des jeunes filles en fleurs*, appeared in 1919). I am not arguing—as did Wyndham Lewis when he identified "the little seed planted by Bergson" as the basis for the "time-book" *Ulysses*—that Joyce "is very strictly of the school of Bergson-Einstein-Stein-Proust" (106), that he was obsessed by Bergsonian or Proustian ideas on time and memory while he was writing *Ulysses*, or that he necessarily thought in terms of Proust's "involuntary memory" or Bergson's "spontaneous memory," but rather that the writings of Bergson and Proust on these subjects embody ideas that were "in the air" at the time Joyce was writing *Ulysses*, and they provide a reasonable and enlightening context and terminology for discussing what Joyce is doing with memory and the past in his writing.[5]

Proust's attitude toward habit is, as Pilkington remarks, "curiously ambiguous" (165). While Proust realized the comforting power of habit's "anaesthetic effect" (1:11), he also felt that "Habit weakens everything" (1:692). "As a rule"—Proust wrote—"it is with our being reduced to a minimum that we live; most of our faculties lie dormant because they can rely on Habit" (1:706). Proust believed that many of the most intense and meaningful moments in life are brought about or allowed to happen through a negation or cessation of habit, and while this disruption of habitual patterns might result in some discomfort or melancholy, the iridescent flash of long-lost memories that can come out of fresh experience brings our consciousness to its highest point:

> Lifting a corner of the heavy curtain of habit (stupefying habit, which during the whole course of our life conceals from us almost the whole universe, and in the dead of night, without changing the label, substitutes for the most dangerous or intoxicating poisons of life something anodyne that procures no delights), such memories would come back to me as at the time itself with that fresh and piercing novelty of a recurring season.... (3:554)

Those who are "blasé par l'habitude," then, cannot capture this freshness, cannot establish this link with what is vital, unless they are able, in Pilkington's words, "to overcome the inertia, the 'vitesse acquise,' and acquired momentum of habit" (165). This Proustian suspicion of habit is sharpened, and perhaps even exaggerated, by Samuel Beckett in his monograph *Proust*, published in 1931. (Beckett's respect for, interest in, and thorough knowledge of Proust's work is especially interesting, considering his close relationship with Joyce, since it suggests that other members of Joyce's circle—and Joyce himself—would likely have been familiar with Proust's writing.)[6] Beckett argues that for Proust,

The laws of memory are subject to the more general laws of habit. Habit is a compromise effected between the individual and his environment, or between the individual and his own organic eccentricities, the guarantee of a dull inviolability, the lightning-conductor of his existence. Habit is the ballast that chains the dog to his vomit. (7–8)

Bergson and Proust both divided memory into two functions or types, and though it would be simplistic to treat Bergson's habit-memory and Proust's voluntary memory or Bergson's spontaneous memory and Proust's involuntary memory as interchangeable, we can generalize enough to say that both writers placed both the superficial memory of habit and conscious recollection in opposition to a more powerful, deeper form of memory that erupts from the subconscious on its own, spontaneously or involuntarily.[7] Proust considered voluntary memory — the conscious attempt to recollect past moments, places, or persons — inferior because it depends on the intellect, which is devoid of the ability to "unlock" the past and because it seeks photographic images rather than the sensations and intuitive reality of lost time. In an interview with Elie-Joseph Bois, Proust claimed:

> For me, voluntary memory, which is above all the memory of the intellect and the eyes, gives us nothing but pictures without truth; but an odor, a taste refound, among totally different circumstances, awakens in us, in spite of ourselves, the past, we feel how much this past was different than that which we believed we remembered, and what our voluntary memory painted, just as bad painters do, with colors without truth. (Quoted in Pilkington, p. 146; my translation)[8]

Similarly, Bergson valued the intensity of spontaneous memory, which though it "is masked by the acquired recollection, may flash out at intervals; but it disappears at the least movement of the voluntary memory" (*Matter* 101).

Thus, both writers view habitual memory and conscious recollection (or voluntary memory) as useful and even necessary for maintaining equilibrium or homeostasis in everyday life, but both of them privilege the more vibrant, explosive, and dangerous (because essentially uncontrollable) involuntary or spontaneous memory, without which, they imply, life would not be worth living.[9] Both view the two types of memory as essentially exclusive of each other. For Bergson, motor-memory or habit-memory inhibits spontaneous memory, which erupts in dreams or other "cases where the sensori-motor equilibrium of the nervous system is disturbed" (*Matter* 98), while for Proust involuntary memory often occurs when the daily, habitual routine is disrupted.[10]

From *Dubliners* through *Ulysses*, Joyce's prose demonstrates a similar privileging of involuntary or spontaneous recollection over habit and voluntary memory. The repressive, paralyzing force of habit is clear in many of the stories in *Dubliners*, but no story in Joyce's collection (except his masterpiece, "The Dead") illustrates the deadening power of habit and the disruptive force of involuntary memory so clearly as "A Painful Case." Patrick Duffy "abhorred anything which betokened physical or mental disorder" (*D* 108); his life centers on the ideals of order, equilibrium, and self-control. In service to these ideals is his daily routine, for Duffy prides himself on restraint, "rectitude," and consistency: "his life rolled out evenly—an adventureless tale" (*D* 109).

In accordance with his desire for equilibrium and homeostasis, Mr. Duffy limits sensual stimulation, as we can see from the description of his bare, unornamented room with which the story opens. Operas and concerts are "the only dissipations of his life," and fittingly it is at the opera that he encounters Mrs. Emily Sinico. Curiously, during this first conversation with Mrs. Sinico, Duffy attempts "to fix her permanently in his memory" (*D* 109), a sign perhaps of his desire to control everything in his life, including his memories. Mrs. Sinico eventually falls between the cracks in Dublin, for she is a warm and vulnerable human being surrounded by what Bergson would call "conscious automata": her husband and daughter are so involved in their own routines that they scarcely know she exists.

The shock and "disillusionment" that Duffy feels when Mrs. Sinico finally touches his hand cause him to "break off their intercourse." He returns "to his even way of life" and the "orderliness of his mind" (*D* 112) until, after four years, he learns by chance that Mrs. Sinico is dead, probably a suicide. Ironically, he tries to explain her sordid death to himself by arguing that she had become "an easy prey to habits," just as the evening paper emphasizes her "habit of crossing the lines late at night" (a subtle insinuation of her addiction to alcohol), her husband explains that she had become "rather intemperate in her habits," and her daughter claims that "her mother had been in the habit of going out at night to buy spirits." Habit has caught up with Mrs. Sinico and, as the paper says, "No blame attached to anyone" (*D* 114–15).

Despite his attempts to maintain control and justify himself ("He had no difficulty now in justifying the course he had taken" [116]), Duffy cannot repress his guilt, and memory begins to take on a life of its own.

Mrs. Sinico, he thinks, "had ceased to exist . . . she had become a memory," and yet, paradoxically, "He began to feel ill at ease" (D 116). Duffy finds that for once he cannot control his thoughts and his memories and realizes that, "His life would be lonely too until he, too, died, ceased to exist, became a memory—if anyone remembered him" (116).

The remorseful, guilty feelings that now begin to haunt him are triggered by his own imagination, in a mode reminiscent of Bergson's "spontaneous memory," which surfaces in moments of reverie when habitual behavior has been disrupted or is in abeyance: "As the light failed and his memory began to wander he thought her hand touched his" (D 116). Appropriately, Duffy's memories come to him in the form of the gesture which first repelled him—the touch of a hand. The remainder of "A Painful Case" is full of sense imagery—touching, feeling, hearing, listening—and the workings of memory, as if Mr. Duffy has been torn open to a new world of sensation: "He felt his moral nature falling to pieces" (D 117). Everything he sees in this mood recalls his dead love, from the lovers lying "in the shadow of the wall of the Park" to the train, "like a worm," which drones "the syllables of her name" (117).

The story ends on a bleak note, for as Mr. Duffy's epiphany fades, he begins "to doubt the reality of what memory told him" (D 117), and his senses, which had become so active, begin to extinguish themselves in nothingness. The story ends in emptiness as memory fades away, yet, though Duffy's epiphany is excruciating and leaves him alone, he *feels* for the first time, and we are justified in regarding the destruction of "his moral nature" as a triumph of involuntary memory. The reader realizes that Duffy has always been alone, but now for the first time he "*felt* that he was alone" (D 117; my emphasis), and such an awakening can be read as one of the few rays of hope or possibility in *Dubliners*—hope that a paralyzed character can break through the habits and behavioral modes that imprison him or her. If the reader hopes that Mr. Duffy will learn to love and to accept human companionship, that goal is more available at the end of "A Painful Case" than it was at the beginning.

Mr. Duffy's awakening or epiphany at the end of "A Painful Case" thus depends on memory, but the kind of memory that works this transformation in his life is not voluntary, hermeneutic memory but an involuntary memory evoked by external stimuli. In "A Painful Case," a newspaper report, the failing light, and perhaps the influence of two very uncustomary glasses of hot punch are enough to shatter Mr. Duffy's routine, allowing repressed remorse and guilt to seep into his conscious mind and making him susceptible—apparently for the first time—to the influence of his own senses.

One particularly destructive form of habit in Joyce's works is the habitual misrepresentation or misrecollection of the past that we call nostalgia, certainly one of the primary features of what Joyce called "that hemiplegia or paralysis which many consider a city" (*SL* 22). Nostalgia derives from the Greek *nostos*—or "return," a term important in the *Odyssey* and consequently important to Joyce, who used it in his correspondence and conversation to label the final chapters of *Ulysses*, in which Bloom returns home to Molly—and *algos*, from the Greek word for pain.[11] Nostalgia is an obsessive return that cherishes the pain of absence, but the return envisioned in the *Odyssey* is less a return to the past than to a state in the future that resembles and completes what once was. Odysseus seeks Ithaca more for the promise that it holds for the future—his son, his old age, reunion with his wife—than for the past and its memories. Nostalgia, on the other hand, like habit, is an orientation toward the past that freezes past experience, preventing rather than encouraging true investigation and dialectic. Nostalgia idealizes and romanticizes the past at the expense of the present and future, and, like habit, it calcifies the past, anesthetizing present experience by robbing it of its uniqueness and immediacy.

The paralyzing power of the past is a central theme throughout *Dubliners*. Joseph Buttigieg rightly claims that in "The Sisters" and "Eveline" we can see the negative effects of what Proust called "voluntary memory." Characters in *Dubliners* often desire stasis and equilibrium—Joyce would say paralysis—above all else, and Buttigieg describes voluntary memory as "a protective screen that keeps reality at bay. It functions both as a fixing agent to secure the pastness of the past and as a safe haven for escape. Through its agency one can postpone almost indefinitely the unpleasantness of facing the real world and defer for as long as possible the necessity to act" (32). The propensity to revert habitually to a nostalgic past as protection against the "dangers" or uncertainties of immediate experience characterizes such Dubliners as the narrator of "The Sisters," Eveline, and the partygoers in "The Dead." As Buttigieg points out, the boy in "The Sisters" tries to "escape into pleasant memory" (33) in his attempt to avoid the mysterious unpleasantness of the priest's life and death, but he finds himself instead drifting "into some pleasant and vicious region" closer to nightmare (*D* 11). Buttigieg claims that the boy's attempt to use voluntary memory as an escape from the present and from his disturbing memories fails because the boy "is not yet a seasoned creature of habit" (33).

The story of the horse Johnny that Gabriel tells the Misses Morkan and Mary Jane in "The Dead" neatly represents the typical Dubliner's attitude toward history and toward the past. Johnny was a creature of habit, employed by Gabriel's grandfather in a mill, "walking round and round in order to drive the mill." When "the old gentleman" finally allowed the horse out of the mill on a carriage ride, the horse went along until it "'came in sight of King Billy's statue: and whether he fell in love with the horse King Billy sits on or whether he thought he was back again in the mill, anyhow he began to walk round the statue'" (D 208). Although the story amuses Gabriel's listeners, the horse that rejects novelty to return to a dull, familiar pattern is not so different from many of the Dubliners we encounter in Joyce's book. Appropriately, Johnny chooses a statue—a frozen image of the past—as his omphalos, and we notice that Johnny has been nostalgically enshrined in family memory as "the never-to-be-forgotten Johnny" (D 207). As Buttigieg remarks, "The inhabitants of Dublin are dead because they are imprisoned and shackled by a fixed and monolithic past. They are paralyzed by their own allegiance to and preservation of a dead tradition" (31).

In the first of his "Five Lectures on Psycho-Analysis," Freud likens neurotics to a Londoner—perhaps not unlike "the never-to-be-forgotten Johnny" in "The Dead"—"who paused to-day in deep melancholy before the memorial of Queen Eleanor's funeral instead of going about his business . . . or instead of feeling joy over the youthful queen of his own heart" or to another "who shed tears before the Monument that commemorates the reduction of his beloved metropolis to ashes although it has long since risen again in far greater brilliance." According to Freud, "every single hysteric and neurotic behaves like these two unpractical Londoners. Not only do they remember painful experiences of the remote past, but they still cling to them emotionally; they cannot get free of the past and for its sake they neglect what is real and immediate" (11:17).

Substitute "Dubliners" for "Londoners" in the above quotation and we have a neat picture of the inhabitants of Joyce's *Dubliners* who escape, when they are able, from the paralyzed present into a past filled with personal or collective monuments. The men gathered in "Ivy Day in the Committee Room" to pay tribute to porter and Parnell illustrate this type of memory well. Sitting in the squalid, dark committee room, bought off with a case of porter, they pay awkward, nostalgic homage to Parnell, attempting to escape the degradation of their day of canvassing in Dublin by turning to the glorious past. Although we can assume that some of these men—Lyons or Crofton, for example—would have opposed Parnell in the flesh, all but Lyons now praise the dead Chief, for, as Mat O'Connor says, "We all respect him now that he's dead and gone" (D 132). The man Parnell has become Parnell the monument, and all pretend to share "One grief—the memory of Parnell" (D 135).

Joyce's Eveline has much—perhaps everything—at stake in her correct assessment of her past, for the way she sees the past affects her decisions about her future. Eveline has to choose between two conflicting visions of the past: her fearful memories of her father's brutality and jealousy versus a desperate attempt to fictionalize the past in order to rationalize passivity. On one hand, she remembers isolated moments of kindness shown to her and her mother by her father:

> Sometimes he could be very nice. Not long before, when she had been laid up for a day, he had read her out a ghost story and made toast for her at the fire. Another day, when their mother was alive, they had all gone for a picnic to the Hill of Howth. She remembered her father putting on her mother's bonnet to make the children laugh. (D 39)

Though Eveline struggles to recall her father's few kindnesses, she is nonetheless powerfully reminded—seemingly by chance—of his cruelty, and it is this wrenching, involuntary memory, triggered by distant music, that tips the scales and impels her to flee:

> Down far in the avenue she could hear a street organ playing. She knew the air. Strange that it should come that very night to remind her of the promise to her mother, her promise to keep the home together as long as she could. She remembered the last night of her mother's illness; she was again in the close dark room at the other side of the hall and outside she heard a melancholy air of Italy. The organ-player had been ordered to go away and given sixpence. She remembered her father strutting back into the sickroom saying:
> —Damned Italians! coming over here!
> As she mused the pitiful vision of her mother's life laid its spell on the very quick of her being . . . . She stood up in a sudden impulse of terror. Escape! She must escape! Frank would save her. (D 39–40)

Although Buttigieg reads this memory of the organ grinder's melody as another example of voluntary memory, it has much more in common with Proust's involuntary memory, triggered as it is by an external, chance stimulus. Eveline tries to convert the melody she hears into yet another reason for staying ("her promise to keep the home together"), but the "melancholy air of Italy" triggers instead a reaction of horror, a true memory of her mother's death and a vision of her own future that touches "the very quick of her being" (D 40).

Although this involuntary memory breaks through the wall of habit and nostalgia that Eveline has tried to create, although it impels her to leave her home and go down to the docks with Frank, she is too much a creature of Dublin and a creature of habit to act, and she remains, at the end of the story, "passive, like a helpless animal" (*D* 41). "Eveline," Buttigieg concludes,

> rendered immobile by the mnemonic ghosts she evokes, joins the company of the dead. . . . Eveline's past and her home are her universe and she dares not disturb that universe by embarking on a journey into an unknown future in an unfamiliar Buenos Aires. She clings to the security of what she "knows": a fabricated past which is rendered more real than her present urges. (36)

An obsession with the past becomes in Dublin a form of habit, a way of habitually or reflexively turning to the past to avoid the present, a habit of forming monumental centers of paralysis in the past that impede involvement with the present. When Mr. Browne and Aunt Kate insist in "The Dead" that the singers of the present day—even Caruso—cannot match those of the past, they exhibit the Dubliner's tendency toward what Nietzsche, in his essay, "On the Uses and Disadvantages of History for Life," calls "the monumental mode of regarding history" (70). Nietzsche argues: "We need history . . . for the sake of life and action, not so as to turn comfortably away from life and action. . . . We want to serve history only to the extent that history serves life: for it is possible to value the study of history to such a degree that life becomes stunted and degenerate. . ." (59).

When Gabriel idealizes Aunt Julia's and Aunt Kate's generation in his speech, we realize that he does it at least partly to denigrate the current generation represented by Miss Ivors. He and most of the other assembled Dubliners ostensibly cherish the "spacious days . . . gone beyond recall" and "the memory of those dead and gone great ones whose fame the world will not willingly let die" (*D* 203), yet earlier, as he rehearsed his praise of "the generation that is now on the wane among us" mentally, he thought to himself "Very good: that was one for Miss Ivors. What did he care that his aunts were only two ignorant old women?" (*D* 192). Gabriel, like Eveline, tries to create a past better than the present in order to avoid facing the present, and in doing so he resembles those ages and societies which, according to Nietzsche, "were quite incapable of distinguishing between a monumentalized past and a mythical fiction, because precisely the same stimuli can be derived from the one world as from the other" (70). Like many of Joyce's Dubliners, Nietzsche's worshippers of the past "do not desire to see new greatness emerge: their means of preventing it is to say 'Behold, greatness already exists!' .... whether they are aware of it or not, they act as though their motto were: let the dead bury the living" (72). Gabriel ends his speech with unconscious irony, claiming that the living must turn away from the "sad memories" of the past in order to "go on bravely with our work among the living." "Therefore," he concludes, "I will not linger on the past" (D 204). This superficial, rhetorical gesture on Gabriel's part shows up the individual's lack of control over the past perhaps more ironically than any other line in Joyce's work. The insufficiency of voluntary memory—the illusion that the "storehouse" of images can be locked, unlocked, and used at will— becomes obvious as we see how Gabriel's life is soon shattered by the past on which he declines to linger. Through the power of Gretta's involuntary memory, released by a chance melody, Gabriel will be drawn ineluctably toward "that region where dwell the vast hosts of the dead" (D 223), a psychic Hades where he learns—as Mr. Duffy did—that the dead can teach him more than he had dreamt of in his after-dinner platitudes.

In *A Portrait of the Artist in Different Perspective*, Joseph Buttigieg offers a brilliant interpretation of "The Dead" based on Beckett's readings of Proust's "voluntary memory" and "involuntary memory." Both Buttigieg and Vincent Pecora—in his essay "'The Dead' and the Generosity of the Word"—read "The Dead" as a story about Dubliners' attempts to control and master the past, to keep it within the realm of the habitual— or, as Joyce would say, the paralytic—through reflexive nostalgia and fictionalization. Pecora and Buttigieg focus on Gabriel's dinner speech as an example of this tendency toward what Pecora calls a "mystified tradition .... a hierarchy of values that places all that must remain unavailable—'our forefathers,' 'those dead and gone great ones,' as well as the legendary, the revelatory, the transcendent—above the sensual, material conditions of their lives" (238). For Pecora, the central issue of the story is Gabriel's inability to control the social situations he encounters at the Misses Morkan's party, which culminates in his failure to escape the paralyzed present with Gretta, "to make her forget the years of their dull existence together and remember only their moments of ecstasy" (D 213-14) and to "be master of her strange mood" (D 217). He is thwarted in his attempts to retrieve the past (or rather, to take refuge in an imagined past) by Gretta's more powerful, involuntary memory of Michael Furey, a memory triggered by an overheard melody from her youth.

This kind of jarring, intense, involuntary memory "is disturbing and painful," Buttigieg writes, "like a birth, for it deprives one of mastery over a world rendered comfortable by habit." According to Buttigieg, Gabriel and Gretta experience the past more intensely after Gretta's cathartic memory of her dead love because they *repeat* it rather than simply recollect it (a notion Freud also would endorse): "The distinction suggested by Joyce in 'The Dead' between a past evoked by a complacent memory and a past that breaks through the complacency to sunder the habitual is a crucial element not only of the final story but of *Dubliners* as a whole" (31). As we will see, Buttigieg's observation obtains not only for *Dubliners*, but for *A Portrait of the Artist as a Young Man* and *Ulysses* as well.

In the final chapter of *A Portrait of the Artist as a Young Man*, Stephen Dedalus, keenly aware of his father's failure and inability to provide money or morale for his family, sarcastically describes his father's occupations: "A medical student, an oarsman, a tenor, an amateur actor, a shouting politician, a small landlord, a small investor, a drinker, a good fellow, a storyteller, somebody's secretary, something in a distillery, a taxgatherer, a bankrupt and at present a praiser of his own past" (P 241). This passage depicts a typical "career" in *Dubliners*—a bit of promise, a bit of success, a bit of liquor, and eventual failure and paralysis—and it fittingly ends with the Dubliner as nostalgiac, turned toward the past in order to avoid the present and future.

We see Simon Dedalus's paralysis by nostalgia most completely in his visit with Stephen to Cork in *A Portrait*. Simon's trip to Cork is a pathetic example of a Dubliner's attempt literally to return to the past, to the scene of his youth, to avoid facing the financial disaster he knows is imminent. Young Stephen feels no sympathy for his father's "evocation of Cork and of scenes of his youth, a tale broken by sighs or draughts from his pocketflask whenever the image of some dead friend appeared in it or whenever the evoker remembered suddenly the purpose of his actual visit" (P 87). Simon tries to bury himself in liquor and nostalgia (which go hand-in-hand in Joyce's writings) throughout his visit to Cork. He and his friends live in the past, cherishing their accomplishments as young men flirting or drinking, thankful that "we lived so long and did so little harm" (P 95). When he talks to a waiter, Simon finds it difficult to reconcile past and present in Cork, for when he brings up a name from the past, the waiter has "in mind the present holder and Mr Dedalus his father or perhaps his grandfather" (P 89). Similarly, their tour through Queens College is continually broken up by more disturbing examples that "times change and we change with them":

> their progress across the gravel was brought to a halt after every dozen or so paces by some reply of the porter's.

—Ah, do you tell me so? And is poor Pottlebelly dead?
—Yes, sir. Dead, sir. (P 89)

While Simon demonstrates the impossibility of reviving the past and the dead through voluntary memory and nostalgia, Stephen has a vision that demonstrates the power of involuntary memory, the tendency of the past to manifest itself intensely and spontaneously because of some unexpected stimulus. As Stephen searches for his father's carved initials in an anatomy classroom, he sees the word "*Fœtus*" cut into the wood of a desk and has an epiphany, a vision or showing-through of the past, "*which his father's words had been powerless to evoke*" (P 89; my emphasis). One of the crucial differences between Stephen's involuntary memory and Simon's attempts to revive the past is the ferment—almost torment—that this vision of dead medical students causes in Stephen. The past has entered Stephen's mind here not as a protective barrier against the present, but as a painful and disturbing stimulus that causes him to explore and question his own recently awakened sexuality.

> It shocked him to find in the outer world a trace of what he had deemed till then a brutish and individual malady of his own mind. His recent monstrous reveries came thronging into his memory. They too had sprung up before him, suddenly and furiously, out of mere words. He had soon given in to them and allowed them to sweep across and abase his intellect, wondering always where they came from, from what den of monstrous images. . . . (P 90)

Stephen can "feel no pity" (P 87) for his father's behavior—his habit of turning to the past in order to forget the present. For Stephen, as for Proust's Marcel, the past is truly alive only when evoked or triggered through involuntary memory. Marcel finds his strenuous efforts to remember Combray powerless, while a sip of tea and the taste of a madeleine can retrieve the past in all its sensual intensity. When Stephen, still disturbed and threatened by his reaction to the word carved in the desk, tries to establish some certainty about his identity, he finds voluntary memory ineffective:

> —I am Stephen Dedalus. I am walking beside my father whose name is Simon Dedalus. We are in Cork, in Ireland. Cork is a city. Our room is in the Victoria Hotel. Victoria and Stephen and Simon. Simon and Stephen and Victoria. Names.
>
> The memory of his childhood suddenly grew dim. He tried to call forth some of its vivid moments but could not. He recalled only

names. . . . He had not died but he had faded out like a film in the sun. (*P* 93)

Memory for Stephen becomes a spur, albeit painful and disturbing, making him conscious of his difference from his father and his father's friends. As he watches his father and "his two cronies" drink "to the memory of their past," he thinks: "An abyss of fortune or of temperament sundered him from them. His mind seemed older than theirs: it shone coldly on their strifes and happiness and regrets like a moon upon a younger earth" (*P* 95). Stephen sees himself as different from others partly because he does not consider himself to be trapped in what he sees as provincial, habitual, and paralytic Irish modes of behavior that cut off the Irish from the European present in favor of an Irish past. In attempting to "fly by those nets" of "nationality, language, religion" that Ireland throws at the soul struggling for freedom (*P* 203), Stephen hopes to escape the past for the future. In a diary entry, he imagines those who remember as feminine and weak: "*6 April:* Certainly she remembers the past. Lynch says all women do. . . . The past is consumed in the present and the present is living only because it brings forth the future. Statues of women, if Lynch be right, should always be fully draped, one hand of the woman feeling regretfully her own hinder parts" (*P* 251).

The Stephen Daedalus of *Stephen Hero* displays a similar repugnance for the stagnant patterns of life that paralyze most Dubliners. When Lynch, defending the institutions of the Catholic Church and marriage, claims, "Still marriage is a custom. To follow a custom is a mark of sanity," Stephen responds that it is rather "a mark of ordinariness" (*SH* 201). He detests the "toy life" or "marionette life" lived by the students and Jesuits at the college, a life that is simply "another variety of the stationary march" (*SH* 187), and he despises "the farce of Irish Catholicism: an island [whereof] the inhabitants of which entrust their wills and minds to others that they may ensure for themselves a life of spiritual paralysis" (*SH* 146). Stephen chooses instead a life of deliberate excess, preferring "the insidious dangers which conceal themselves under the guise of extravagance" to "a dull discharge of duties, neither understood nor congenial, [which] was far more dangerous and far less satisfactory" (*SH* 179).

As we have seen, however, Stephen is not as free from the past as he would like to think. Not only is he unable to escape his personal memories, but as an artist he falls into the verbal habits—or clichés—of his contemporaries too quickly and too easily. The passage quoted above in which Stephen thinks of the "abyss" that separates him from Simon and his cronies drifts immediately into the sort of clichéd, exaggerated, fin de siècle style that Leopold Bloom derides when he thinks of AE and Lizzie Twigg in the "Lestrygonians" episode of *Ulysses:* "Those literary etherial people they are all. Dreamy, cloudy, symbolistic. Esthetes they are" (*U*8.543-44). Again, when Stephen sets out to write a poem for "E. C." earlier in *A Portrait*, he begins by writing the Jesuit motto on top of the page "From force of habit" and then writes vague verses full of "balmy breezes," "the maiden lustre of the moon," and "Some undefined sorrow . . . hidden in the hearts of the protagonists" (*P* 70). Much of the irony that readers sense at the end of *A Portrait* derives from Stephen's assumption that he can leave behind the past and its patterns of behavior so easily, setting out freely into the future—like Daedalus and Icarus—with no baggage, only wings.

As barriers to memory, habit and nostalgia are predictably present as themes in *Ulysses*, and nowhere do these paralyzing forces display themselves more fully than in the tenth episode, "Wandering Rocks." "Wandering Rocks" is centrally placed within the book's eighteen episodes and represents Dublin in much fuller detail than any other chapter in the novel. In 1906, Joyce explained to Grant Richards that he chose Dublin as the scene for *Dubliners* "because that city seemed to me the centre of paralysis" (*SL* 83); in *Ulysses*, Joyce chooses this central episode to once again present his native city as "the centre of paralysis."

The *symplegades petrai*—literally, the "justling" or "striking" rocks (Liddell and Scott 763)—belong not to the *Odyssey*, but to the *Argonautica*. Circe alludes to them briefly in Book XII of Homer's epic, calling them the "Planctae" or "wanderers," and warning Odysseus of their dangers, explaining that only Jason managed to pass through, and then only because of Hera's assistance. In the detailed "schemas" to *Ulysses* that Joyce provided to his friends Carlo Linati, Herbert Gorman, and Stuart Gilbert,[12] he labeled the "Technic" of the episode as "Labyrinth moving between two banks." In the schemas he gave to Gorman and Gilbert he indicated that the "European Bank" is symbolized in the episode by the Viceroy, while Father Conmee represents the "Asiatic Bank." At the same time, he wrote that the *symplegades* corresponded to "Groups of Citizens." These correspondences share an implied view of human institutions as sinister objects or forces[13] that frustrate, halt, and destroy any human beings trapped by their frequent collisions. Other elements of Joyce's schemas reinforce this view: he listed the "Persons" of the episode as "Objects, Places, Forces, Ulysses," indicating that "Ulysses"—

here represented presumably by both Bloom and Stephen—is the only human person among the "Wandering Rocks"; he called "The Hostile Environment" the "Sense" or "Meaning" of "Wandering Rocks"; and he designated "Mechanics" as the "Science" or "Art" of the chapter.

"Wandering Rocks," then, presents a picture of Dublin as hostile environment, labyrinth, and destructive machine—a mechanism that paralyzes and frustrates the desires of its residents. The banks of the Bosporus between which Ulysses must sail are the Church and State, represented by Conmee at the beginning of the episode and the Viceroy's procession at the end. As the groups of citizens move around the city, "Dublin asserts itself as micropolis, with petty debts, petty spies, petty rebellions, petty lives and deaths, as if to deny the artist's effort to make it into Bloomusalem" (Ellmann, *Liffey* 91). The church, the state, and the groups of citizens represent forms or patterns of social discourse that lead to paralysis and smash lives. Destruction between the "Wandering Rocks" in *Ulysses*, then, means losing one's identity and becoming part of the social mechanism that is the "centre of paralysis." At one point in the episode, Stephen articulates this vision of the world as an impersonal machine he is caught in, not unlike the Deistic vision of the universe as a clock:

> The whirr of flapping leathern bands and hum of dynamos from the powerhouse urged Stephen to be on. Beingless beings. Stop! Throb always without you and the throb always within. Your heart you sing of. I between them. Where? Between two roaring worlds where they swirl, I. Shatter them, one and both. But stun myself too in the blow....
>
> Yes, quite true. Very large and wonderful and keeps famous time. (*U*10.821–24)

Much has been written about the narrative voice in "Wandering Rocks" and the ways in which it parallels the mechanistic and paralytic themes of the episode. Karen Lawrence, in *The Odyssey of Style in "Ulysses,"* compares the narrator to Dickens's Gradgrind, obsessed with "fact," yet like Gradgrind, unable to synthesize or use the facts compiled (83). Lawrence attributes "a curiously mechanical quality to the narrative, as if a writing machine, rather than a human imagination, produced it" (85). Clive Hart describes the episode as "a relatively static moment" in the course of the novel ("Wandering Rocks" 186), "a chapter full of traps for everyone, readers and characters alike. Things are not what they seem, and most of the characters are a prey to illusion or frustration. For them, the city is continually disappointing and evasive" ("Wandering

Rocks" 188). Here Hart refers to the ironic fact that while the narrator of "Wandering Rocks" is obsessed with "documentary reality," with the details of everyday life in Dublin, many of the details in the episode are erroneous. Hart outlines "four types" of traps or errors in "Wandering Rocks" (189), including geographical errors so blatant that Joyce, as a native Dubliner, could not have committed them unintentionally.

Critics interpret these narrative lapses or errors in various ways. Ellmann sees them as an assertion of doubt, or what he calls the "uncertainty principle" (*Liffey* 92). Lawrence sees the narrative uncertainty and discontinuity of the episode as the beginning of "the breakdown of the initial style and a departure from the novelistic form of the book's first half" (80). While conceding the value of both these perspectives, can we also see the narrative lapses of "Wandering Rocks" as examples of what the narrator of "Ithaca" will call "defective mnemotechnic" (*U*17.766)? When we read *Ulysses* as a book of memory, this chapter illustrates the defects of voluntary memory, of the assumption that the past is a collection of facts and details that can be easily and simply reassembled. In "Wandering Rocks," memory breaks down, as if in mockery of Joyce's own statement to Frank Budgen that *Ulysses* would "give a picture of Dublin so complete that if the city one day suddenly disappeared from the earth it could be reconstructed out of my book" (*James Joyce* 69).

"Wandering Rocks" is full of characters from the earlier episodes of *Ulysses* as well as from *Dubliners* and *A Portrait of the Artist as a Young Man*, yet the narrator's attempts to "remember" these other texts—to get the past straight—is doomed to failure because of the mechanistic, objective, and obsessive qualities of this view of the world. Karen Lawrence describes the "narrative mind" of "Wandering Rocks" as a "paratactic imagination" (83), a description that can be applied just as well to Hume's epistemology and psychology, parataxis in this sense referring to the refusal to concede relation and causality between moments in time.[14] The narrator in this episode, then, represents the passivist view of memory and displays the weaknesses of voluntary memory by "forgetting" the very facts that he seems so obsessed with.

Joyce's "groups of citizens" or "wandering rocks" are thus trapped and paralyzed by the same stagnating forces that operate in *Dubliners* and *A Portrait:* religion, politics, language, and the various paralyzing habits that Dubliners are prone to. We can see these paralyzing forces at work in other chapters of *Ulysses* as well: "Lotus-Eaters," for example, is an episode dealing—at least in part—with the paralyzing effects of Catholicism, while "Cyclops" reveals the deleterious effects of alcohol and nationalist mythologizing of the Irish past, "still there for us today rendered more beautiful still by the waters of sorrow which have passed over them and by the rich incrustations of time" (U12.1462–64). The Irish nationalist approach to history threatens to become a "Nightmare from which you will never awake" (U7.678), as Stephen thinks in "Aeolus," when he listens to the newsmen reminiscing about the Phoenix Park murders. "Sirens," which immediately follows "Wandering Rocks," provides a picture of Dubliners anaesthetizing themselves with alcohol, nostalgia, and sentiment (here in the form of music).

But if we consider the possible meanings implied by the relationship between *Ulysses* as an odyssey of memory and the classical parallel (here as much Apollonius as Homer), what are we to make of Joyce's "Wandering Rocks" and "Sirens"? Certainly Joyce's Ulysses (be it Stephen or Bloom) must pass these dangers if he is to continue toward Ithaca: no paralyzed Dubliner, in other words, could be capable of fully coming to terms with the past in the way that Stephen and Bloom must in order to move through and beyond the memories that obstruct them.

Much evidence in *Ulysses* supports the notion that Stephen and Bloom are somehow different from other Dubliners, and at times the text hints that they may be different enough to be exempt from some forms of the Dublin paralysis that surrounds them. Stephen's connection to his own culture is a complicated issue, and certainly we cannot take at face value his own sense of himself as a voluntary outcast from all things Irish. After all, he has returned to Dublin from the Continent after his failed flight, and at times his longing for acceptance seems almost to match his apparent disdain for his surroundings. And yet, he remains convinced of his own separateness, proud, alienated, aloof. As a Jew, Bloom is an outcast in Dublin, and we can see in the "Hades" and "Cyclops" episodes that he is treated as such. Frank Budgen notes that Joyce once commented on Bloom's "loneliness as a Jew who finds no warmth of fellowship either among Jews or Gentiles" (*Further* 4).

Clive Hart notes the isolation of Stephen and Bloom in "Wandering Rocks," and he implies that this isolation is a problem for them, a failure to successfully integrate inner and outer worlds. Hart feels that Stephen and Bloom need to learn to belong more fully to their environment, claiming that "Although discouraged by his fellow Dubliners from being one, it is as burgher that Bloom would be most effective and most comfortable" ("Wandering Rocks" 188). Hart correctly points out that "Neither Bloom nor Stephen belongs, wholly and vitally, to this meticulously evoked city environment" ("Wandering Rocks" 183) and that "Even their interactions with their physical circumstances are minimal" ("Wandering Rocks" 186). He adds that Bloom "is shown in this chapter less conscious of his surroundings than at almost any other point in the book. . . . He and the city are less at one here than at any other time. . . . It almost seems as if this climactic presentation of the urban world were irrelevant to him" ("Wandering Rocks" 187). Perhaps, however, the isolation and alienation that Hart notes are not signs of a need or a failing in Bloom and Stephen, but are instead signs that the two are literally "singled out" in the text, allowed to remain free from the kinds of defective mnemotechnic that other Dubliners are prone to. Ellmann argues for the symbolic evidence that Stephen and Bloom are the only Dubliners in "Wandering Rocks" who manage to negotiate between the rocky shores of church and state at the end of the episode by pointing out, "The special status of Bloom and Stephen here is confirmed in that they, alone among the many people mentioned, take no notice of either the viceroy or Father Conmee" (*Liffey* 101).

Another hint that Stephen and Bloom are somehow different, somehow resistant to the paralyzing effects of their environment, comes near the end of the "Wandering Rocks" episode, when we follow a crumpled piece of paper floating out to sea on the River Liffey, "eastward by flanks of ships and trawlers, amid an archipelago of corks, beyond new Wapping street past Benson's ferry, and by the threemasted schooner *Rosevean* from Bridgwater with bricks" (*U*10.1096–99). This piece of paper is a throwaway advertising a religious revival, placed in Bloom's hand by a "somber Y.M.C.A. young man" in the "Lestrygonians" episode. Among other things, the flyer apparently proclaims, "Elijah is coming" (*U*8.13), a phrase that develops into a motif associated with Bloom throughout the novel. Although we must suspect irony and deception in all that occurs in "Wandering Rocks," the plot of the novel continues through the episode just as surely as the Argo passed through the *symplegades*, and this passage of the throwaway, of "Elijah," down the Liffey toward the sea (like Anna Livia in *Finnegans Wake*) is remarked upon three times in the episode.[15] This final passage outlining the throwaway's escape is also significant in describing a movement "eastward," for this is the symbolic direction of escape and renewal: to the east lies Europe, the rising sun, Eden, and Jerusalem. Adding to the symbolic "weight" of this passage is the inclusion of the *Rosevean*, the "silent ship" that Stephen Dedalus sees at 11 A.M. at the end of the "Proteus" episode, a "threemaster, her sails brailed up on the crosstrees" (*U*3.504). The three crosstrees, Elijah, and the religious symbolism of the East, as well as the triple repetition of the throwaway's journey through the "Wandering Rocks" episode, help to balance the doubt created by the deceptive narrator and argue for a reading of this passage as a hint that Stephen and Bloom are somehow linked and may somehow avoid the paralysis of Dublin life.

In a letter to Harriet Shaw Weaver dated August 6, 1919, Joyce defended the stylistic eccentricities of "Sirens" by claiming, "I did not know in what other way to describe the seductions of music beyond which Ulysses travels" (*SL* 242). Here, certainly, Joyce meant by "the seductions of music" the power of music to carry and intensify sentiment and sentimentality, including nostalgic longings. Joyce must also have been familiar with Victor Bérard's fascinating etymology for the word "siren," which Bérard provides in *Did Homer Live?* Bérard claims that "siren" derives from the Semitic *sir* + *en*, *sir* meaning "song, canticle," and *en* meaning "to fasten, to hold in." Bérard explains:

> The Sirens are singers, but they are enchantresses too—fascinators, taking the word in its fullest and earliest sense, which means the women who *bind* by their *enchantments*. Such is the meaning of the Latin *fascinare, fasciare*, or of the Greek *thelgo* which the Poet uses. The Sirens *charm* men; they *bind, enchain* them with their magic songs....
>
> This ... must, I think, make the etymological derivation *sir-en:* "a song of fascination." (202; original emphasis)

While the barmaids who wreck men on the bar with alcohol certainly correspond to the Homeric Sirens, the men who sing so beautifully of the past, of lost love, and of the Croppy Boy, are Sirens as well. Joyce's emphasis, then, like Bérard's, is not on death—which is what Homer's Sirens bestow—but on stasis, binding, and paralysis. And yet Joyce writes to Harriet Weaver that his Ulysses, like Homer's, must travel "beyond" this enchanting music, insinuating that Bloom, unlike the other men in the bar, is able to avoid the typical Dublin obsession with the past, even though it may momentarily appeal to him. Bloom does not drink, and he seems to recognize the dangerous attractions of nostalgia and sentiment more fully than the other men in the bar do. Although at one point, trying to avoid thoughts of Molly and Boylan, he thinks, "Wish they'd sing more. Keep my mind off" (*U*11.914), Bloom also realizes the danger of such thinking: "Cowley, he stuns himself with it: kind of drunkenness. Better give way only half way the way of a man with a maid. Instance enthusiasts. All ears. Not lose a demisemiquaver. Eyes shut. Head nodding in time. Dotty. You daren't budge. Thinking strictly prohibited" (*U*11.1191–94).

Of course, Stephen and Bloom still suffer from their own individual defective mnemotechnics compounded of repression, resistance, habit, and nostalgia. I already have discussed how each character tends to live in the past despite his attempts to avoid unpleasant memories, since each of them has failed to come to terms with buried problems in his own history. This set of individual problems has led each to his own impasse in the present: Stephen's bitterness, inability to write, alienation, and rejection of community along with authority; and Bloom's sexual alienation, which manifests itself most obviously in his tendency to idealize women as "goddesses" or reduce them to masturbatory fantasies. Hart perhaps unwittingly marks these individual obsessions when he notes the ways in which Bloom and Stephen are isolated from the mechanisms of Dublin life: "Bloom, adrift on the swell of his sexual imagination, and Stephen, trapped in the dust of the burial earth, are surrounded by the working parts of a physical and social machine of great intricacy" ("Wandering Rocks" 201).

As I have argued, Bloom's repression of the trauma of Rudy's death has led to the formation of a complex set of problems and habits, primarily related to his sexuality and relationships with women. Bloom's tendencies toward a habitual, sterile idealization of women are first represented in the "Calypso" episode in the form of the framed picture *The Bath of the Nymph* that he has cut out of *Photo Bits* and hung above the bed he shares with Molly. Although we may be tempted to view Molly as the counterpart of Calypso in this episode—lying in bed, holding Ulysses captive to her whims—as Richard Ellmann and others do,[16] the Nymph is a better symbol of the mental and sexual habits that keep Bloom/Ulysses from progressing toward his Ithaca. The Nymph, unlike Penelope, is immortal, static, and absolutely sterile. Trapped by the nymph Calypso, Homer's Odysseus longs for the human love and companionship of his wife Penelope far away in Ithaca; ironically, the photo of the Nymph above Leopold and Molly Bloom's bed symbolizes just how far our modern Ulysses will have to "travel" to return to his wife who waits only inches away. In his reading of Victor Bérard's *Les Phéniciens et l'Odyssée,* Joyce noted that the name Calypso derives from the Greek verb "Καλυπτω—I hide" (Rose 25); the *Photo Bits* Nymph as Calypso provides an idealized image of woman that allows Bloom to hide from Molly and from problems of memory and sexuality that he must somehow face.

As Adaline Glasheen notes, while Bloom may consider the Nymph safer than Molly—this ideal image of woman cannot threaten him and his masculinity by bearing another deformed child—"she proves to be most lethal" (62). The *Photo Bits* Nymph is the first in a series of "ideal," unattainable female figures that intrigues Bloom in *Ulysses*. These images of unattainable, sterile womanhood form a central motif for Bloom, culminating in his cathartic confrontation with the Nymph herself in "Circe."

Bloom's habitual way of imagining women allows him to avoid a full consideration of and confrontation with his sexual and marital problems. As the chameleon narrator of the "Oxen of the Sun" episode puts it,

> Or is it that from being a deluder of others he has become at last his own dupe as he is, if report belie him not, his own and his only enjoyer? . . . Unhappy woman, she [Molly] has been too long and too persistently denied her legitimate prerogative. . . . Has he not nearer home a seedfield that lies fallow for the want of the ploughshare? A habit reprehensible at puberty is second nature and an opprobrium in middle life. (*U*14.913–31)

"In "Nausicaa," Bloom and Gerty engage in masturbation and mystification; although they never speak to each other, each uses the other as a canvas for a sexual fantasy. Gerty thinks of Bloom as a stereotyped, dark, mysterious stranger, wondering "if she could make him fall in love with her, make him forget the memory of the past" (*U*13.437–39). Bloom thinks of himself, after he has come and she has gone, as Rip Van Winkle: "Twenty years asleep in Sleepy Hollow. All changed. Forgotten. The young are old. His gun rusty from the dew" (*U*13.1115–16). Bloom's need for sexual satisfaction without the risk of physical involvement with another human being reflects his desire to forget Rudy's death and Molly's adultery with Boylan as well as his related fears of sexual inadequacy ("His gun rusty from the dew").[17]

The ending of "Lotus-Eaters" underscores Bloom's recourse to masturbatory fantasy as a habitual substitute for sexual involvement. Joyce's "Lotus-Eaters," based on the Homeric parallel of a land paralyzed and befuddled by narcosis, depicts a city paralyzed by habit—here, especially, the habits of religious devotion. Bloom, as usual, is set apart from the culture surrounding him and is able to observe and identify the social opiates of the Irish masses at work in their daily lives. As we have seen, however, Bloom has his own special problems—his own "nosebag" like the horses in "Lotus-Eaters"—in his habitual avoidance of the problems of the past and in his escapist tendency to indulge in sexual fantasy. Thinking of Molly as he shops for her at the chemist's, Bloom shifts quickly into a fantasy of masturbating in the Turkish baths and ends the episode imagining or "foreseeing" himself lying in the bath, his penis now ironically "the limp father of thousands, a languid floating flower" (U5.571–72), one of the lotus flowers of habit that keeps Bloom from proceeding toward his goal in the novel.

Both Stephen Dedalus and Leopold Bloom remember happier—or at least less troubled—times before the deaths of May Goulding and Rudy Bloom, yet neither of them seems able to unravel and heal the traumas of the past through voluntary memory. Stephen has tender memories of his mother in the "Telemachus" episode, but his feelings for her are too involved with his religious guilt and resentment to prevent these potentially healing memories from shading quickly into terrifying visions of his mother as vengeful ghost. Similarly, Bloom remembers the days before Rudy was born as happier times, but he thinks, "I was happier then. Or was that I? Or am I now I? Twentyeight I was. She twentythree. When we left Lombard street west something changed. Could never like it again after Rudy. Can't bring back time. Like holding water in your hand. Would you go back to then? Just beginning then. Would you?" (U8.608–12).

Bloom characteristically shifts away from this troubling question into thoughts of his correspondence with Martha Clifford, but he knows that the past is "All changed. Forgotten. The young are old" (U13.1115–16). This tension between the irretrievable past and the paralyzed present is most clearly and poignantly evident in the "Lestrygonians" episode, when Bloom tastes a glass of Burgundy: "Glowing wine on his palate lingered swallowed. Crushing in the winepress grapes of Burgundy. Sun's heat it is. Seems to a secret touch telling me memory. Touched his sense moistened remembered" (U8.897–99). Like Marcel's sip of tea-soaked madeline in *Du côté de chez Swann*, this sip of wine stimulates a sensuous, involuntary memory, here of Bloom's lovemaking with Molly on Howth Hill years ago, kissing and passing "seedcake warm and chewed" from mouth to mouth (a scene that she also remembers tenderly at the end of the novel), yet Bloom's final comment on this vision of the past is the simple and hopeless "Me. And me now" (U8.917). The narrative emphasizes the desolation of the present in contrast to the past by framing this involuntary memory at the beginning and end with the image of two flies, perhaps in the act of copulation: "Stuck on the pane two flies buzzed, stuck" (U8.896) and "Stuck, the flies buzzed" (U8.918).

Perhaps to avoid the pain of this powerful memory of happier times, Bloom again shifts immediately away from the images of physical love between man and woman presented to him by the past into a vision:

Shapely goddesses, Venus, Juno: curves the world admires.... Quaffing nectar at mess with the gods golden dishes, all ambrosial. Not like a tanner lunch we have .... Nectar imagine it drinking electricity: gods' food. Lovely forms of women sculped Junonian. Immortal lovely. And we stuffing food in one hole and out behind: food, chyle, blood, dung, earth, food: have to feed it like stoking an engine. They have no. Never looked. I'll look today. Keeper won't see. Bend down let something drop. See if she. (*U*8.920-32)

Bloom flees from his memory of love on Howth to a correspondent idealization that filters out the physical, replacing the "seedcake warm and chewed" with nectar, replacing the real woman with a goddess free from the gross properties and processes of the flesh. That this flight represents a desperate avoidance of his past and his problems becomes clearer at the end of this episode when he sees Blazes Boylan and flees into the Museum to avoid meeting his wife's suitor: "Quick. Cold statues: quiet there. Safe in a minute" (*U*9.1176-77). The "Lestrygonians" episode ends appropriately, as Bloom, entering the Museum, stuck in the habits that keep him "safe" from sexual risk, reaches into his pocket and feels "tepid paper stuck. Ah soap there I yes. Gate. Safe!" (*U*8.1192-93). The repetition of "stuck" here echoes the flies, "stuck on the pane," that frame Bloom's spontaneous memory of better times with Molly. Here, we see the workings of the book's textual memory, which has appropriately taken up "stuck" as a motif to be remembered and repeated throughout the novel, often linked to an object or situation reflective in some way of Bloom's sexual problems with Molly.[18]

The insufficiency of voluntary memory is demonstrated in "Oxen of the Sun" when Bloom and Stephen simultaneously encounter the difficulty of controlling the past and of avoiding the problems that they have buried there. A long passage in indirect free style in the manner of Charles Lamb follows Bloom's reminiscences, as "in a retrospective arrangement" he imagines himself in the past—"a mirror within a mirror"—as a boy. His pleasant memories, where presumably he hopes to find solace and escape from the disturbing conversations about misbirths he has just heard, gradually become unpleasant and turn—predictably—to the death of his son:

What is the age of the soul of man? As she hath the virtue of the chameleon to change her hue at every new approach, to be gay with the merry and mournful with the downcast, so too is her age changeable as her mood. No longer is Leopold, as he sits there, ruminating, chewing the cud of reminiscence, that staid agent of publicity and holder of a modest substance in the funds. A score of years are blown away. He is young Leopold. There, as in a retrospective arrangement, a mirror within a mirror (hey, presto!), he beholdeth himself. (U14.1038-45)

The recollections that follow are stylized and sentimental, as the parody of Lamb's style (described appropriately by Gifford and Seidman as "gentle pathos and nostalgia" [432]) dictates, emphasizing the sentimentality of Bloom's return into this construction of his past. Bloom, however, begins to lose control over his reminiscences, as "hey, presto, the mirror is breathed on and the young knighterrant recedes, shrivels, dwindles to a tiny speck within the mist. Now he is himself paternal and these about him might be his sons" (U14.1060-62). Bloom then drifts into a memory of his first sexual encounter with a young prostitute named Bridie Kelly:

He thinks of a drizzling night in Hatch street .... Bridie! Bridie Kelly! He will never forget the name, ever remember the night: first night, the bridenight.... but—hold! Back! It must not be! In terror the poor girl flees away through the murk. She is the bride of darkness, a daughter of night. She dare not bear the sunnygolden babe of day. No, Leopold. Name and memory solace thee not. That youthful illusion of thy strength was taken from thee—and in vain. No son of thy loins is by thee. There is none now to be for Leopold, what Leopold was for Rudolph. (U14.1063-74)

Bloom's attempt to find comfort by means of voluntary memory fails as his memory returns him once again to his failure to produce a son. Recollection simply entangles him once again in the webs of the past.

At the same time, Francis Costello is

reminding Stephen of years before when they had been at school together in Conmee's time.... You have spoken of the past and its phantoms, Stephen said. Why think of them? If I call them into life across the waters of Lethe will not the poor ghosts troop to my call? Who supposes it? I, Bous Stephanoumenos, bullockbefriending bard, am lord and giver of their life. (U14.1110-16)

Ironically, moments later Lenehan callously jokes that Stephen "could not leave his mother an orphan" and Stephen, visibly hurt, "would have withdrawn from the feast had not the noise of voices allayed the smart"

(U14.1123–26). Clearly, Stephen has less control of the "poor ghosts" and "phantoms" of his own past than he has pretended to Costello.

At its most powerful, memory is not subject to volition and control in *Ulysses*. The models of mind and memory implied in *Ulysses* include too many baffles and blocks for memory to work this easily. We have seen that Stephen and Bloom for various reasons are unable to control or cure the past through voluntary or hermeneutic memory. Memory, then, must work its own cure. Joyce, like his contemporaries Proust and Bergson, imagined other modes of memory, among them an involuntary or epiphanic memory capable of bursting out of the past, carrying the freshness and power of original experience back up through the layers of obscurity, repression, and habit that voluntary memory cannot penetrate. Involuntary memory is thus dynamic, transforming the present by driving or rising out of the past into the future and forcing the characters toward narrative goals that they seem unable or unwilling to reach by themselves. Joyce may have found a paradigm for this powerful, motive, and purposive form of memory in contemporary debates about memory, especially the role of memory in evolution. At times in *Ulysses* the presence of this powerful involuntary force, embedded in shared memories and in the textual memory of the novel, seems to imply that Bloom and Stephen may set the past right, purge it of its ghosts, and proceed out of the paralyzed present into the future. The central themes of recall and return in *Ulysses* underscore this possibility, as does the Homeric parallel. This potentially healing, dynamic, teleological memory is a primary constituent of the cultural unconscious of the book, a holistic drive in tension with the modernist or postmodernist surface of the novel.

As Stephen helps young Sargent with his lessons in the "Nestor" episode, he reflects:

> Like him was I, these sloping shoulders, this gracelessness. My childhood bends beside me. Too far for me to lay a hand there once or lightly. Mine is far and his secret as our eyes. Secrets, silent, stony sit in the dark palaces of both our hearts: secrets weary of their tyranny: tyrants, willing to be dethroned. (U2.168–72)

As we have seen, neither Bloom nor Stephen is willing or able to master the past and dethrone the secrets that tyrannize their hearts. Yet, as I have argued, other levels and modes of memory are available in *Ulysses*, and despite their unwillingness or inability we will see that slowly, inevitably, and unconsciously, Bloom and Stephen will be drawn toward the confrontations with the past that they have hitherto avoided. Just as Homer's Odysseus was unable to return to Ithaca on his own and required the aid of Athena, and just as Hera's love allowed Jason to sail unscathed through the Wandering Rocks, Stephen and Bloom will require more than their own voluntary and hermeneutic powers of memory to continue on toward their goals.

3 Memory, Destiny, and the Limits of the Self

The Past—the dark unfathom'd retrospect!
The teeming gulf—the sleepers and the shadows!
The past—the infinite greatness of the past!
For what is the present after all but a growth out of the past?
(As a projectile form'd, impell'd, passing a certain line, still keeps on,
So the present, utterly form'd, impell'd by the past.)
—Walt Whitman, "Passage to India"

Earlier chapters have shown how personal memory and voluntary memory are insufficient for establishing sure knowledge of the self or the past. For Joyce, as for his contemporaries Bergson and Proust, voluntary memory is often thwarted by the obscurity of the past, by bad mnemonic "habits" such as repression, resistance, and nostalgia, and by the everyday deadening of experience caused by habitual patterns of life. Something additional is required, then, if Ulysses is to continue on toward Ithaca, something more subtle that moves toward the implied narrative goals of the novel—proleptic, dynamic modes of memory that hint at resolution and acknowledge memory as a force rather than a faculty. Like Proust and Bergson, Joyce realized the continual power of the past to drive us involuntarily into the future, and involuntary memory clearly plays a great role in bringing Bloom and Stephen closer to the confrontations with the past expected by many readers of *Ulysses*, confrontations prerequisite to an end of mourning and a continuation of the self's development or unfolding.

Involuntary memory does not lead us back into the past in any simple way. At the close of "The Dead," for example, we sense that Gretta's involuntary memory of Michael Furey has somehow worked a change in Gabriel. Just as Mr. Duffy begins to *feel* at the end of "A Painful Case" because of the rupture that memory has made in his restricted, patterned life, so Gabriel's encounter with his wife's long-embalmed love threatens to shatter the complacency and self-control that he has struggled so hard to maintain. Mr. Duffy may never achieve much with his newfound feelings,[1] and Gabriel's life will not necessarily be "fixed" or perfected by his confrontation with the power of the past. What is central here is the sense of possibility, of uncertainty, of uncontrollability that such events convey. If habit can suppress receptivity to difference and newness, involuntary memory has the *potential* to break down such barriers to perception and to reopen the mind and the self to a sense of potential and change. Whether we conceive of the self as unfolding entelechy or as consciousness within duration, it is clear that habit, repression, and fixation on the past direct the mind back upon itself and prevent or obstruct the creative interaction of self and experience.

One function of memory, elaborately articulated in the late nineteenth and early twentieth centuries, is its role as a powerful, active, and involuntary disruptive force. This active, dynamic memory has the power to get the ego—what Bergson would have called the "superficial self"—out of the way of the "profound self" (Kolakowski 17)—including unconscious mental processes and reactions—so that we are able to perceive the possibility and newness of each moment.

Before we can examine the workings of involuntary memory in Joyce's novel, however, we must inquire into its sources, for here Joyce differs significantly from his contemporaries. Proust, for example, never indicates that the resources of involuntary memory extend any further or involve anything other than the personal memory of the individual, the experiences—albeit unconscious and unavailable to voluntary memory—that the rememberer has had in his or her lifetime. Freud, who developed the most complex, metaphorical, and "literary" modern conception of mind, hesitated to publicly consider or acknowledge the possibility that the individual mind has access to information beyond the personal experience of the individual. In Freud's earlier writings, at least, even the darkest nooks of the unconscious can be inscribed only by personal experience.[2] However, just as Ulysses cannot succeed in his *nostos* by relying on his own powers, Bloom and Stephen do not proceed within the boundaries of conventional, empiricist, passivist models of mind and memory. *Ulysses* shows that the boundaries of the mind may be less definite and more extensive than those imagined by Locke and empiricist philosophy.

John Paul Riquelme notes that *Ulysses* "is a drama of mimesis," meaning that the text is engaged in "the mimesis of consciousness" (151). Writing of *Finnegans Wake* as well as *Ulysses*, Riquelme rightly claims:

> The sort of consciousness these books evoke is not an empiricist one that functions primarily metonymically by association. . . . *We require a more supple theory of mind*, one that includes some recognition of the unconscious, of memory, of imagination, of what is sometimes called the imaginary than any empiricist view can muster. I am not suggesting that a Freudian notion of the unconscious operates in Joyce's writings or that a Freudian critical perspective is necessary for explaining Joyce's works. But repression, repetition, forgetting, and the return to or return of the repressed are helpful notions in describing the complicated representations of mind in Joyce's fiction . . . . These related notions, especially repression as Freud used it, express the complications of an ambivalence that may include remembering and forgetting, *forgetting as prelude to remembering and to working through or acting out*. (150; my emphasis)

Though Riquelme suggests that the general Freudian model of consciousness and the unconscious is one "theory of mind" that provides a necessary supplement to the understanding of how Joyce's later texts mirror mind, we can argue further that many older, metapersonal models of mind were at least as available or even more easily available as models for the mimesis of consciousness in the text of *Ulysses*.

Since Stephen and Bloom do not consciously move toward their confrontations with the past, Joyce himself must set the scene for the hallucinatory encounters that will occur in the subconscious nightworld of "Circe." Joyce liked the image of the artist as a god, and certainly in terms of the plot of *Ulysses*, Joyce functions as a god—not, perhaps, by direct intercession, as Athena does in the *Odyssey*, but by creating a world that allows his characters to find the resources that they need for their journey "home." As Joyce allegedly told Jacques Mercanton while he was writing *Finnegans Wake*, "I reconstruct the nocturnal life . . . as the Demiurge goes about the business of creation, starting from a mental outline that never varies. The only difference is that I obey laws I have not chosen. But he?" (208). The world that Joyce creates in *Ulysses* leads the characters (and the reader) toward this subconscious setting by gradually loosening the boundaries of personality and memory. As the power of memory expands beyond the boundaries of individual personality in *Ulysses*, the characters unconsciously begin to draw on each other's thoughts and on deeper levels of memory and suggestion, moving closer and closer to the confrontations of "Circe." In *Ulysses*, Joyce creates a textual memory and a model of mind that allow for the intervention of involuntary, metapersonal memory.

In the *Odyssey*, Ulysses learns that his passage home depends on forces beyond his control: fate and the favor, disfavor, and intervention of the gods. He runs afoul of Poseidon and Apollo, for example, but receives constant attention and aid from Athena and direction from Circe. The reader of *Ulysses* finds that Stephen and Bloom must also depend on forces beyond their control—even beyond their awareness—if they are to move beyond the past into the future. In *Ulysses*, the text itself becomes both a proleptic and dynamic force—a textual memory—anticipating and building toward an eventual confrontation with the past through its preservation and repetition, developing a sense of destiny that subtly links Stephen and Bloom and gives what is to come in the text an added resonance and meaning. The text, as a model of mind, also becomes a source of metapersonal memory that provides material needed by the characters in their journey toward their necessary confrontations with the past.

As I argued in chapter 2, Stephen and Bloom seem singled out in *Ulysses*, not only by the throwaway that floats past the obstacles in the Liffey, but by many other conjunctions, similarities, and synchronicities. We learn in "Ithaca," for example, that both men had simultaneously been aware of a cloud passing overhead earlier in the day (U17.40–42). Strangely, even the tone and content of their responses to the cloud parallel each other. When the cloud's shadow covers Stephen in the "Telemachus" episode, it provokes a reverie on his mother's death that begins with a comparison of the bay beneath him to the "bowl of bitter waters" next to his mother's deathbed and leads to a terrifying vision of "Her glazing eyes, staring out of death, to shake and bend my soul" (U1.248–73) before Mulligan distracts him and the sunlight returns. Early in "Calypso," when the same cloud darkens the sky above Bloom, he imagines "the dead sea," "poisonous foggy waters," "the grey sunken cunt of the world," and desperately tries to avoid the "Grey horror" of this vision until the sunlight returns (U4.218–30).

This and other examples of synchronicity and shared mind, as well as the similarities in the characters' situations already discussed, contribute to a sense of shared fate. An obscure destiny—the suggestion of a textual entelechy—develops within the cultural unconscious of *Ulysses* and is strongly suggested by the text. In the similarities and synchronicities that make up this destiny, we can find a proleptic intimation of and a dynamic movement toward one possible narrative goal of *Ulysses*—an atonement with the past that will free the self from a painful and unproductive obsession with the nightmares of its own history, the agenbite of inwit. Two modes of metapersonal memory—shared memory and universal memory—operate to bring Stephen and Bloom closer together and to suggest the possibility of an atonement with the past.

Bloom and Stephen share many strange coincidences of thought and memory in *Ulysses*, seemingly telepathic exchanges that imply the ability of one mind to draw on the experiences of another. Some of these shared memories are very recent—thoughts or events that occur to one character appearing in the mind of the other only hours later—and are shared memories only in the sense that any nonsimultaneous shared thoughts must involve memory. Other shared memories go much deeper, allowing the characters to access more distant memories, events that happened years ago but still have a crucial significance for Stephen and Bloom on June 16, 1904.

The late nineteenth century witnessed a great interest in spiritualism and the study of alleged psychic phenomena by such groups as the Society for Psychical Research. Seances purported to contact the spirits of the dead, while others investigated such mysteries as telepathy and shared mind. This interest extended far beyond the eccentric circles of the Spiritualists themselves and prompted widespread discussion of the scientific validity and possibility of such claims by philosophers and psychologists. William James, for example, wrote extensively about spiritualistic phenomena and was fascinated by telepathy. James attended seances and conducted research for the Society for Psychical Research and often expressed interest in sources of mental content beyond the conscious mind of the individual. In *The Principles of Psychology*, he wrote: "Whether all sub-conscious selves are particularly susceptible to a certain stratum of the *Zeitgeist*, and get their inspiration from it, I know not; but this is obviously the case with the secondary selves which become 'developed' in spiritualist circles" (394). And in a remarkable passage from a 1909 essay, "The Final Impressions of a Psychical Researcher," James writes:

> Out of my experience, such as it is (and it is limited enough), one fixed conclusion dogmatically emerges, and that is this, that we with our lives are like islands in the sea, or like trees in the forest. The maple and the pine may whisper to each other with their leaves, and Conanicut and Newport hear each other's foghorns. But the trees also commingle their roots in the darkness underground, and the islands also hang together through the ocean's bottom. Just so there is a continuum of cosmic consciousness, against which our indi-

viduality builds but accidental fences, and into which our several minds plunge as in to a mother-sea or reservoir. Our "normal" consciousness is circumscribed for adaptation to our external earthly environment, but the fence is weak in spots, and fitful influences from beyond leak in, showing the otherwise unverifiable common connection. Not only psychic research, but metaphysical philosophy, and speculative biology are led in their own ways to look with favor on some such "panpsychic" view of the universe as this. (324)

My point here is not that Joyce knew of James's writings on telepathy—though he may have—but rather that an interest in metapersonal memory, in sources of memory outside one's personal experience, was part of the zeitgeist within which *Ulysses* was composed. Accepting the commonplace that every work of art, every human creation, reflects the time and place in which it is created and indeed is to some extent created by that matrix of cultural discourses, we must remember that the turn of the century was much more hospitable to models of mind that transgressed or violated the empirical model which dominates us today. This widespread interest in telepathy and shared mind among Joyce's contemporaries provides a context for the telepathic exchanges between Stephen and Bloom, shared memories that suggest mysterious and complex bonds between the characters, allowing a sense of destiny, of importance, to build up around their meeting and to prepare for the climactic "Circe" episode, in which memories and symbols relevant to one character's experience become available and useful to the other.

We begin to discover one of the most crucial examples of shared memory in the "Proteus" episode of *Ulysses*, as Stephen Dedalus walks along Sandymount Strand pondering deep questions on the nature of time and space. When Stephen sees two old women descending a flight of steps onto the sand, he thinks: "Number one swung lourdily her midwife's bag, the other's gamp poked in the beach. . . . One of her sisterhood lugged me squealing into life. Creation from nothing. What has she in the bag? A misbirth with a trailing navelcord, hushed in ruddy wool" (U3.32–37). We learn in "Nausicaa" that Bloom and Stephen are "Strandentwined" in the sense that both walk alone along the same Strand during the day. Bloom later picks up a piece of paper that may have been left on the beach by Stephen (U13.1246). Memories also form a "strandentwining cable" between Bloom and Stephen, for in his fantasy in "Proteus," Stephen has unknowingly used images particularly relevant to Bloom's past. "Ruddy wool" conjures for the careful reader an image of Bloom's son, Rudy, who was a "misbirth" and, as we later learn, was buried in a "little woolly jacket" (U18.1448), "a fair corselet of lamb's wool" (U14.269) that Molly knitted for him.

Stephen remembers the two midwives later in the day, using them as characters in his riddling "Parable of the Plums" in "Aeolus," yet, significantly, when he consciously recalls them and speaks of them to his companions in that episode, the image of the misbirth "hushed in ruddy wool" does not occur to him. The hint of Bloom's life carried into his mind when he sees them walking on the Strand does not form part of his memory of the two women, who have now become caricatures to be played with and re-created artistically in his "Parable of the Plums." Stephen does not think of the women again after "Aeolus," yet through them a connection to Bloom's dead son has been created in text associated in the reader's imagination with Stephen's mind.

The narrator of "Wandering Rocks" underscores this connection between Rudy and Stephen's imaginary misbirth in "Proteus" by describing the same "two old women fresh from their whiff of the briny," one carrying the umbrella and the other a "midwife's bag in which eleven cockles rolled" (U10.818–20). This image is repeated at the end of the episode, as the Viceroy's cavalcade passes "two sanded women" carrying "an umbrella and a bag in which eleven cockles rolled" (U10.1275–76). A complex juxtaposition of symbols in the twice-repeated phrase "bag in which eleven cockles rolled" suggests not only the misbirth that Stephen previously imagined in the bag, but also the beginning of a more extensive, more profound, and more puzzling link between Stephen and Bloom related to the number eleven and the figure of William Shakespeare. Stephen's fantasy has been taken up by the narrator, enhanced, and invested with a new significance.

In "Scylla and Charybdis," Stephen claims that Shakespeare wrote *Hamlet* to exorcise (or at least to exercise) the ghosts in his own memory. Imagining Shakespeare playing the part of the Ghost in *Hamlet*, Stephen thinks:

> It is the ghost, the king, a king and no king, and the player is Shakespeare who has studied *Hamlet* all the years of his life which were not vanity in order to play the part of the spectre. He speaks the words to Burbage, the young player who stands before him beyond the rack of cerecloth, calling him by a name:
> *Hamlet, I am thy father's spirit,* bidding him list. To a son he speaks, the son of his soul, the prince, young Hamlet and to the son

of his body, Hamnet Shakespeare, who has died in Stratford that his namesake may live for ever. (U9.165-73)³

Hamnet Shakespeare lived eleven years; in Stephen's reading of Shakespeare's life and work, Hamnet and Hamlet are one and the same to the mourning father.⁴ Both are linked more closely to the contents of the midwife's bag through the cockle, which Stephen has already associated with Hamlet in "Proteus," where, alluding to Ophelia's mad song in *Hamlet*, Stephen describes himself: "My cockle hat and staff and hismy sandal shoon" (U3.487-88).⁵

Shells in *Ulysses* are often associated with emptiness, hollowness, and absence of life.⁶ The "eleven cockles" in the midwife's bag suggest the eleven days of Rudy Bloom's life and the eleven years that Shakespeare's son Hamnet lived. The materialistic Mr. Deasy, who likes to put matters "in a nutshell" (U2.321), collects shells, and among them Stephen notices "this, the scallop of saint James. An old pilgrim's hoard, dead treasure, hollow shells" (U2.214-16). Stephen twice imagines "the two maries" (U3.297) as devotees of the shrine at Lourdes (U3.32 and 7.949), so it is fitting that they carry symbols of pilgrimage and that Stephen first sees them as he walks on the "crackling wrack and shells" (U3.10-11), the "Wild sea money" (U3.19) of Sandymount. By a simple substitution, the narrator of "Wandering Rocks" has changed the contents of the midwife's bag to suggest not only Bloom's dead son, but Shakespeare's dead son, Hamnet. The two different versions of what the midwife carries serve to link Rudy Bloom, Hamnet Shakespeare, and Stephen Dedalus through three simple but highly charged words: misbirth, eleven, and cockles.

Shared memories link Stephen, Bloom, and Shakespeare at other points in *Ulysses*, as we can see in the comparison of two passages, one in Stephen's thoughts and one in the mind of Leopold Bloom. In "Scylla and Charybdis," which takes place in the early afternoon, Stephen shifts from his ingenious defense of his interpretation of *Hamlet* into a curious, disconnected vision centered on Shakespeare: "Do and do. Thing done. In a rosery of Fetter lane of Gerard, herbalist, he walks, greyedauburn. An azured harebell like her veins. Lids of Juno's eyes, violets. He walks. One life is all. One body. Do. But do. Afar, in a reek of lust and squalor, hands are laid on whiteness" (U9.651-54). Later in the afternoon, Bloom, sitting in the bar of the Ormond Hotel, thinks of a letter he has written to Martha Clifford:

> Too poetical that about the sad. Music did that. Music hath charms. Shakespeare said. Quotations every day in the year. To be or not to be. Wisdom while you wait.

> In Gerard's rosery of Fetter lane he walks, greyedauburn. One life is all. One body. Do. But do.
> Done anyhow.... (U11.904-9)

Curiously, what seems a "normal" chain of associations in Bloom's thoughts—that is, one bounded by the limits of individual experience that we tend to see as the limits of the individual mind—moves from Shakespeare into a nearly verbatim repetition of phrases that had occurred to Stephen hours earlier. Much later, when Stephen and Bloom are together in "Eumaeus," Stephen "launched out into praises of Shakespeare's songs, at least of in or about that period, the lutenist Dowland who lived in Fetter lane near Gerard the herbalist" (U16.1761-63), and Bloom shows no sign of remembering the shared phrases.

The relationship of Shakespeare, Stephen, and Bloom is, like much of *Ulysses*, more suggestive than conclusive, and readers, following the relationship as it grows in the novel, tend to be frustrated by the strange scene in "Circe" in which Stephen and Bloom see in a mirror the beardless face of Shakespeare, "rigid in facial paralysis, crowned by the reflection of the reindeer antlered hatrack in the hall" (U15.3822-24).[7] Although the correspondences that link Stephen, Bloom, and Shakespeare are shadowy, we can isolate some pieces of this perhaps finally unsolvable or incomplete puzzle that are useful for the present discussion. First, Stephen equates Shakespeare's son Hamnet with the character of Prince Hamlet and identifies Shakespeare with the Ghost. Second, although Stephen at times seems to identify himself with the Ghost of King Hamlet,[8] he also sees himself at times as Prince Hamlet, wearing his "Hamlet hat" (U3.390). This identification with Hamlet/Hamnet allows Stephen to represent some of his anger at his father, who, like Stephen's vision of Shakespeare acting King Hamlet, is "a ghost by absence" (U9.174), and at his mother, "the guilty queen" (U9.179-80), who, like Gertrude, is to blame for her son's anguish. Third, there is a striking resemblance between Shakespeare's marital and familial situations as Stephen describes them and Bloom's current situation: both are cuckolds, both are troubled by guilt over the death of an only son,[9] both are insecure in their sexuality.[10] For example, when Stephen says of Shakespeare, "Belief in himself has been untimely killed.... Assumed dongiovannism will not save him" (U9.455-59), the reader may naturally think of Bloom's attempts at creating a romantic image of himself for Martha Clifford and Gerty MacDowell as well as Bloom's recurring thoughts about Mozart's *Don Giovanni* during the day.[11] Fourth, just as there is a suggested relationship between Stephen and Hamlet/Hamnet, so there is, as we have seen above, a link between Hamnet and Rudy Bloom. This complex network of correspondences and suggestions becomes even more puzzling when set into the context of larger themes such as paternity: if Bloom equals Shakespeare and Stephen equals Hamlet/Hamnet and Hamnet equals Rudy, then does a father/son relationship between Bloom and Stephen exist through these parallels? If Rudy is the son of Bloom's body, is Stephen "the son of his soul" (U9.171)?

Whatever the nature of the connections that Stephen and Bloom share through their relationships to Stephen's narrative of Shakespeare's life, clearly Joyce goes to great lengths to establish a system of subtle correspondences between them through shared memories and a number of similarities in personalities and situations. Just as the similarities between characters lie beneath the surface of the novel, available to the careful reader but not, for the most part, to the characters themselves, so the shared memories serve to link the characters subconsciously rather than consciously, giving us access to a deeper level of significance than the characters are consciously aware of and providing material for the workings of "Joyce's mnemotechnic," an involuntary textual memory in *Ulysses* carefully constructed to suggest one possible model for the working-through or entelechy of identity.

The shared memories and thoughts in *Ulysses* suggest a strong, albeit murky, sense of a common destiny or fate shared by Stephen and Bloom. Discussing Shakespeare's life in "Scylla and Charybdis," Stephen recalls that "A star, a daystar, a firedrake, rose at his birth. It shone by day in the heavens alone, brighter than Venus in the night, and by night it shone over delta in Cassiopeia . . ." (U9.928–30). Much later, after the fireworks of "Circe," the narrator of "Ithaca" tells us of Bloom's consideration of this star, "a new luminous sun generated by the collision and amalgamation in incandescence of two nonluminous exsuns" (U17.1120–21). We then learn of another star "of similar origin but of lesser brilliancy which had appeared . . . about the period of the birth of Leopold Bloom" (U17.1123–26) and of two other stars "of (presumably) similar origin which had (effectively or presumably) appeared in and disappeared from the constellation of Andromeda about the period of the birth of Stephen Dedalus, and in and from the constellation of Auriga some years after the birth and death of Rudolph Bloom, junior . . ." (U17.1126–30). Admittedly, we must read anything presented in "Ithaca" in the context of the episode, allowing for the ironic, facetious tone of the narration. The narrative technique of "Ithaca" creates a gulf between the reader and the character that is difficult to bridge. For example, do the astronomical details presented above actually occur to Bloom or has the intrusive narrator taken over by the end of this long passage? Almost all of the episodes in *Ulysses* after "Hades" present similar questions about the effects or repercussions of narrative eccentricities on the meaning of the occurrences in each episode and how these occurrences presumably fit into the larger reading of the plot of *Ulysses* as a *novel* rather than a collection of episodes. My reading of *Ulysses* presumes that the eccentricities of individual narrators do not extend deep enough to distort fully what is "going on" in each episode and hence in the plot of the novel; rather, the narrative voices affect how we hear about what is going on and how much we are able to learn about what is going on. From this perspective we can assume that the correspondences developed in the course of Bloom's contemplation of the constellations in "Ithaca" are congruent with Stephen's earlier thoughts about Shakespeare's star in "Scylla and Charybdis." Thus, while the exact meaning of the stellar affinities among Shakespeare, Stephen, Rudy, and Bloom may elude us (as does any exact meaning of the other correspondences between these four persons), the fact that these correspondences are established and reinforced through so much of the novel suggests that these relationships transcend irony, coincidence, and mere similarity, that they are "written in the stars" or governed by some sort of special destiny.

This sense of fate or destiny presents itself again in a dream that Stephen remembers in the morning as he walks along the beach:

> After he woke me up last night same dream or was it? Wait. Open hallway. Street of harlots. Remember. Haroun al Raschid. I am almosting it. That man led me, spoke. I was not afraid. The melon he had he held against my face. Smiled: creamfruit smell. That was the rule, said. In. Come. Red carpet spread. You will see who. (*U*3.365–69)

Stephen's memory of the dream is provoked when he imagines the cocklepickers' dog digging in the sand as "a pard, a panther, got in spousebreach, vulturing the dead" (*U*3.363–64), which reminds him of Haines's dream in the tower the night before.[12] This memory of Haines's dream triggers his own involuntary memory of a dream he cannot quite remember; voluntary memory will not yield the secrets of the dream up to him, but the reader who remembers Stephen's dream later in the novel comes to see its occult relation to Bloom.

Later in the day, when Stephen feels someone passing behind him as he stands on the steps of the National Library, he moves aside and thinks about his destiny in the same spot where in *A Portrait* he had "watched the birds for augury" (*U*9.1206; *P*224–26). The man who has passed him is Bloom, and as Mulligan greets the "wandering jew," Stephen remembers: "Last night I flew. Easily flew. Men wondered. Street of harlots after. A creamfruit melon he held to me. In. You will see" (U9.1206–9).

Stephen's dream is, like many dreams, obscure, ambiguous, and difficult to recall. Its full meaning is unclear, yet there is more to Stephen's dream than is first apparent. We learn later that Bloom has also dreamed the night before, and that Bloom's dream, though not identical to Stephen's, bears some intriguing resemblances to it. Furthermore, Stephen's dream is not only a memory shared with Bloom, but also a prophecy, for many of the seemingly meaningless phrases he remembers become clear to the reader only in the later chapters of *Ulysses*.

Is it simply chance or coincidence that Bloom first recalls his dream on Sandymount Strand, just as Stephen has done? This first recollection is involuntary; a phrase pops into Bloom's mind as he is thinking of something else and disappears so quickly that he is hardly aware of it: "Come in, all is prepared. I dreamt. What?" (U13.878). As he sits on the rocks at the end of the episode, Bloom recalls a practical joke played on Dennis Breen, which causes him to worry about his sexual ability and then, like Stephen, to think of fate: "U.p:up. Fate that is. He, not me. Also a shop often noticed. Curse seems to dog it. Dreamt last night? Wait. Something confused. She had red slippers on. Turkish. Wore the breeches. Suppose she does? Would I like her in pyjamas?" (U13.1239–42).

Both men's dreams of the night before, while similar in tone, contain some elements particularly appropriate to their own situations. Bloom thinks of Molly wearing the pants, while Stephen dreams of Daedalian flight. Yet both dreams evoke images of the East, a motif that runs through Bloom's mind all day. Bloom associates melons with the East, and he associates Molly's buttocks with melons and the odors of the East. Musing about fruit transported from "Orangegroves and immense melonfields north of Jaffa" (U4.194) through the Mediterranean and Gibraltar (where Molly was born) to Ireland, Bloom remembers "Molly in Citron's basketchair. Nice to hold, cool waxen fruit, hold in the hand, lift it to the nostrils and smell the perfume. Like that, heavy, sweet, wild perfume" (U4.206–8). Near the end of "Ithaca," we find Bloom in bed with Molly, satisfied

> at the ubiquity in eastern and western terrestrial hemispheres, in all habitable lands and islands explored or unexplored (the land of the midnight sun, the islands of the blessed, the isles of Greece, the land of promise), of adipose anterior and posterior female hemispheres,

redolent of milk and honey and of excretory sanguine and seminal warmth.... (U17.2229-33)

Thus satisfied, Bloom turns to his wife and kisses "the plump mellow yellow smellow melons of her rump, on each plump melonous hemisphere, in their mellow yellow furrow, with obscure prolonged provocative melonsmellonous osculation" (U17.2241-43).

Stephen's dream of a man who held a melon with a "creamfruit smell" up to him thus suggests a connection with associations in Bloom's mind regarding Molly, the Mediterranean, and the East. This connection is established more firmly in "Eumaeus" when Bloom goes out of his way to emphasize Molly's passionate southern nature to Stephen, even displaying a soiled photograph of his wife "with her fleshy charms on evidence in an open fashion as she was in the full bloom of womanhood in evening dress cut ostentatiously low for the occasion to give a liberal display of bosom" (U16.1428-30). "Do you consider," Bloom asks Stephen, "that a Spanish type?" (U16.1426)

The characters' dreams, then, provide more shared, unconscious memories, more common associations that tie them closer and closer together subliminally as the day goes on. These shared memories and shared thoughts imply a special relationship between Stephen and Bloom that exists on a level which the characters are not consciously aware of, and, in doing so, they suggest a model of mind that depends on some larger, unconscious form of memory than the personal memory of the limited, empiricist subject. The phrase "street of harlots" in Stephen's dream (U3.366 and 9.1209), for example, looks forward and announces what is to come, for Bloom and Stephen encounter the ghosts of their pasts, the representations of buried traumas, on a "street of harlots" in "Nighttown"; there the two minds merge most fully, there each has more access to the other's mind than at any other point in the novel. The shared memory of the dream thus prepares the characters subconsciously for the eventual confrontations with the past that they will face in "Circe" and verifies for the reader the existence of some sort of occult and unusual relationship between the two men.

The implied "destiny" buried in Stephen's dream depends on the eventual revelation of more correspondences and links to the reader. As *Ulysses* proceeds, and as Stephen and Bloom move into and through the nightworld of Nighttown, we see many of these links continued and reinforced. For example, as Stephen nears his vision of his mother, he realizes confusedly that the setting of his dream has been realized:

"Mark me. I dreamt of a watermelon. . . . It was here. Street of harlots. In Serpentine avenue Beelzebub showed me her, a fubsy widow. Where's the red carpet spread?" (U15.3922 and 3930-31). Haroun al Raschid, who figures in Stephen's dream, turns up in "Circe" in one of Bloom's fantasies (U15.3113). Later, after Bloom has impressed Bella with his knowledge of her personal life, she asks, "(*almost speechless*) Who are. Incog!" (U15.4308).[13] Bloom does not answer, but as he leaves the house he "draws his caliph's hood and poncho and hurries down the steps with sideways face. Incog Haroun al Raschid he flits behind the silent lechers and hastens on . . . with fleet step of a pard" (U15.4324-26). Though the narrative tone is ironic, the inclusion of details from Stephen's dream earlier in the day (Haroun al Raschid, the pard) stimulates the reader to consider a shared mind that lies beyond what we are accustomed to accept as the limits of the personal mind and individual memory.

By the time Bloom and Stephen reach Nighttown there seems to be no limit to what the characters may know, for they are able to draw on symbols and memories far beyond their own experience. These shared memories can best be explained in the context of what I will call "universal memory"—the idea that all mind is linked in a universal psychic medium, a vast repository of knowledge that transcends the limitations of time and space which normally dominate the consciousness of the individual human mind, bound as it is in a physical body. Universal memory forms a backdrop for the telepathy that takes place in *Ulysses* when one character shares the contents of another's mind, and it also helps explain the deeper networks of meaning that often lie behind the characters' shared thoughts and memories.

Joyce had many sources—both modern and ancient—for a tradition that posited the idea of a repository of information much larger than one individual's personal experience—essentially, the "innate ideas" that Locke's theory of mind so successfully rejected. While, as I noted, the content of the Freudian unconscious is generally limited to individual experiences, many pre-Freudian thinkers wrote of what we now call the unconscious as a far less restricted, more open form of universal memory. This idea of universal memory underlies Joyce's conceptions of personal and shared memory and provides more symbolic and associative material for the use of involuntary memory as it attempts to work out the destinies of Stephen and Bloom in *Ulysses*.

The idea of memory as a link to a prenatal, metapersonal mind or source of knowledge goes back at least as far as Plato's concept of *anamnesis*. In the *Meno*, for example, Socrates coaxes a young servant boy through a geometrical equation, demonstrating that the boy is able to "remember" innate knowledge—in this case, mathematical forms—that he could not possibly have learned in his lifetime. Learning in the *Meno* thus becomes a "recollection in this life of realities and truths seen and known by the soul before its incarnation" (Cornford 2). R. S. Bluck argues in his commentary on Plato's *Phaedo* that the *Meno* illustrates Plato's belief in the Pythagorean and Orphic doctrines of reincarnation and the transmigration of souls, or metempsychosis:

> The suggestion is that if the Orphic doctrine of the immortality and transmigration of souls is correct, then the soul will behold all things in this world and the next, and so must acquire knowledge of everything; and if that is so, it should be capable of being reminded of what it once knew. Further, since all nature is a coherent system, if the soul is reminded even of only one thing, it ought to be able to discover everything else by what we should call association of ideas. (8)

The fact that Joyce's library contained three of the Platonic dialogues most concerned with *anamnesis*—the *Meno*, the *Phaedo*, and the *Phaedrus* (Gillespie, *Trieste* 185)—and the presence of two references to the *Phaedo* in *Ulysses* (U6.578 and 9.1139) reinforce the supposition that he was familiar with this Platonic conception of knowledge hidden "in the nights of prenativity and postmortemity" (U14.386-7).[14] Certainly, Joyce encountered similar ideas about the vastness and all-inclusiveness of memory in the Tenth Book of St. Augustine's *Confessions*, where Augustine dwells at length on memory and its nature as he describes his search for God.[15] Augustine concurred with the Platonic doctrine of innate ideas, claiming, for example, that the memory

> contains the innumerable principles and laws of numbers and dimensions. None of these can have been conveyed to it by means of the bodily senses, because they cannot be seen, heard, smelled, tasted, or touched. . . . We know them simply by recognizing them inside ourselves without reference to any material object. (219)

Asking himself how these concepts can exist in the mind even before they are learned, Augustine answers: "It must have been that they were already in my memory, hidden away in its deepest recesses, in so remote a part of it that I might not have been able to think of them at all, if some other person had not brought them to the fore by teaching me about them" (218).

It is within the memory that Augustine finds innate knowledge of happiness and blessedness and, finally, the dwelling of God himself.

Memory, then, is potentially the most powerful psychic force, for Augustine's memory allows us to transcend our own personal experiences, including all material things, and ties us to divinity:

> The power of the memory is great, O Lord. It is awe-inspiring in its profound and incalculable complexity. Yet it is my mind: it is my self. What, then, am I, my God? What is my nature? A life that is ever varying, full of change, and of immense power. The wide plains of my memory and its innumerable caverns and hollows are full beyond compute of countless things of all kinds. Material things are there by means of their images; knowledge is there of itself; emotions are there in the form of ideas or impressions of some kind, for the memory retains them even while the mind does not experience them, although whatever is in the memory must also be in the mind. My mind has the freedom of them all. I can glide from one to the other. I can probe deep into them and never find the end of them. This is the power of memory! This is the great force of life in living man, mortal though he is! (223-24)

Augustine's view that the psyche transcends the individual ego, that it in fact contains universal knowledge is echoed by Joyce's contemporary, Carl Gustav Jung, and was one of the wedges that drove Freud and Jung apart. Jung in a 1934 essay, "The Soul and Death," discusses the difficulties that modern science has in understanding or even recognizing telepathic phenomena. Jung says:

> The nature of the psyche reaches into obscurities far beyond the scope of our understanding. It contains as many riddles as the universe with its galactic systems, before whose majestic configurations only a mind lacking in imagination can fail to admit its own insufficiency. . . . If, therefore, from the needs of his own heart, or in accordance with the ancient lessons of human wisdom, or out of respect for the psychological fact that "telepathic" perceptions occur, anyone should draw the conclusion that the psyche, in its deepest reaches, participates in a form of existence beyond space and time, and thus partakes of what is inadequately and symbolically described as "eternity"—then critical reason could counter with no other argument than the "non liquet" of science. Furthermore, he would have the inestimable advantage of conforming to a bias of the human psyche which has existed from time immemorial and is universal. (414)

When Stephen imagines the misbirth in the midwife's bag in "Proteus," he thinks of its "trailing navelcord" as a connection to "Edenville": "The cords of all link back, strandentwining cable of all flesh. That is why mystic monks. Will you be as gods? Gaze in your *omphalos*. Hello! Kinch here. Put me on to Edenville. Aleph, alpha: nought, nought, one" (*U*3.37–40). Stephen's playful image of the umbilicus as a telephonic link to his ancestors resembles conceptions of race memory, similar in some ways to universal memory, current in Joyce's time. This idea of racial or ancestral memory suggests itself to Stephen later in the same episode in a strange "memory" of an actual historical event that occurred in Dublin in the fourteenth century, according to Thornton, when, "During a famine in 1331, a school of whales was caught in the shallows of Dublin Bay. The Dubliners killed and ate the whales, temporarily relieving the famine" (58). In one sense, Stephen is merely re-creating in his imagination an event he has read about, but his involvement with and relationship to the people in his revery suggests closer ties:

> A school of turlehide whales stranded in hot noon, spouting, hobbling in the shallows. Then from the starving cagework city a horde of jerkined dwarfs, my people, with flayers' knives, running, scaling, hacking in green blubbery whalemeat. I moved among them on the frozen Liffey, that I, a changeling, among the spluttering resin fires. I spoke to no-one: none to me. (*U*3.303–9)

Stephen's phrase "that I, a changeling" can be read not only in terms of ancestral or racial memory, but also in relation to the doctrine of metempsychosis, which becomes in *Ulysses* a motif suggesting psychological transformation, even within one individual, a metaphor for psychic transmigration or transformation. True, when Bloom first explains the idea in response to a question from Molly, he tries to give the orthodox definition: "It's Greek," he says, "from the Greek. That means the transmigration of souls." Molly's response—"O, rocks! . . . Tell us in plain words"—leads him to try again: "—Some people believe, he said, that we go on living in another body after death, that we lived before. They call it reincarnation. That we all lived before on the earth thousands of years ago or some other planet. They say we have forgotten it. Some say they remember their past lives" (*U*4.362–65).[16] Much later, in the "Oxen of the Sun" episode, Bloom adapts his definition of metempsychosis to apply to changes in one psyche through time as he observes the blasphemous medicals:

Singular, communed the guest with himself, the wonderfully unequal faculty of metempsychosis possessed by them that the puerperal dormitory and the dissecting theatre should be the seminaries of such frivolity, that the mere acquisition of academic titles should suffice to tranform in a pinch of time these votaries of levity into exemplary practitioners of an art which most men anywise eminent have esteemed the noblest. (U14.896–902)

The most obvious source for this interest in metempsychosis, reincarnation, and the memory of other existences in *Ulysses* is the Theosophical Society and the writers that associated themselves with it. Theosophy was popular with the intelligentsia in Dublin and London at the turn of the century, attracting to its teachings such writers as AE, W. B. Yeats, and Maurice Maeterlinck. Contact with Theosophical literature and with its adherents exposed Joyce to a "secret doctrine" that mixed challenging and provocative philosophical and religious assertions with pomposity, vagueness, and intellectual confusion. Joyce's reading in Theosophical literature was extensive; his brother Stanislaus wrote in *My Brother's Keeper* that James first approached Theosophy "as a kind of interim religion," reading "with serious intent expository works on theosophy by Madame Blavatsky, Colonel Olcott, Annie Besant, and Leadbeater." While the skeptical Stanislaus felt that his brother's "serious interest in theosophy lapsed very quickly" (131), Joyce's readers face the continued presence of his ambivalent involvement with Theosophy in his writings. In Richard Ellmann's appraisal, Joyce, "like Yeats and unlike George Russell, was attracted more by the symbology than by the pious generalizations of Theosophy" (*JJII* 75–76). According to Ellmann, this interest extended deeper into Joyce's work than the mockery of his tone toward the Theosophical Society itself indicates: "Nevertheless he was genuinely interested in such Theosophical themes as cycles, reincarnation, the succession of gods, and the eternal mother-faith that underlies all transitory religions. *Finnegans Wake* gathers all these up into a half-'secret doctrine'" (*JJII* 99).

Thus, while Joyce publicly scorned and mocked the cliquishness, the embarrassing jargon, and the eccentric behavior of the Theosophists and their hangers-on, he privately explored those parts of Theosophical doctrine that seemed interesting or useful to him, incorporating them into his writing as early as his 1902 essay on James Clarence Mangan and as late as *Ulysses* and *Finnegans Wake*.[17] Although Joyce was put off by what he perceived as the silliness of Madame Blavatsky and some of her followers, his abiding, though not always evident, respect for Yeats and his serious interest in the Belgian playwright and mystic Maeterlinck[18] must have convinced him to consider Theosophical ideas more seriously. Thus, while the characters and narrative voices in *Ulysses* often mock and parody Theosophy, occult and mystical themes such as metempsychosis and universal memory borrowed—in part—from Theosophy function as serious thematic elements.

One feature of Theosophical doctrine Joyce was certainly aware of is the importance of what Theosophists call Akasic memory. As believers in reincarnation, Theosophists hold that the individual personality is composed, as Helena Blavatsky writes, of two fundamental parts: "There are two *Selves* in men—the Higher and the Lower, the Impersonal and the Personal Self. One is divine, the other semi-animal" (*Key* 364). The Higher Self, according to Theosophists, survives the death of the body and goes on to continual rebirth in a succession of lives as it struggles to return to the Universal Soul that it and all other matter is part of. On the other hand, just as the body disintegrates after death, the Personal Self dissipates, yet the memories associated with the single life that it lived do not disappear, but are absorbed by the Universal Memory or imprinted on the Akasic Memory (a sort of film that surrounds the earth). In *Isis Unveiled*, Madame Blavatsky writes of a "vast repository," "the MEMORY OF GOD," which "keeps an unmutilated record of all that was, that is, or ever will be. The minutest acts of our lives are imprinted on it, and even our thoughts rest photographed on its eternal tablets" (1:178–79).[19] Maurice Maeterlinck, much influenced by Theosophy, maintained the existence of a cosmic consciousness and wrote in *The Unknown Guest* (1914): "We can find more or less everywhere in nature that prodigious faculty of storing away inexhaustible energies and ineffaceable traces, memories and impressions in space. There is not a thing in this world that is lost, that disappears, that ceases to be, to retain and to propagate life" (91).

In 1901, W. B. Yeats, already expelled from the Theosophical Society for experimenting with practical magic, published an essay on "Magic" outlining

> three doctrines, which have, as I think, been handed down from early times, and been the foundations of nearly all magical practices. These doctrines are: —
>
> (1) That the borders of our mind are ever shifting, and that many minds can flow into one another, as it were, and create or reveal a single mind, a single energy.
>
> (2) That the borders of our memories are as shifting, and that our

memories are a part of one great memory, the memory of Nature herself.

(3) That this great mind and great memory can be evoked by symbols. (28)[20]

Joyce demonstrated an early familiarity with this essentially passivist conception of memory in his 1902 essay on James Clarence Mangan, in which he said, "In those vast courses which enfold us and in that great memory which is greater and more generous than our memory, no life, no moment of exaltation is ever lost. . ." (CW 83). Similarly, in his 1912 lecture on William Blake, Joyce told his audience he would try to "recall his [i.e., Blake's] spirit from the twilight of the universal mind, to detain it for a minute and question it" (CW 219). In "Telemachus," Stephen Dedalus thinks of his dead mother, "Folded away in the memory of nature" (U1.265), and in the "Aeolus" episode, Stephen considers the possibility that the words of John F. Taylor's famous speech on the Irish language as well as his own furtive encounter with a prostitute are preserved in the "Akasic records of all that ever anywhere wherever was" (U7.882–83 and 7.928).

Theosophists hold that this "vast repository" of universal memory is rarely accessible to normal consciousness, but rather, as Annie Besant argues in *The Ancient Wisdom*,[21]

> Nothing is really forgotten; but much is hidden out of sight of the limited vision of our waking consciousness, the most limited form of our consciousness, although the only consciousness recognized by the vast majority. Just as the memory of some of the present life is indrawn beyond the reach of this waking consciousness, and makes itself known again only when the brain is hypersensitive and thus able to respond to vibrations that usually beat against it unheeded, so is the memory of the past lives stored up out of reach of the physical consciousness. (261–62)

In the same vein, Madame Blavatsky argues that the "Spiritual Ego," or Higher Self, which is potentially omniscient, "rebecomes *quasi* omniscient during those hours on earth when certain abnormal conditions and physiological changes in the body make the *Ego* free from the trammels of matter" (*Key* 133). Coincidentally, the "abnormal conditions" listed by Blavatsky include dreams, hypnotic states, and somnabulism, all of which Bloom is susceptible to.[22] Suggesting that Madame Blavatsky had a serious effect on Joyce's thinking about the nature of mind and memory may seem farfetched, especially considering the ridicule with which he usually referred to Theosophy and Theosophists, but Theosophical writings participated in a wide culture of belief in paranormal phenomena. For example, no less a thinker than William James echoed these Theosophical notions when, in explaining the ideas of the German psychologist and physicist Gustav Theodor Fechner in a report to the Society for Psychical Research, he argued:

> If an act of yours is to be consciously remembered hereafter, it must leave traces on the material universe such that when the *traced parts of the said universe systematically enter into activity together* the act is consciously recalled. During your life the traces are mainly in your brain; but after your death, since your brain is gone, they exist in the shape of all the records of your actions which the outer world stores up as the effects, immediate or remote, thereof, the cosmos being in some degree, however slight, made structurally different by every act of ours that takes place in it. (*Essays* 358; original emphasis)[23]

The notion of psychic access to some form of universal memory is clearly related to the undercurrent of shared memory and distant memories in *Ulysses*, providing a context for these strange occurrences, a model of mind that exceeds the psychic resources normally granted by the empiricist model of mind. Under the right conditions, universal memory as envisioned by Yeats, Maeterlinck, and the Theosophists can expand the associative power and significance of symbols, allow access to other minds, and even grant access to the memories or spirits of the dead. These notions of universal memory are thus useful in considering the loosening of the boundaries of mind and experience that occurs in the "Circe" episode, in which powerful memories and symbols call up the specters of the past to bring Stephen and Bloom to the confrontations with the past that they have avoided. As Yeats wrote in the passage from "Magic" quoted above, "this great mind and great memory can be evoked by symbols." In "Circe," seemingly simple, homely objects, words, and actions strike chords in the personal memories of Stephen and Bloom, in part because of the resonance that these symbols gather from the deeper, common mental territory which Joyce has established between them through shared memories and from a still deeper Great Memory in which—at least, according to Theosophy—all meanings and associations are stored. Certainly, one can argue that prevailing cultural discourse forms a "cultural memory" that provides such common associations without the need for a Great Memory; all I claim here is that

Joyce's writings give us reason to suppose that notions of universal memory current in his time supplement other forms of memory in his work, providing another thread in the cultural unconscious of *Ulysses*. One could even argue that this model of memory underlies a complex textual memory in the novel, in that virtually every notable occurrence, every word of significance in *Ulysses* is "remembered" by the text and becomes available to the characters—not only to the character who originally experienced the event, but to other characters and to the various, often limited, narrative voices in the novel. Thus, the text of *Ulysses* becomes a sort of Akasic memory "of all that ever anywhere wherever was" (*U*7.882–83).

Critics working with the "Circe" episode have been puzzled by certain textual anomalies in the chapter, passages that go beyond shared memory between one character and another and defy or violate traditional novelistic limits assigned to character, narrator, and even to the author of a work of fiction. In these anomalous passages, the characters and the specters that they encounter demonstrate knowledge not only far beyond their own experience, but even beyond the experience of other characters.

The hallucinations in "Circe" often include unusual, random bits of material that have occurred previously only in narrative digressions in earlier chapters. One example is Black Liz, a hen that appears in a strange narrative parody in "Cyclops" that arises from the nameless narrator's sarcastic thought that Bloom would "have a soft hand under a hen": "Black Liz is our hen. She lays eggs for us. When she lays her egg she is so glad. Gara. Klook Klook Klook. Then comes good uncle Leo. He puts his hand under black Liz and takes her fresh egg" (*U*12.845–49). When Zoe reads Bloom's palm in "Circe" and suggests that he is a "henpecked husband,"[24] Black Liz reappears as "a huge rooster hatching in a chalk circle" (*U*15.3706–7). The seemingly chance combination of symbols in the text—Bloom's hand, "henpecked," and even a suggestion of Madame Blavatsky's interest in magic[25]—forms a matrix that evokes Black Liz, significantly transformed into a cock to reflect Bloom's sexual fears.

Another unsettling anomaly in "Circe" involves the appearance of the "ghouleaten" Paddy Dignam. Dignam's death has been on Bloom's mind all day—when he defines metempsychosis for Molly in "Calypso," for instance, he thinks to himself, "That we live after death. Our souls. That a man's soul after he dies, Dignam's soul . . ." (*U*4.352–53)—so the fact that Bloom "sees" Dignam and speaks to him in the hallucinatory palace of "Circe" is not strange in itself. If Dignam's ghost in "Circe" is simply a manifestation of the subconscious mind, however, it is more than a manifestation of *Bloom's* personal, subconscious mind, for Joyce inserts a phrase into the specter's speech that ties it to an earlier appearance of Dignam's specter in—appropriately—a parody of Theosophy and spiritualism in "Cyclops" that has no clear connection to Bloom's thoughts or concerns. In "Cyclops," the apparition of Dignam's "etheric double" (*U*12.341) is related by a remote and sarcastic narrative voice, clearly not by a character in the novel. Accompanied by "ruby light" and "orangefiery and scarlet rays" and describing life in "the great divide beyond," Dignam's spirit is said to remark that "the highest adepts were steeped in waves of volupcy of the very purest nature. Having requested a quart of buttermilk this was brought and evidently afforded relief" (*U*12.340–57). Poor Dignam's relief is short-lived, however, for when we meet him in "Circe" he says, "I must satisfy an animal need. That buttermilk didn't agree with me" (*U*15.1234–35).

Other anomalies link Dignam's ghost with Stephen as well as Bloom, for when Bloom explains to the Watch that Dignam's voice "is the voice of Esau" (*U*15.1220), he unconsciously alludes to Stephen's thought in "Scylla and Charybdis": "I am tired of my voice, the voice of Esau" (*U*9.981). When the Watchmen ask, "How is that possible?," Dignam responds, "By metempsychosis. Spooks" (*U*15.1222–26). Finally, the seance parody in "Cyclops" has its links with Stephen's mind as well, for in the "Oxen of the Sun" episode Stephen's attempt to parody Theosophical jargon incorporates a number of the words identical or similar to those used for the same purpose in the "Cyclops" passage:

> Theosophos told me so, Stephen answered, whom in a previous existence Egyptian priests initiated into the mysteries of karmic law. The lords of the moon, Theosophos told me, an *orangefiery* shipload from planet Alpha of the lunar chain would not assume the *etheric doubles* and these were therefore incarnated by the *rubycoloured* egos from the second constellation. (*U*14.1168–73; emphasis indicates echoes of the earlier passage)

If we append "drunk" to Madame Blavatsky's list of "abnormal conditions and physiological changes in the body," Stephen is certainly "free from the trammels of matter" (*Key* 133) and prepared for contact with the universal mind by this point in *Ulysses*.

What are the implications of this sort of textual anomaly in *Ulysses*? Is the reader to assume that the minds and thoughts of characters and narrators can overlap? Is it possible that what appears to the narrator of "Cyclops" and to Bloom in "Circe" is really Dignam's spirit, called forth from the night of "postmortemity"? Critics explicating these anamolous passages in *Ulysses* at times broach the argument that through this technique "*Ulysses* itself becomes one great 'character'" (Groden 55), or, as Karen Lawrence suggests, that "it is the *book's* past that provides the material for the drama" (152; original emphasis). Often such passages are seen as part of a narrative experiment on Joyce's part that has more to do with the relationship between author and reader than with the situations of the characters themselves. Thus, Arnold Goldman claims that breaches of character in "Circe" can be explained only by the assumption that "the whole is the surrealistic fantasy of a man who knows what went on in Nighttown on June 16, 1904, and who has read (or written) the fourteen previous chapters of *Ulysses*. 'Circe' is, if we will, The Dream of James Joyce" (96).

Rather than assume that Joyce is demonstrating narrative virtuosity, let us consider the possibility that he is attempting to represent a model of mind that violates and exceeds the normally accepted limits of empiricist philosophy and science by violating the normally accepted conventions of fiction. Here, narrative recapitulates Theosophy: in the nightworld of "Circe" all thought and all experience is potentially accessible. The shared memories and textual anomalies in *Ulysses* allow the reader to see that there are no limits to what Stephen and Bloom can remember, and yet, this sort of remembering, like involuntary memory, is not a controllable faculty, but rather an uncontrollable force. How are these shared memories and glimpses of vaster memory useful for Stephen and Bloom? How do they move the characters forward toward the visions of "Circe"?

I have already argued that destiny in *Ulysses* is a dynamic force indicated in the text by proleptic signs that anticipate and assume movement into the future rather than a turning-back into the past. While hermeneutic and voluntary modes of memory are conscious and analeptic, referring or turning back into the past, the examples of shared and universal memory outlined above are primarily unconscious and partake of an involuntary movement forward in the plot and, by imaginative reflection, in the lives of the characters.

Although destiny is a proleptic, dynamic force in the novel, what appears superficially as destiny in *Ulysses* is obscure and often dependent for its meaning on its context. For example, when Bloom wants to avoid responsibility for his problems with Molly, he uses a rigid "fate" as his excuse. Remembering their first meeting, he thinks, "First night when first I saw her at Mat Dillon's in Terenure. Yellow, black lace she wore. Musical chairs. We two the last. Fate. After her. Fate." And "First I saw.

She thanked me. Why did she me? Fate" (*U*11.725–26 and 11.732). Similarly, when Stephen first confronts the apparition of May Goulding in "Circe," he responds, "(*choking with fright, remorse and horror*) They say I killed you, mother. He offended your memory. Cancer did it, not I. Destiny" (*U*15.4185–86). The horrified Stephen has his own reasons here for wanting to lay the blame on "destiny," yet the destiny hinted at by the text, by the deep links between Bloom and Stephen, seems much more subtle and indeterminate than any rigid scheme of predestination.

The coincidences, synchronicities, and telepathic exchanges in *Ulysses* suggest possibilities for the characters and set the stage for an intermingling of destiny and chance that may lead to what is apparently desired by the plot (and, presumably, the reader) of *Ulysses*: confrontation of the "sins of the past." An interest in various forms of "evolutionary" destiny, in the sense of a purposive or teleological force, flourished in the intellectual milieu of the late nineteenth and early twentieth centuries, and certainly Joyce was conversant with Bergson's élan vital, Samuel Butler's evolutionary instinct, and Theosophical karma as well as Maeterlinck's notion of destiny. Shared by all of these conceptions is a sense of movement into the future based on the accumulation of the past, a movement dependent not on predestined "fate," but on the inevitable influence of the past on experience in the present and future, the influence of forces beyond the control of any individual organism that predispose it toward events. As Stephen entertains his audience in the Library with his biographical interpretation of Shakespeare, he provides them with a version of destiny different from the sense of predestination that he later takes refuge in to escape responsibility for his mother's death:

> He found in the world without as actual what was in his world within as possible. Maeterlinck says: *If Socrates leave his house today he will find the sage seated on his doorstep. If Judas go forth tonight it is to Judas his steps will tend. Every life is many days, day after day. We walk through ourselves, meeting robbers, ghosts, giants, old men, young men, wives, widows, brothers-in-love, but always meeting ourselves.* (*U*9.1041–46; original emphasis).[26]

As Weldon Thornton has noted, Stephen here alludes to Maeterlinck's *Wisdom and Destiny*, where the author develops a theory of destiny and its workings that pervades most of his work. Maeterlinck's destiny depends on the notion of *nature*—the idea that each of us has a unique nature that predisposes or inclines us to act or not act in a given way—rather than fate or predestination. Maeterlinck's recurrent references in *Wisdom and Destiny* to "the instinct of our planet" (16), "the secret intention of life" (18), and "the secret instinct" are countered or balanced by "the influence that wisdom can have upon destiny" (22). "It is true," Maeterlinck writes, "that on certain external events our influence is of the feeblest, but we have all-powerful action on that which these events shall become in ourselves" (29). Maeterlinck here suggests an interplay between what Stephen Daedalus calls "fate or her stepsister chance" (*SH* 168), the idea that while we cannot control or understand the purpose behind what happens to us, our nature to some extent determines the nature of what will occur to us. According to Maeterlinck, our response is not rigidly prescribed, but rather is influenced by our natural inclinations, or "instinct." The passage from *Wisdom and Destiny* that Stephen alludes to in "Scylla and Charybdis" contains such an assertion, one similar in its implications about the self to the Aristotelian sense of entelechy:

> Let us always remember that nothing befalls us that is not of the nature of ourselves. There comes no adventure but wears to our soul the shape of our everyday thoughts . . . . If Judas go forth to-night, it is towards Judas his steps will tend, nor will chance for betrayal be lacking; but let Socrates open his door, he shall find Socrates asleep on the threshold before him, and there will be occasion for wisdom. (31–32)

One's destiny in this sense becomes the fulfilling of one's nature, and this fulfillment becomes the "one great goal" toward which one's personal history moves. Stephen rejects Mr. Deasy's pompous assertion in the "Nestor" episode that "All human history moves towards one great goal, the manifestation of God" (*U*2.380–81) by reducing God to a more truly human scale: "A shout in the street" (*U*2.386). In Nighttown, however, as the two men's destinies seem to pull them closer, Stephen perceives links between himself and Bloom as Zoe reads Bloom's palm and exclaims, "See? Moves to one great goal. I am twentytwo. Sixteen years ago he was twentytwo too. Sixteen years ago I twentytwo tumbled. Twentytwo years ago he sixteen fell off his hobbyhorse" (*U*15.3718–20). Our fulfillment of our "destiny," then, depends in part upon our receptivity to novelty—the sort of receptivity envisioned in Bergson's and Proust's notions of a kind of memory that breaks through the deadening effects of habit to make each moment new.

The Theosophical interpretation of karma fits in well with this loose sense of destiny in *Ulysses* and clearly must form part of Maeterlinck's views on destiny as well. Bloom muses that karma was responsible for the disastrous sinking of the American steamer *General Slocum:* "All those women and children excursion beanfeast burned and drowned in New York. Holocaust. Karma they call that transmigration for sins you did in a past life the reincarnation met him pike hoses" (*U*8.1146–48). For Theosophists, karmic destiny is no more than the effects of the accumulation of the past in the present, the working-out of what has happened on the stage of what is happening and what shall happen. Madame Blavatsky illustrates this view of karma by quoting E. D. Walker's book *Reincarnation* in *The Key to Theosophy*: "the doctrine of Karma is that we have made ourselves what we are by former actions, and are building our future eternity by present actions. There is no destiny but what we ourselves determine" (209). Just as Maeterlinck posits an external and an internal destiny to represent the interplay between what happens and how our natures respond to these occurrences, so Blavatsky claims:

> from the remotest antiquity *mankind* as a whole. . . . believed that *there are external and internal conditions which affect the determination of our will upon our actions*. They rejected fatalism, for fatalism implies a blind course of some still blinder power. But they believed in *destiny*, which from birth to death every man is weaving thread by thread around himself, as a spider does his cobweb. . . . When the last strand is woven, and man is seemingly enwrapped in the net-work of his own doing, then he finds himself completely under the empire of this *self-made* destiny. It then either fixes him like the inert shell against the immovable rock, or like a feather carries him away in a whirlwind raised by his own actions. (*Isis* 2: 593; original emphasis)

The law of karma, Blavatsky argues, "predestines nothing and no one" (*Key* 211).

Although the line between predestination and a more flexible, less definite destiny is unclear in *Ulysses*, the characters seem to sense a gathering force as their meeting nears. When Stephen feels Bloom pass behind him in "Scylla and Charybdis," he thinks, "Part. The moment is now. Where then? If Socrates leave his house today, if Judas go forth tonight. Why? That lies in space which I in time must come to, ineluctably" (*U*9.1199–1201).

Various ideas of evolutionary memory current in Joyce's time also incorporate prenatal, metapersonal memory and a sense of destiny based on the accumulation of the past. In "Passage to India," for example, Walt Whitman celebrated the unity of past, present, and future in racial development and expansion, seeing movement forward in space and time as a simultaneous "voyage" of the soul back into the past: "Passage indeed

O soul to primal thought. . . . Of man, the voyage of his mind's return, / To reason's early paradise, / Back, back to wisdom's birth" (*Complete* 537).²⁷ Similarly, Bergson's concept of the élan vital, or vital force, developed in *Creative Evolution*, depends on "the continuous progress of the past which gnaws into the future and which swells as it advances" (7). Arguing that Darwin's system of random variation and natural selection fails to account for the complexity of the evolutionary process, Bergson countered with a process in which an "original impulse" (Kolakowski 57) or "initial movement" (*Creative Evolution* 116) works itself out in the development of life. Bergson views this process of evolution as purposeful, not as a predestined or teleological process, but rather as a "creative" process in which "the past presses the present to give birth to a new form which is incommensurable with its antecedents" (*Creative Evolution*; quoted in Kolakowski 56). Much of the work of creative evolution in mankind is carried on unconsciously by instinct and intuition, which Bergson distinguishes from intelligence, or the pragmatic functioning of the conscious mind.

Another writer on evolution, chance, and destiny with whom Joyce was familiar is Samuel Butler, who—like Bergson—developed his views on evolution as an optimistic and purposeful alternative to Darwin's random natural selection. Objecting to the idea that the origin and development of species depends on chance variations and comparing natural selection to "the shuffling of cards, or the throwing of dice without the play," Butler nonetheless also rejected "the teleology that saw all adaptation to surroundings as part of a plan devised long ages since by a quasi-anthropomorphic being." Butler opted instead for the Lamarckian notion of the accumulation and hereditary transmission of individually acquired characteristics, arguing that the "older men" of evolutionary theory realized that "cards did indeed count for much, but play counted for more" (253-54).

Butler based his explanation of evolution on an examination of the nature and origin of instinct and habit—in other words, of innate knowledge. In polemical works such as *Life and Habit, Luck or Cunning*, and *Unconscious Memory*, Butler maintains that "All the main business of life is done unconsciously or semiconsciously." This "business" includes everything from embryonic development to breathing to "the action of the brain, which goes on prior to our realizing the idea in which it results. . . . So also all the deeper springs of action and conviction. The residuum with which we fret and worry ourselves is a mere matter of detail" (*Life* 44). Butler ascribes the unconscious performance of complex activities to "habit," that is, to the repetition of an activity to the point where an unconscious memory of its mechanics takes over and performs the action for us. According to the Lamarckian model of evolution, Butler argues that habits and knowledge acquired by one generation are passed on to offspring and over many generations acquire the force of instinct. Thus, fetal development and other complex processes carried out by an organism even before birth must be the result of unconscious or racial memory. This theory of innate knowledge has tremendous implications for personal identity, for as Butler argues in *Unconscious Memory*, we are dependent for the most basic elements of our beings on memories inherited from our progenitors.

> If a man of eighty may consider himself identical with the baby from whom he has developed, so that he may say, "I am the person who at six months old did this or that," then the baby may just as fairly claim identity with its father and mother, and say to its parents on being born, "I was you only a few months ago." By parity of reasoning each living form now on earth must be able to claim identity with each generation of its ancestors up to the primordial cell inclusive. (18)

Stephen Dedalus's vision of the umbilicus as the "strandentwining cable of all flesh" in *Ulysses* (U3.37) may allude to Butler's most famous work, *The Way of All Flesh*, which embodies some of Butler's ideas on heredity and memory. Bloom is, of course, also susceptible to the influence of his ancestors in *Ulysses*, mostly by way of the bizarre, troubling, suspect, humorous hallucinations of his immediate progenitors in "Circe." Bloom's racial past influences him more generally, however, in passages such as his vision of Agendath Netaim, a Zionist colony in Palestine, a vision evoked by the passage overhead of the cloud that affects Stephen at the same time: "A dead sea in a dead land, grey and old. Old now. It bore the oldest, the first race.... The oldest people. Wandered far away over all the earth, captivity to captivity, multiplying, dying, being born everywhere. It lay there now. Now it could bear no more. Dead: an old woman's: the grey sunken cunt of the world" (U4.222–28). This notion of Agendath Netaim as wasteland is repeated in a cryptic passage in "Oxen of the Sun," when "swiftly, silently the soul is wafted over regions of cycles of cycles of generations that have lived.... Agendath is a waste land, a home of screechowls and the sandblind upupa. Netaim, the golden, is no more" (U14.1079–87). Bloom's alienation from his racial past is similar to his general alienation or repression of his personal past, for he cannot avoid thoughts of his ancestors and his race. Despite his conversions to other faiths and his marriage to a Gentile,

Bloom cannot deny or erase his racial past—as the Citizen proves for him in "Cyclops."

This notion of ancestral memory is found not only in Butler's writings, but in Maeterlinck's "Land of Memory" in *The Blue Bird* (1909) and later in "The Abode of the Ancestors" in *The Betrothal* (1918). Carl Jung's collective unconscious, filled with "the deposits of all our ancestral experiences" in the form of archetypal categories ("Relations" 190), represents another attempt to provide an inherited, ancestral source for metapersonal memories. Jung, dividing the unconscious into two "layers," claims in his essay "On the Psychology of the Unconscious": "The personal layer ends at the earliest memories of infancy, but the collective layer comprises the pre-infantile period, that is, the residues of ancestral life" (77). Joyce was reading Jung's work as early as 1911 (*JJII* 340n.) and may have been familiar with Jung's developing ideas on the nature of this hypothetical, unconscious repository of innate knowledge; whether Joyce knew of Jung's collective unconscious or not, he clearly cannot have been ignorant of the general drift toward the various concepts of metapersonal, prenatal memory present in the works of so many of his contemporaries and near contemporaries.

My point here is not to reduce *Ulysses* to a representation of counter-Darwinian theories of evolution nor to claim that Joyce had Theosophical, Jungian, Bergsonian, or Butlerian notions of unconscious memory, evolution, and destiny in the forefront of his mind when he wrote his novel. As Shiv Kumar argues in *Bergson and the Stream of Consciousness Novel:* "What is of real importance to note is that Bergson and Joyce . . . were . . . manifestations of the same *Zeitgeist*" (107). Bergson and Butler, Maeterlinck and Yeats, all represented strains of thought that colored the climate of opinion which Joyce lived in, maintaining a belief in a mysterious, purposeful force that works itself out in life based upon the influence of the past. These various versions of a purposeful force moving into the future by means of the power of memory operate within the cultural unconscious of the novel to continually suggest the possibility of bringing Stephen and Bloom to their necessary confrontations with the past, of using the power of involuntary memory to somehow dissolve or break the paralyzing mental blocks that keep the characters from fulfilling their own destinies, whatever they may be. This does not mean that such destinies, needs, or goals are clear or must be achieved by the end of the novel, in much the same sense as Kolakowski argues that for Bergson life "has no goal in the sense that human actions have goals, in other words, no one can anticipate its future course, which is more similar to an artistic creation than to the operation of a machine" (58).

In *Ulysses*, then, the reader senses a goal or a set of needs on the part of the characters, as well as a destiny, a sense of involuntary motion toward these goals that works itself out through the mysterious and extensive power of memory, the power of the individual mind to draw upon sources of meaning independent even of individual experience and beyond the understanding of the conscious mind. All of these resources contribute to the transformative power of involuntary memory, which awaits in Circe's dark palace.

4 Joyce's Mnemotechnic: Textual Memory in *Ulysses*

Coming events cast their shadows before. —(U8.526)

When the apparition of Bloom's Hungarian grandfather, Lipoti Virag, appears in Bella Cohen's brothel in *Ulysses*, he tells Bloom to "Stop twirling your thumbs and have a good old thunk. See, you have forgotten. Exercise your mnemotechnic" (U15.2383-85). "Mnemo?" Bloom asks, and Virag answers, "(*excitedly*) I say so. I say so. E'en so. Technic" (U15.2390-92).

Though Bloom has already lamented his fear of sexual inadequacy to his grandfather by complaining "(*regretfully*) When you come out without your gun" (U15.2348), Virag seems convinced that sexual intercourse would be for Bloom an act of memory—of mnemotechnic—a method of gaining a sense of potency in the present by reestablishing a link with the past. Virag's message to his grandson seems to be that only by means of the past—only through memory—can one reestablish control over the present and future. This sense of the need for memory's regenerative power suffuses the text of *Ulysses*, yet as we have seen, Bloom and Stephen seem unable to avail themselves consciously of memory's transformative powers.

Despite the insufficiency of conscious, voluntary memory, however, the text of *Ulysses* develops its own memory, a textual repository of words, phrases, objects, and sounds charged with power by the associations they carry on a number of levels of memory. This construction of a textual memory in *Ulysses* may have been Joyce's response to a number of theories of memory that competed with and sometimes contradicted each other—notions that he may well have encountered in his readings of Aristotle, Augustine, Bruno, Freud, Bergson, Samuel Butler, the Theosophists, and others. Many of these theories—from Aristotle's entelechy to the Theosophical notion of Karma to Bergson's creative evolution to George Bernard Shaw's Life Force—deal in some way with the existence of an unconscious, evolutionary drive within all life. As my discussions of Bergson and Butler in chapter 3 indicated, a significant strand of the cultural unconscious of *Ulysses* may well have been generated by Joyce's reading in and general awareness of debates about evolution and its meaning that were current in the intellectual culture of his time. In the writings of such contemporaries as Samuel Butler, Bergson, and Shaw, in particular, Joyce found repeated assertions of a Lamarckian, purposive, teleological theory of evolution put forward as a counter to the perceived anarchy or randomness of Darwin's theory of natural selection.[1] Just as *Ulysses* may be approached as a site of tension between chaos and cosmos, disorder and order, or postmodernism and more holistic earlier cultural frameworks, so this conflict between differing theories of evolution and their implications may serve as a more specific example of the way that *Ulysses* negotiates this cultural tension within modernism by incorporating it into the workings of the text itself.

Scholars of Victorian literature—for example, Gillian Beer and George Levine—have noted the explosive cultural effects of what Daniel C. Dennett has called *Darwin's Dangerous Idea*, especially on the novel.[2] As Beer has argued in *Darwin's Plots*, "Evolutionary ideas shifted in very diverse ways the patterns through which we apprehend experience and hence the patterns through which we condense experience in the telling of it" (8). Among other possible effects, Darwin forced a cultural paradigm shift away from the conviction of design, purpose, and teleology—to chance and inconclusiveness. As noted, the evidence of this disruption in fundamental patterns of thought was all around Joyce, not only in his reading of Butler and Bergson, but even among writers he knew personally or professionally. The Irish writer John Millington Synge, for example, was devastated by his first reading of *The Origin of Species* at age fourteen; he recalled in his autobiographical notes that when he picked up Darwin's book, it opened to a passage that explores the homologies between the human hand and the bat's wings. "I flung the book aside," he writes,

> and rushed out into the open air . . . the sky seemed to have lost its blue and the grass its green. I lay down and writhed in an agony of doubt. My studies showed me the force of what I read, [and] the more I put it from me the more it rushed back with new instances and power. Till then I had never doubted and never conceived that a sane and wise man or boy could doubt. . . . It seemed that I was become in a moment the playfellow of Judas. . . . (Skelton 10)

This sense of Darwinian evolution as a disturbingly random process that robs human life of its purpose and uniqueness is the primary objection to Darwinism in the counter-Darwinian writings that Joyce owned. Although Darwin himself attempted to play down these disturbing implications of natural selection, Darwin's theory is, as both friendly and hostile commentators have noted since the publication of *The Origin of Species*, fundamentally aleatory, or dependent on chance. As George Levine writes:

> "Progress" is an imposition on Darwin's argument (sometimes, it is true, by Darwin himself). There is no perfection in Darwin's world, no intelligent design, no purpose. Fact may not be converted to meaning.
> This is a very tough sort of "chance," and its toughness helps account for the century of opposition the theory of "natural selection" has provoked, regardless of the evidence. (269)

The evidence shows that Joyce, too, was situated, either consciously or unconsciously, within this debate. While the novel foregrounds stylistic disruptions and metafictional innovations, reflecting "a micro and a macrocosm ineluctably constructed upon the incertitude of the void" (U17.1014–15), a core element of the cultural unconscious of *Ulysses* is a contra-Darwinian tendency that would subsume chance into design and chaos into telos. The novel enacts the paradigmatic tension created within the culture by the struggle to assimilate or resist the implications of natural selection, with its emphasis on constant change as the result of random variation, with no goals, no progress, no final resting place. This struggle of ideas surrounded Joyce—in his education, his reading, and the general intellectual climate of his time; and in his writing, his process of composition and his sense of plot and closure bear the marks of this evolutionary cultural struggle to adapt to the new, nonteleological worldview implied by Darwinism.

Darwin and evolution do make overt appearances in Joyce's novels. In chapter 5 of *A Portrait of the Artist as a Young Man*, for example, Stephen Dedalus opposes his neo-Thomist notions of beauty to the "drearier" views of sexual selection propagated by Darwin, according to which "every physical quality admired by men in women is in direct connection with the manifold functions of women for the propagation of the species." This distasteful idea of beauty, Stephen argues, "leads to eugenics rather than to esthetics. It leads you out of the maze into a new gaudy lectureroom where MacCann, with one hand on *The Origin of Species* and the other hand on the new testament, tells you that you admired the great flanks of Venus because you felt that she would bear you burly offspring" (208-9). In contrast, Stephen's "applied Aquinas" directs us toward "the phenomena of artistic conception, artistic gestation and artistic reproduction" (209).

Darwin is explicitly present in *Ulysses* as well. Most notably, of course, the "Oxen of the Sun" episode uses evolution as a structural trope, and in that episode we encounter speculation that the revolting Mr. Costello is "that missing link of creation's chain desiderated by the late ingenious Mr Darwin" (U14.858-59). Later, in the "Ithaca" episode, the narrator provides proof "that [Bloom] loved rectitude from his earliest youth" (U17.1634) by noting that "in 1882 during a juvenile friendship . . . he had advocated during nocturnal perambulations . . . the evolutionary theories of Charles Darwin, expounded in *The Descent of Man* and *The Origin of Species*" (U17.1640-45).

Most of the counter-Darwinian texts in Joyce's Trieste library (with the exception of Maher's *Psychology*) acknowledge the fact of species evolution but attempt in different ways to mitigate the great cultural shock or disruption that Darwinism caused.[3] While they reject the more threatening cultural implications of Darwinism—particularly the role that chance or accident play in evolution and the abandonment of a goal or telos in evolution—they attempt to stake out a middle ground between the official Christian rejection of evolution and Darwinian chaos (as they saw it). This debate provides a possible model for the workings of textual memory in *Ulysses* and ultimately has important ramifications on questions of artistic design, authorial control, and closure in the novel.

"Oxen of the Sun" is the first episode in which Bloom and Stephen are together for a significant time, and appropriately, in this episode we see the text and characters continually raising issues that lead toward the dark questions and anxieties which Stephen and Bloom will face in "Circe." The structure of the episode itself raises questions about entelechy, evolution, and teleology, as Joyce famously organized the "Oxen of the Sun" on the model of ontogeny recapitulating multiple phylogenies. Joyce conceived of the episode developing along the lines of parallel courses of evolution: individual (developed through references to the various stages of fetal development), linguistic (parodies of historical styles of English literature), and biological evolution in general. At one point in the episode, Lynch

> [makes the] ingenious suggestion . . . that both natality and mortality, as well as all other phenomena of evolution, tidal movements,

lunar phases, blood temperatures, diseases in general, everything, in fine, in nature's vast workshop from the extinction of some remote sun to the blossoming of one of the countless flowers which beautify our public parks is subject to a law of numeration as yet unascertained." (U14.1267–73)

And yet, considering the source, we cannot be comfortable taking such a suggestion too seriously. As Robert Spoo notes, Joyce's explanation of the episode in a letter to Frank Budgen is undeniably full of "organicist metaphors," such as "progression," "natural stages of development," "periods of faunal evolution," and others (141). Spoo argues that the presence of these organicist phrases in Joyce's writing about the episode demonstrates the importance of "the developmental hypothesis, the master narrative of organic growth which, with the rise of the biological sciences and theories of evolution, increasingly shaped the larger discourse of history in this period" (142). The central role of various evolutionary models in shaping this episode, combined with its explicit references to the Aristotelian idea of the *"nisus formativus"* (a synonym for entelechy; U14.1238), to the Theosophical evolutionary notion of "plasmic memory" (U14.988), and to "the late ingenious Mr Darwin" (U14.858–59), highlight the struggle in the cultural unconscious of *Ulysses* between different models of evolution immediately prior to the climactic "Circe" episode. These conflicting models of evolution present in the text preserve a tension between chance and entelechy or chaos and cosmos that exists throughout the book, for while the episode itself and Joyce's comments on the episode to friends such as Budgen imply a reliance on ideas of "progress" and development, the parodic tone of the episode and its ending in what Joyce, in his letter to Budgen, called "a frightful jumble" (*JJII* 475) seem to refute or mock any sense of teleological development, any confidence that the evolutionary models incorporated into the text lead to any sort of perfection or resolution.

The setting of "Oxen of the Sun" in a maternity hospital of course makes the appearance of topics related to life and death likely, but Bloom and Stephen often steer the resulting discussions toward their own areas of insecurity. Stephen directs conversation into contrasts between "our holy mother" and "our earthly mother which was but a dam to bear beastly" (U14.248–50) and wonders whether "an omnivorous being which can masticate, deglute, digest and apparently pass through the ordinary channel ... such multifarious aliments as cancrenous females emaciated by parturition ... might possibly find gastric relief in an innocent collation of staggering bob" (U14.1287–92). Stephen here unconsciously unites his own central anxiety (his feelings about his mother's death from cancer) with one of Bloom's deepest problems—the deaths of infants ("staggering bob"), and, more specifically, Bloom's unresolved anxiety about the responsibility that he may bear for Rudy's death.

Other forces operate as well to bring up these issues and thrust them back into the characters' minds again and again, forming a textual drive or entelechy, a subtle collusion between fate and "her stepsister chance," as Stephen Daedalus puts it in *Stephen Hero* (*SH* 168). Subtly and subliminally, through other characters or seemingly chance occurrences, the text provides objects, sounds, words, and events that trigger memories in Stephen and Bloom, leading them toward the questions they have avoided so long. In "Oxen of the Sun," for example, a thunderbolt becomes, for Stephen, "A black crack of noise in the street," reminding him of the angry *dio boia* that he hates and fears and of the "crack" of the pandybat in *A Portrait of the Artist as a Young Man* (*U*14.408). Similarly, when Mulligan enters the conversation, he introduces topics that the narrator casts in terms related to Bloom's anxieties about his dead son, his marriage, and his sexuality. Considering "the causes of sterility, both the inhibitory and the prohibitory," Mulligan wonders "whether the inhibition in its turn were due to conjugal vexations or to a parsimony of the balance as well as whether the prohibition proceeded from defects congenital or from proclivities acquired" (*U*14.668-72). These problems and the succeeding phrase—"womanly bloom" (*U*14.676)—adumbrate Bloom's anxieties; over and again, the medicals raise questions of maternal death, infant mortality, and birth defects. As we will see, Joyce's process of composition was partly directed toward adding, organizing, and focusing these and other triggers to memory.

In the "Circe" episode, we see Stephen and Bloom confront representations of the traumas in their pasts. Jacques Mercanton claimed Joyce once told him that "the hallucinations in *Ulysses* are made up out of elements from the past, which the reader will recognize if he has read the book five, ten, or twenty times" (207). As John Gordon puts it, hallucination in *Ulysses* "becomes a Trojan horse by which the memory gets into the landscape and takes it over, making it personify the deepest images of either the individual or his inherited culture, or both" (29).

In "Circe," Bloom confronts the Nymph, who symbolizes his fears of sexual impotency arising from the guilt that he feels over Rudy's death. The Nymph represents the idealized, sterile, distanced, and "perfect" female sexuality that Bloom has tried to substitute for actual human sexuality; the figure of the Nymph and the vision of the feminine that she embodies allow Bloom to avoid the threat of sexual reproduction.

In "Circe," Stephen confronts "The Mother"—much more than a figure for his own mother, but a representation of the guilt, anger, and fear he associates with the Catholic Church. These confrontations with the past and its ghosts occur as a result of an extensive textual memory—Joyce's mnemotechnic—that brings the characters to the hallucinations of "Circe" through the agency of involuntary memory.

Involuntary memory depends on the assumption that the past is not stored passively in the mind but rather is an active force, pressing constantly against the present and released through repetition (of past situations, sensations, and words, for example). Joyce's mnemotechnic combines an involuntary, spontaneous evocation of memory with meta-personal sources of mind, memory, and signification as well as the hint of a destiny that drives toward resolution.

Involuntary memory works its transformations in the earliest of Joyce's writings—in "Eveline" and "A Painful Case," for example—as well as in "The Dead," and *A Portrait of the Artist as a Young Man*. From Gretta's chance encounter with Bartell D'Arcy's rendition of "The Lass of Aughrim" to Stephen's disturbing vision of the past in response to the word *"foetus,"* we see the power of memory and imagination to intrude unbidden into the life of the present. Like Proust's involuntary memory, the shattering recollections that break through into the lives of Joyce's characters are carefully composed compositions of place and time in which the full force of experience rises out of the past through the agency of a triggering object, sensation, or event. (Odors and tastes seem to be the most powerful triggers for Proust; words for Joyce.)

We can see this power of word and scene to trigger memory at work in *A Portrait*, for example, when Wallis and Heron demand that Stephen acknowledge his interest in E. C. Heron begins to strike Stephen's calf with his cane while repeating the word, "Admit." Stephen playfully begins the confiteor, but as he recites it, he is drawn into another, involuntary memory of a similar incident in which his classmates struck him with a cane in an attempt to force him to "Admit that Byron was no good" (*P*82). This recollection is brought on by a collocation of memory triggers:

> The confession came only from Stephen's lips and, while they spoke the words, a sudden memory had carried him to another scene called up, as if by magic, at the moment when he had noted the faint cruel dimples at the corners of Heron's smiling lips and had felt the familiar stroke of the cane against his calf and had heard the familiar word of admonition:—Admit. (*P* 78)

We can see Joyce developing his technique of setting up and manipulating the memories of his characters through a careful composition of scene in his notes to *Exiles*, where he compiles long lists of associated symbols designed to work as memory triggers. In a meditation conflating images of Nora's early suitors Michael Bodkin and Willie Mulvey with Shelley's grave in Rome, Joyce writes, presumably of Bertha, but perhaps as much of Gretta Conroy and Nora.

> Rahoon her people. She weeps over Rahoon too, over him whom her love has killed, the dark boy whom, as the earth, she embraces in death and disintegration. He is her buried life, her past. His attendant images are the trinkets and toys of girlhood (bracelet, cream sweets, palegreen lily of the valley, the convent garden). His symbols are music and the sea, liquid formless earth, in which are buried the drowned soul and body. . . . She is Magdalen who weeps remembering the loves she could not return. (*E* 118)

In another passage in the same notebook, Joyce provides a more extensive and associative list of triggers, suggesting the way that his process of composition would carefully incorporate memory triggers into the text:

> Blister — amber — silver — oranges — apples — sugarstick — hair — spongecake — ivy — roses — ribbon.
> The blister reminds her of the burning of her hand as a girl. She sees her own amber hair and her mother's silver hair. This silver is the crown of age but also the stigma of care and grief which she and her lover have laid upon it. This avenue of thought is shunned completely; and the other aspect, amber turned to silver by the years, her mother a prophecy of what she may one day be is hardly glanced at. Oranges, apples, sugarstick—these take the place of the shunned thoughts and are herself as she was, being her girlish joys. Hair: the mind turning again to this without adverting to its colour, adverting only to a distinctive sexual mark and to its growth and mystery rather than to its mystery. The softly growing symbol of her girlhood. . . . Ivy and roses: she gathered ivy often when out in the evening with girls. Roses grew then a sudden scarlet note in the memory which may be a dim suggestion of the roses of the body. The ivy and the roses carry on and up, out of the idea of growth, through a creeping vegetable life into ardent perfumed flower life the symbol of mysteriously growing girlhood, her hair. . . . A proud and shy instinct turns her mind away from the loosening of her bound-up

hair—however sweet or longed for or inevitable—and she embraces that which is hers alone and not hers and his also—happy distant dancing days, distant, gone forever, dead, or killed? (*E* 119–20)

Lists such as this one demonstrate the care that Joyce took in tracing the workings of memory and association, and they indicate the intensity that Joyce is able to build up in his writing through an accumulation of words that are "charged" with the power of the past. Another list in the same set of notes illustrates how Joyce attempted to control "the flow of ideas" (*E* 121) in his prose by incorporating mnemonic triggers related to all the senses that work as keys to forgotten passageways of memory and association. He follows two lists of images—one associated with snow ("frost, moon pictures, holly and ivy, currant-cake, lemonade, Emily Lyons, piano, window sill") and one associated with tears ("ship, sunshine, garden, sadness, pinafore, buttoned boots, bread and butter, a big fire")—with a vignette in which he imagines a young girl grieving over the loss of her best friend and concludes:

> Homesickness and regret for dead girlish days are again strongly marked. A persistent and delicate sensuality (visual: pictures, adorned with holly and ivy; gustatious: currant cake, bread and butter, lemonade; tactual: sunshine in the garden, a big fire, the kisses of her friend and grandmother) runs through both series of images. . . . The boots suggest their giver, her uncle, and she feels vaguely the forgotten cares and affection among [which] she grew up. She thinks of them kindly, not because they were kind to her but because they were kind to her girlself which is now gone and because they are part of it, hidden away from herself in her memory. (*E* 121–22)

Joyce best describes the working of his mnemotechnic in a passage based on the prose style of Cardinal Newman in the "Oxen of the Sun" episode. Joyce emphasized the special significance of this passage when he told Jacques Mercanton that he considered Newman "the greatest of English prose writers" and said that in the "Oxen of the Sun," "where all the authors are parodied, Newman alone is rendered pure, in the grave beauty of his style. Besides," Joyce added, "I needed that fulcrum to hold up the rest" (217). The passage reads like a preview of the essential action of the "Circe" episode:

> There are sins or (let us call them as the world calls them) evil memories which are hidden away by man in the darkest places of the heart but they abide there and wait. He may suffer their memory to grow dim, let them be as though they had not been and all

but persuade himself that they were not or at least were otherwise. Yet a chance word will call them forth suddenly and they will rise up to confront him in the most various circumstances, a vision or a dream, or while timbrel and harp soothe his senses or amid the cool silver tranquility of the evening or at the feast, at midnight, when he is now filled with wine. Not to insult over him will the vision come as over one that lies under her wrath, not for vengeance to cut him off from the living but shrouded in the piteous vesture of the past, silent, remote, reproachful. (U14.1344-55)

This description of involuntary memory addresses many elements of memory already discussed: repression and resistance, chance, and involuntary memory as a function of "abnormal conditions" or the relaxation of everyday psychic defenses. As Shiv Kumar notes, "In tone and presentation, this passage will recall Bergson's theory of memory, or Proust's treatment of *mémoire involuntaire* in *A la recherche du temps perdu*" (122), but it is much more interesting and significant as a gloss to Joyce's own ideas about memory and how the power of memory can be worked into a text.

In Joyce's text, repressed memories, no matter how vehemently one denies them or attempts to ignore them, can be evoked instantly by "a chance word," or, put more broadly within the context of the "Circe" episode, a chance symbol, whether this be a phrase, a snatch of song, or a seemingly insignificant object. Just as no events or thoughts escape the mind but rather "abide there and wait," Joyce's text in *Ulysses* represents a memory that—like the Theosophical Akasa—retains all that has happened in the course of the novel as well as wider cultural associations. This "remembered" material is not static, however, but forms part of a textual dynamic. The past continually intrudes into the text, active and motive rather than passive or simply stored. "A chance word," therefore, recalls other words and other memories, spinning a web of association and affect. As Daniel Ferrer writes, "every word in Circe has its own past and must be considered, individually, as a kind of ghost, haunting the text, returning with a whole network of associations, woven during its previous occurrences in *Ulysses*" (133).

The paragraph immediately following the imitation of Newman illustrates the mnemotechnic outlined there, for as Bloom studies Stephen's face and listens to Stephen's words, "A scene disengages itself in the observer's memory, evoked, it would seem, by a word of so natural a homeliness as if those days were really present there (as some thought) with their immediate pleasures" (U14.1359-62). Involuntary memory presents Bloom with a peaceful, but vivid, recollection of Stephen as a boy in which Bloom sees "A lad of four or five in linseywoolsey" (*U*14.1371), suggesting the "little woolly jacket" that Rudy was buried in. This memory serves to link Stephen with Rudy in Bloom's mind and thus helps to establish the paternal feeling he develops for Stephen. Bloom's memory ends with an echo of the Newman passage, as Stephen's mother "watches from the *piazzetta* . . . with a faint shadow of remoteness or of reproach (*alles Vergängliche*) in her glad look" (*U*14.1376–79).[4]

"Yet a chance word will call them forth. . . ." Proust's involuntary memory is fully dependent on chance, while in Joyce's works chance remains "stepsister" to fate. The coincidences that repeatedly provide Stephen and Bloom with triggers for their involuntary memory—especially in "Circe"—are too frequent and too complex to be ascribed fully to simple chance. In a letter to Budgen, Joyce listed "chance" as one possibility for his counterpart to the *moly* given to Odysseus by Hermes in the *Odyssey*. Strangely, he writes that *moly* "is the invisible influence . . . which saves in case of accident," a seemingly paradoxical suggestion that chance and accident are not identical. He goes on to describe Hermes' appearance to Odysseus as "an accident of providence" (*Letters* I, 147–48), a suggestively ambiguous phrase that insinuates the close relationship that Joyce felt between seemingly chance events and deeper patterns of meaning. *Moly*, after all, is a gift of the gods, and thus something *provided*, not simply accidental. According to Budgen, Joyce described his own process of composition as a similar collaboration of chance and providence, begging Budgen for "a catchword" that would "set him off" in his composition of "Circe" (*Letters* I, 147). In *Myselves When Young*, Budgen claimed that Joyce "believes nature, chance, or something provide him with illustrative incidents for what he's writing" (201). Jacques Mercanton claimed that Joyce once told him: "Why should I regret my talent? I haven't any. I write with such difficulty, so slowly. Chance furnishes me what I need. I am like a man who stumbles along; my foot strikes something, I bend over, and it is exactly what I want" (213).

While Proust's involuntary memory relies on a combination of chance occurrence and psychic susceptibility resulting from a relaxation of habitual patterns, the pattern of chance occurrences in *Ulysses* and the ways that Joyce carefully builds these occurrences into the text indicate that something more than simple chance guides the experiences of Joyce's characters. Stephen and Bloom encounter memory triggers— "chance" occurrences of objects, words, events—repeatedly in the text, and at crucial points in "Circe," Joyce went back through the text over and over again, adding more of these memory triggers at every stage of composition.

Whereas in Proust's novel extensive, conscious explorations of the meaning of involuntary memories concern themselves with a few important experiences—the madeleine, stumbling on a curbstone, etc.—in *Ulysses*, at least up until the end of "Circe," memory seems to serve an irresistible, purposive force reflected in the textual repetition of memory triggers that evoke repressed content, building a web of associative motifs into the texts of the characters' experience to force them unconsciously toward that which they will not willingly explore. As Shiv Kumar writes, Stephen and Bloom

> do not go, like Proust's Marcel, in search of lost time: memory is co-extensive with their perceptions, manifesting itself in a thousand elusive forms. It may, in fact, be said that *mémoire involontaire* is a permanent aspect of their mental processes, and it is rarely that they have to evoke past images by a deliberate effort of the will. (119)

Joyce's mnemotechnic is thus deeper than involuntary memory in Proust's terms and more comprehensive than Bergson's spontaneous memory because it incorporates the force of metapersonal memory and is fueled by a textual dynamic or entelechy. When Marcel tastes the madeleine-soaked tea in *A la recherche du temps perdu*, for example, he finds the effects of involuntary memory immediate, powerful, and transformative—life at its most intense—and yet this surge of memory is purely personal. Marcel is consciously aware of the recollection of Combray that floods his mind and at least partly understands its association with the taste of the madeleine. As chapter 3 has shown, in Joyce's mnemotechnic memory triggers—symbols or images that stimulate involuntary memory on the parts of Stephen and Bloom—gain their power to evoke the past not only through associations with the past life of the individual character responding to the mnemonic stimulus, but also through shared associations (for example, words that come to have strong associations for Stephen also stimulate Bloom's memory) and through a larger, cultural—in effect, universal or collective—network of associations that increases the numinosity or charge of the symbol, even though the characters themselves may not be aware of these associations.

Seemingly chance symbols appear in the text of *Ulysses* not by chance, but rather by design—not only in the obvious sense that they were put where they are by a designing author, but in the sense that the text of *Ulysses* models a sort of destiny or *nisus formativus* in the lives of the characters. Chance and destiny collaborate in the text of *Ulysses* in a manner similar to the workings of repression and repetition in Freud's model of psychology. The energy created by the repression of traumatic memories works itself out in a repetition of the elements of repressed trauma—a return of the repressed—and the locus for this repetition is the text itself. As Peter Brooks explains in *Reading for the Plot:*

> If we can accept the idea of a textual energetics, we can see that in any well-plotted novel the energies released and aroused in the text, especially in its early moments, will not be lost: the text is a kind of thermodynamic plenum, obeying the law of the conservation of energy (as well, no doubt, as the law of entropy). Repetition is clearly a major operative principle of the system, shaping energy, giving it perceptible form, form that the text and the reader can work with in the construction of thematic wholes and narrative orders. (123)

Thus, as "Memories beset his brooding brain" (*U*1.265–66) in "Telemachus," Stephen struggles with a disturbing memory of a dream of his dead mother: "Her glazing eyes, staring out of death, to shake and bend my soul" (*U*1.270-72). The dream is itself a repetition of what has been repressed—Stephen's horror and guilt over his mother's death and his religious apostasy—and this collection of repressed matter in Stephen's memory generates much energy as it festers, animating much of his response to his environment—the "chance" occurrences he encounters—throughout the day. Accordingly, while (or perhaps since?) Stephen attempts to repress or banish this vision of his mother with the phrase "Ghoul! Chewer of corpses!" (*U*1.278), cannibalism and other forms of corpse-chewing become a motif in the text that preserves the repressed material, saving it for later confrontations with the past.[5] Freud claims in "Remembering, Repeating and Working-Through" that repetition is the way in which repressed content manifests itself "as a present-day force" (12:150–51). Brooks clearly explains this combination of dynamic and analeptic energies in *Reading for the Plot:*

> As Kierkegaard writes near the beginning of *Repetition,* 'Repetition and recollection are the same movement, only in opposite directions; for what is recollected has been, is repeated backwards, whereas repetition properly is repeated forwards.' Freud . . . considers repetition to be a form of recollection, brought into play when conscious mental rememoration has been blocked by repression. Lacan argues that Freud distinguishes between repeating (*wiederholen*) and reproduction (*reproduzieren*): reproduction would be the full reliv-

ing, of the original traumatic scene, for instance, that Freud aimed at early in his career, when he still believed in "catharsis"; whereas repetition always takes place in the realm of the symbolic—in the transference, in language—where the affects and figures of the past are confronted in symbolic form. (124)

This is not to say, as some have, that "Circe" is *Ulysses* psychoanalyzing itself, or that Joyce carries on his self-analysis in *Ulysses*, or, as Jay A. Wentworth argues, that Bloom's experience in "Circe" is a "courageous act of self-therapy" (127), thus implying that Bloom is in control of what happens, that he is engaged in "Jung's technique of active imagination" (128). I use Freud's model here only as an illustration of or analogy for what happens in the text of *Ulysses* rather than as an implied plan or blueprint for either the novel or the "Circe" episode. While I do not agree with Hélène Cixous's claim that "Circe" is "an immense debacle of representation which bursts all logical chains, divisions, differences" ("At Circe's" 388; quoted in Wentworth, 127–28), that is, a series of random, meaning-shattering absurdities, Wentworth's claim that Bloom is consciously in control—that he "puts himself on trial" (132), for example—is not borne out by the text.

Memory is a force in "Circe," not a tool; Stephen and Bloom are not consciously and carefully exploring their pasts for therapeutic purposes. Most of what happens in "Circe" is chaotic and confusing, balanced as it is between destiny and chance, between conscious and unconscious. Nor does Cixous's offer of another extreme satisfy; just because events, thoughts, and dreams are unclear does not mean they are meaningless, as we will see when we look into the same riddle in "Nestor" that Cixous reads (in "Joyce: The (R)use of Writing") as an emblem of Joycean "discouragement," as part of "this farce of breaking-up which interferes directly with the order of *Ulysses*, indicating the vulnerability of that order" (21).

The evolution of plot in *Ulysses* seems subject—at least, up to the point of "Circe"—to a hidden teleology, a destined development that operates outside the characters. Joycean mnemotechnic would find no fault with Marcel's dictum that "The past is hidden somewhere outside the realm, beyond the reach of intellect, in some material object (in the sensation which that material object will give us) of which we have no inkling," yet *Ulysses* differs from Marcel's subsequent observation that "it depends on chance whether or not we come upon this object before we ourselves must die" (1: 47–48), for in *Ulysses* what seems to be chance is actually part of a textual entelechy, a dynamic process of development created, within the text, by the constant, ineluctable recurrence of powerful symbols.

If chance and destiny collaborate in *Ulysses*, the characters appear unable to see beyond or beneath the level of chance occurrence to grasp firmly the action or pattern of the dynamic force in their lives. William Beatty Warner, in *Chance and the Text of Experience*, writes that Christian theology marginalized chance by insinuating all aleatory occurrence into a larger framework of divine intention and pattern, so that "an event which from a divine vantage point must appear necessary appears chance to the single person" (225). The divine vantage point of Joyce's concept of the godlike author may have led him to embed hints of shared experience, of a destined meeting, into the text of *Ulysses*. The question of whether anything significant results from this "destined" conjunction is not central here; what matters is that the careful reader of *Ulysses* can see a pattern behind the seemingly accidental or chance events of *Ulysses* that is not clearly visible to the characters themselves, a pattern that reflects the cultural unconscious of *Ulysses* and helps to create a tension between frustration and fragmentation and meaning in the text.

A remarkable analogy to the difference that I have noted between Proust and Joyce on matters of chance is the debate noted above—still current in Joyce's time—between Darwinian and neo-Lamarckian theories of evolution. Two of the most notable proponents of neo-Lamarckism during Joyce's lifetime were Samuel Butler and Henri Bergson.[6] Neo-Lamarckians tended to view chance as subordinate or incidental to larger, often teleological forces such as Bergson's élan vital. Samuel Butler often criticized what he perceived as the Darwinians' obsession with "sports and happy accidents" as the basis of evolutionary change ("Deadlock" 249). Butler preferred Lamarck's emphasis on patterns of species development controlled by acquired characteristics developed through habitual behaviors of use and disuse that are encoded genetically and passed on to offspring through what Butler called "unconscious memory." The older and more established the "habitual" pattern, the more unconscious the behavior—Butler gives breathing and digestion as examples—while more recently acquired behaviors need a certain amount of stimulation, learning, and practice before they can become "unconscious" (here Butler cites musical ability as an example). The sense of design and teleology inherent in Butler's view of evolution is apparent, as this passage from his essay "The Deadlock in Darwinism," which Joyce had in his library and appears to have read,[7] demonstrates:

Variations on the other hand, that are ascribed to mere chance cannot be supposed as likely to be accumulated, for chance is notoriously inconstant, and would not purvey the variations in sufficiently unbroken succession . . . . It is vital therefore to the theory of evolution . . . that variations should be supposed to have a definite and persistent principle underlying them . . . . The existence of such a principle and its permanence is the only thing that can be supposed capable of acting as rudder and compass to the accumulation of variations, and of making it hold steadily on one course for each species, till eventually many havens, far remote from one another, are safely reached. (250)

Joyce's fellow Irishman, George Bernard Shaw, was also a prominent exponent of neo-Lamarckian theories of evolution and a vocal secular critic of Darwin. Shaw—whose writings also formed part of Joyce's library[8]—developed this Bergsonian idea of the élan vital in such plays as *Man and Superman*, where he posited a Life Force directing the evolution of all living things.[9] In a letter to Charles Trevelyan written in 1918, Shaw gives us a sense of the spirit of the times and the general power of these various attempts to accept evolution while rejecting Darwin and natural selection (or, as Shaw called it, Circumstantial Selection). Seeking a new "common religion, which nowadays means a philosophy and a science," Shaw proclaimed that he had found "such a nexus" between philosophy and science in creative evolutionism:

> Out of the mere destruction and confusion and excitement about mere Bible smashing, and the emptying out of mind and soul and spirit along with Jehovah, which Darwin produced, there has come a quite sufficiently definite and inspiring religion of evolution. Its crystallization has been taking place everywhere: you will find it in Thomas Hardy's poems at one extreme of literature and in the blitherings of Christian Science at the other. But take two expositions that may be known to you: the third act of Man and Superman and Bergson's Creative Evolution. These are totally independent of one another: Bergson and I would have written as we did, word for word, each if the other had never been born. . . . Our very catchwords, Life Force and Élan Vital, are translations of one another. The Irishman & the Frenchman find their thoughts in focus at the same point; and both of them had the way pointed out by that intensely English Englishman, Samuel Butler. I can now, when asked what my religion is, say I am a creative-evolutionist. . . . Well, why not a creative-evolutionist party?" (*Collected Letters* 3: 542–43)

One of Shaw's sharpest attacks on natural selection came in his lengthy preface to *Back to Methuselah*, the first performance of which occurred in February 1922, the same month in which *Ulysses* was published. In this preface, Shaw continues to articulate his ideas concerning the Life Force and Creative Evolution, and in the process he provides a clear picture of the sense of chaos and disruption caused even among proponents of evolution by the implications of Darwin's emphasis on accident in evolution:

> as compared to the open-eyed intelligent wanting and trying of Lamarck, the Darwinian process may be described as a chapter of accidents.[10] As such, it seems simple, because you do not at first realize all that it involves. But when its whole significance dawns on you, your heart sinks into a heap of sand within you. There is a hideous fatalism about it, a ghastly and damnable reduction of beauty and intelligence, of strength and purpose, of honor and aspiration, to such casually picturesque changes as an avalanche may make in a mountain landscape, or a railway accident in a human figure. To call this Natural Selection is a blasphemy, possible to many for whom Nature is nothing but a casual aggregation of inert and dead matter, but eternally impossible to the spirits and souls of the righteous. If it be no blasphemy, but a truth of science, then the stars of heaven, the showers and dew, the winter and summer, the fire and heat, the mountains and hills, may no longer be called to exalt the Lord with us by praise: their work is to modify all things by blindly starving and murdering everything that is not lucky enough to survive in the universal struggle for hogwash. (xxxii)

In *Creative Evolution*, we can see Bergson linking his activist view of the past constantly forcing its way into and through the present to the evolutionary idea of an élan vital, a powerful generative force behind change and development. Bergson's complex theory of evolution sought to find an acceptable middle ground between pure determinacy and pure indeterminacy, between the mistake of what Bergson called "radical finalism" or the rigid belief "that things and beings merely realize a program previously arranged" (*Creative Evolution* 45) and the Darwinian emphasis on accidental variation as the primary basis for evolutionary change. While evolutionary change must include a certain amount of accident and indetermination, and while the end point of evolution is not predetermined, Bergson believed that all evolution springs from "an *original impetus* of life" (*Creative Evolution* 95; original emphasis), a "limited force, which is always seeking to transcend itself and always remains inadequate to the work it would fain produce" (*Creative Evolution* 140). Despite this limitation, however, despite the presence of occasional accidents and the absence of a predetermined terminus, Bergson insisted upon a non-Darwinian belief in

> the *continuous progress* indefinitely pursued, an invisible progress, on which each individual organism rides during the short interval of time given it to live.
>
> Now, the more we fix our attention on this continuity of life, the more we see that organic evolution resembles the evolution of a consciousness, in which the past presses against the present and causes the upspringing of a new form of consciousness, incommensurable with its antecedents. (*Creative Evolution* 32)

My point here is not that Joyce was a neo-Lamarckian or even that he was particularly concerned with such a debate, but rather that the terms of this debate were all around him in his library in the works of Bergson and Butler, but also in Shaw, Herbert Spencer, and even the Russian anarchist Peter Kropotkin, who struggled to substitute the force of cooperative, progressive, purposeful "mutual aid" in place of the competition at the heart of Darwin's system. All these writers offered Joyce models for the operation of unconscious, purposive, and supraindividual forces that direct and control not only chance occurrence, but even the course of individual life itself. Chance for neo-Lamarckism is subservient to design.

We can include Freud among Joyce's influential contemporaries willing to credit Lamarck's theory of evolution in *Moses and Monotheism*, where he argued that "the archaic heritage of human beings comprises not only dispositions but also subject-matter—memory-traces of the experience of earlier generations." Freud went on to acknowledge that "My position, no doubt, is made more difficult by the present attitude of biological science, which refuses to hear of the inheritance of acquired characters by succeeding generations," but he asserted that "I cannot do without this factor in biological evolution." This belief led Freud to the conclusion: "If we assume the survival of these memory-traces in the archaic heritage, we have bridged the gulf between individual and group psychology: we can deal with peoples as we do with an individual neurotic" (23:99–100). Most startling is the discovery, in 1983, of an unpublished manuscript by Freud stored in an old trunk belonging to Sandor Ferenczi in which he works through a "phylogenetic fantasy" of human behavior based on Lamarck's evolutionary theories. Freud believed it possible that neuroses observable in modern individuals are in fact by-products of evolution, learned behaviors, that are no longer necessary but which persist in the genetic inheritance of modern humans. As Axel and Peter T. Hoffer explain:

> Freud ultimately concludes that each individual contains somewhere within himself or herself the history of all mankind; further, that mental illness can usefully be understood as a vestige of responses once necessary and highly adaptive to the exigencies of each era. Accordingly, mental illnesses can be understood as a set of formerly adaptive responses that have become maladaptive as the climatic and sociological threats to the survival of mankind have changed. (*Phylogenetic* xii)

In the end, Freud decided not to publish this material as one of his essays on metapsychology ("Mourning and Melacholia" was one of the metapsychological papers he did choose to publish), but it is clear that in his later work he sought to locate the origins of mental illness in a Lamarckian framework of inherited ideas.

In the controversy between Darwinian and neo-Lamarckian ideas concerning the bases for the development or evolution of animal life we can find an analogy to the ways chance and destiny work in *Ulysses*, where the text bombards Stephen and Bloom with chance or accidental occurrences that jog their memories, preparing their confrontations with the past through the accumulation of the affect and anxiety created by these subconscious (though at times consciously perceived) associations. Careful reading demonstrates that more than chance is at work here, for the memory triggers in the text often work interchangeably in the minds of Bloom and Stephen and occur too often and too strategically at points of stress and conflict in the text to be simple accidents or coincidences. Some force seems to be "behind" these textual events—a force akin to entelechy, instinct, destiny, evolution—that develops what, left to chance, might never occur.

The point of this analogy is to indicate that in *Ulysses*, chance operates in tandem with or even in subservience to larger movements or forces working themselves out. That which appears accidental to the limited individual consciousness may actually be a function of an unconscious will, a view reflected in Stephen's paradoxical assertion in "Scylla and Charybdis" that "A man of genius makes no mistakes. His errors are volitional and are the portals of discovery" (U9.228–29). Clearly, the sort of volition implied here is unconscious and even vitalist, a sense of unconscious will closely related to the Aristotelian notion of entelechy, or self-unfolding, that interests Stephen so much. Stephen's statement suggests the existence of an unconscious force within one's life or "nature" that moves inexorably toward a goal that one may not even be aware of, so that what appear to the conscious mind as "errors" are in fact vital expressions of an unconscious volition. This subordination of chance to destiny also occurs in the motif that Stephen introduces in the same episode when he considers that Shakespeare "found in the world without as actual what was in his world within as possible. Maeterlinck says: *If Socrates leave his house today he will find the sage seated on his doorstep. If Judas go forth tonight it is to Judas his steps will tend*" (U9.1041–44).

Stephen's apparent endorsement of Maeterlinck's idea that "nothing happens to us which is not of the same nature as ourselves" (*Wisdom* 28) implies a stronger sense of self and personal nature than some of his earlier musings about identity do. One's destiny in this sense can be interpreted as the fulfilling of one's nature, and chance occurrences, coincidences, and synchronicities may thus appear fated, teleological, or proleptic rather than random. Whereas Proust's Marcel derives great satisfaction and insight from his chance encounters with involuntary memories, we do not sense in reading *A la recherche du temps perdu* that these isolated experiences are part of a intricate pattern of destiny in the text. Marcel is generally pleased to rediscover the immediacy and power of the past, and he tries to "follow," to maintain and magnify, his recollections, while involuntary memory in *Ulysses* represents the repressed and unpleasant traces and phantoms of the past following Stephen and Bloom until they must finally turn and acknowledge them.

The "Circe" episode, then, is the enchantress of *Ulysses*, the sorceress who uses the magic of memory to transform the characters—to degrade them to their lowest, most animalistic psychic levels in order to force them to face and overcome that which they have buried deepest in their memories. The symbols that make up Joyce's mnemotechnic are magical in the sense that they strike chords in the characters' minds, leading them further toward their deepest traumas, calling up the apparitions that they encounter, and working the psychic transformations of "Circe."

Many magical systems seek some sort of transformation as their goal, whether it be a transformation of lead to gold or of intentions to physical realities. Transformation is also a central trope in *Ulysses*, where strange metamorphoses occur not only in the style of the book, but in the thoughts and daydreams of Bloom and Stephen. In "Proteus," for example, Stephen imagines the decomposition of a drowned man's body, thinking, "God becomes man becomes fish becomes barnacle goose becomes featherbed mountain" (U3.477–79).[11] The drowned man's "metempsychosis," his resurrection from the depths of the sea, ironically parallels the physical transformation of his body into a "bag of corpsegas sopping in foul brine" (U3.476). By the time that the "Circe" episode is reached, metempsychosis becomes a metaphor for psychic transformation. Homer's Circe is a daughter of the Sun, while Joyce's is a "woman of the night," but Bella Cohen presides over a palace where all is as liable to shift and change and blend (at least in the minds of Stephen and Bloom) as it is in Circe's palace on Aiaia. In the "Circe" episode, psychic transformation or metempsychosis—consisting, at least in part, of a breaking down of barriers to memory, of resistance and repression—comes about through the effects of Joyce's mnemotechnic by means of the appearance of seemingly chance words and phrases, objects, and events in the text that affect Stephen and Bloom by connecting them with their repressed pasts.

Numinous, magical qualities thus attach to ordinary objects, and metempsychosis becomes in part a metaphor for the ability of the inanimate to incorporate or represent the animate, an idea perhaps more closely related to the Celtic folk tradition of shape-shifting than the Pythagorean doctrine of reincarnation. Proust describes the workings of involuntary memory in *A la recherche du temps perdu* in terms reminiscent of Bloom's definition of metempsychosis for Molly in the "Calypso" episode ("you could be changed into an animal or a tree, for instance" [U4.376]):

> I feel that there is much to be said for the Celtic belief that the souls of those whom we have lost are held captive in some inferior being, in an animal, in a plant, in some inanimate object, and thus effectively lost to us until the day (which to many never comes) when we happen to pass by the tree or to obtain possession of the object which forms their prison. Then they start and tremble, they call us by our name, and as soon as we have recognised their voice the spell is broken. Delivered by us, they have overcome death and return to share our life. (1: 47)

In much the same way, objects, words, and sounds come to be associated with the dead in *Ulysses*, and they jog the unconscious memories of Bloom and Stephen when they occur seemingly by chance in the text. Joyce's mnemotechnic, then, consists of symbolically charged images and phrases subtly embedded in the text that surface as if by chance to move the protagonists unconsciously toward their "destined" confrontations with the past, or at least with their memories of the past.

As noted in chapter 3, W. B. Yeats maintained that the idea of a Great Memory is fundamental to "nearly all magical practices," adding that this Great Memory "can be evoked by symbols" (28). Yeats goes on to explain that these symbols can be "inherent" or "arbitrary" (49), that is, that their power can derive either from universal (i.e., inherent) associations or personal (and hence, arbitrary) associations. Finally, however, such distinctions are unimportant to Yeats, for all symbols

> act, as I believe, because the Great Memory associates them with certain events and moods and persons. Whatever the passions of men have gathered about, becomes a symbol in the Great Memory, and in the hands of him who has the secret it is a worker of wonders, a caller-up of angels or of devils. The symbols are of all kinds, for everything in heaven or earth has its association, momentous or trivial, in the Great Memory, and one never knows what forgotten events may have plunged it, like the toadstool and the ragweed, into the great passions. (50)

For Yeats, even the most humble object—the potato that Bloom carries, for example—could become a powerful symbol if it accumulated enough of the weight of the past, if it were to become "charged" with affect and association. Moreover, even the personal associations gathered around a symbol partake of and participate in a deeper, more general significance, be it archetypal, magical, cultural, or mythic. In *Further Recollections of James Joyce*, Frank Budgen emphasizes the impact that Yeats's essay had on Joyce's use of language, arguing that we must remember:

> Joyce lived among the believers and adepts in magic gathered around the poet Yeats. Yeats held that the borders of our minds are always shifting, tending to become part of the universal mind, and that the borders of our memory also shift and form part of the universal memory. Joyce pointed this out to me, and added that in his own work he never used the recognized symbols, preferring instead to use trivial and quadrivial words and local geographical allusions. The intention of magical evocation, however, remained the same. (12)

This idea of Joyce's seems to have rubbed off onto Budgen, for at the beginning of his essay Budgen makes the following apology to the reader:

> Below I set forward a few more such recollections with the same end in view. They follow no plan, unless there is a concealed plan in the seemingly haphazard operations of memory; and should any

of them appear trivial, I entrench myself in advance behind Joyce's own doctrine wherein the trivial (a place where three ways meet, as he often pointed out) rightly apprehended may be a showing forth of spiritual substance. (3)

Budgen's phrase—"a showing forth of spiritual substance"—recalls Joyce's theory of the epiphany. Although Joyce's epiphanies are more properly part of a theory of perception than a theory of memory, they bear some similarities to the working of Joyce's mnemotechnic. In *Stephen Hero*, we learn that for Stephen an epiphany is "a sudden spiritual manifestation, whether in the vulgarity of speech or in a memorable phrase of the mind itself" (*SH* 211). For Stephen, epiphanies are "the most delicate and evanescent of moments" (*SH* 211). The central difference between Joyce's epiphanies and his evocations of involuntary memories is the content of each event, for while the epiphany involves a moment of insight into the *quidditas* of an object or scene present to the senses, the epiphanic memories brought about through Joyce's mnemotechnic reveal the past or fantasies composed of repressed emotions that have become part of the character's memories.

Richard Ellmann has suggested that sometimes Joyce's epiphanies are "eucharistic" (*JJII* 83), and perhaps the best model for Joyce's moments of epiphanic memory is the Roman Catholic concept of anamnesis. Anamnesis, originally a Platonic term for memory, was incorporated into the Catholic mass as part of the communion ritual, in which the priest says, "Do this in remembrance of me" (1 Cor. 11.24). The anamnesis, as part of the celebration of the Eucharist, symbolically and ritualistically re-creates the scene of the Last Supper, and in doing so acquires the *actual* spiritual power of that earlier event; it is not merely a subjective memory, but an objective re-creation that invokes, receives, and renews the power of the original event. In the mass, anamnesis involves "the sense not merely of remembering something absent but of recalling or representing before God an event of the past so that it becomes present and operative" (*New Catholic Encyclopedia* 1: 175–76). Anamnesis, then, is a direct link to the power of God, and like a magical ritual, it assists in a transformation, the transubstantiation of bread and wine into the Body and Blood of Christ. Similarly, the Joycean artist—the "priest of eternal imagination, transmuting the daily bread of experience into the radiant body of everliving life" (*P* 221)—composes, through a textual mnemotechnic, scenes that recall the past in all its power, though with the important difference that Joycean anamneses need not recall "truth" to achieve power.

In letters written while he was composing "Circe," Joyce referred to the episode as "the last adventure" of Ulysses before he begins his *nostos* (*Letters* I, 141 and 142). In his schemas and letters and in a chart he made for John Quinn (*Letters* I, 145), Joyce clearly designates "Circe" a turning point—the end of the Odyssey, the start of the "return." Why should Circe's palace be the center of Joyce's *Odyssey?* In Homer's epic, Circe is a magician and a sexual figure—Odysseus stays with her for a year as her lover—as well as a dynamic force in the narrative: she gives Odysseus directions that enable him to continue his journey. In Joyce's "Circe," Bloom and Stephen confront various images of woman—as whore, goddess, and mother—that reflect their respective problems with women—dead mother, dead marriage.

Most important, however, is Circe's magic. Without doing violence to Joyce's novel by attempting to find absolute correspondences for Circe's potions and wand and Odysseus' *moly*, we can read "Circe" as a textual "place" where men become swine and then become men again. "Think of that," Joyce is said to have remarked as he was writing the "Circe" episode, "swine and yet with men's memories" (*JJII* 495).[12] The "Linati schema" that Joyce provided for *Ulysses* identifies the "art" of the episode as "Magic," and the magic that produces the phantasmagorical, cathartic changes of "Circe" is the magic of memory.

Joyce's choice of the goddess Circe as presiding spirit for his chapter of memory and transformation may be explained by a comment that James Hillman makes in reference to Frances Yates's exposition of the classical "art of memory," a mnemonic system in which the images of mythical figures—gods and heroes—were used as mental headings:

> Under the rubric of this or that God can be classified a vast assortment of passions, ideas, events, objects, all of which "hang together" because the archetypal configuration to which these details belong gives them inherent intelligibility. The archetype permeated the events grouped under it, and the numinous power of the divine figures gave to each trivial fact in the halls of the mind a charge of emotional value. (178-79)[13]

Joyce's climactic chapter is thus placed under the aegis of the goddess Circe, and her "numinous power" of transformation charges even the most trivial objects and events in the episode. The concept that Hillman explains above—the memory theater—bears further examination as an analogy to the ways that memory works in *Ulysses*. In *Stephen Hero*, Stephen Daedalus says of the clock of the Dublin Ballast Office, "I will pass it time after time, allude to it, refer to it, catch a glimpse of it. It is only an item in the catalogue of Dublin's street furniture. Then all at once I see it and I know at once what it is: epiphany" (*SH* 211). In *A Portrait*, as Richard Ellmann notes, "Stephen Dedalus, after protesting to the rector that he has been unjustly pandied, leaves the rector's room and walks down the long corridor. At the end of it he bumps his elbow against the door. I am told that generations of Clongowes pupils have bumped their elbows against this same door" (*Four Dubliners* 68).

Joyce's interest in such seemingly trivial details of local geography as an inconvenient door illustrates their power both to capture and evoke memory in his works. In *A Portrait*, for example, Stephen realizes as he walks through Dublin how the various parts of the city evoke in him memories of the works of Gerhart Hauptmann, Newman, Guido Cavalcanti, and Ibsen (*P* 176). In *Ulysses*, the "street furniture" continues to heighten mnemic force, but almost always with the focus on the particular and the "trivial." Ellmann argues: "Other novelists are . . . much more likely to present a city in reconstructable form. Joyce offers no architectural information, only places to bump elbows, or to lean them, to see out of the corner of an eye, to recognize by a familiar smell. The city rises in bits, not in masses" (*Four Dubliners* 68).

Joyce's awareness of the mnemonic potential of trivial or ordinary objects and places may have been heightened by Tommaso Campanella's *City of the Sun* (*Città del Sole*), a copy of which Joyce owned. In *The Art of Memory*, Yates argues that this Renaissance Utopian work

> could be used as an occult memory system through which everything could be quickly learned, using the world "as a book" and as "local memory." The children of the Sun City were instructed by the Solarian priests who took them round the City to look at the pictures . . . . The pedagogic method of the highly occult Solarians, and the whole plan of their City and its images, was a form of local memory, with its places and images. (377–78)

While the mnemonic systems or memory theaters that Yates describes in *The Art of Memory* were mental or imaginary apparatuses for *voluntarily* remembering, the memory theater—an imagined correspondence of place and image that trapped or held memory for the rhetorician until it was needed—also serves well as an analogue for the way that Joyce embodies mnemic power throughout his text in the objects, sounds, and language that make up the city of Dublin. Joyce took great interest in the minute details of Dublin's landscape, telling Budgen that he wanted *Ulysses* to be so exact that Dublin could be re-created from its pages (*James Joyce* 69), and Richard Ellmann tells us that Joyce "delighted in testing his memory" against those of his Irish visitors in Trieste "by naming all the shops in order along O'Connell Street, or by questioning them about other people and places he had known. When a shop had changed hands he was a little disgruntled, as if a picture had been removed from his museum" (*JJII* 579). Joyce's Dublin is a memory theater in which the most trivial details matter. Although the characters are often unaware of the effects and associations of the symbols they encounter, the Dublin of *Ulysses* (and, by embodying the city, the text itself) functions as a loaded landscape in which virtually every detail seems to be connected to the past and, through the past, to every other detail.[14]

Another Renaissance writer who practiced the art of memory was the Renaissance occultist Giordano Bruno, the hero of Joyce's adolescence and a figure of continuing fascination for him. References to Bruno in Joyce's works from "The Day of the Rabblement" to *Finnegans Wake* suggest not only his interest in the man, but also his familiarity with Bruno's writings. An important part of Bruno's hermetic philosophy was his development of a magical "art of memory." Bruno's method went a step beyond the Classical tradition, which viewed mnemonics as a valuable organizing aid for the orator, while Bruno saw it as a means of attracting and using magical power. As Yates explains it in *Giordano Bruno and the Hermetic Tradition*, the Renaissance occultist appropriated the earlier tradition of the memory theater

> by imprinting archetypal, or magically activated, images on the memory. By using magical or talismanic images as memory-images, the Magus hoped to acquire universal knowledge, and also powers, obtaining through the magical organisation of the imagination a magically powerful personality, tuned in, as it were, to the powers of the cosmos. (192)

Joyce certainly knew that Bruno's investigations into the magical uses of memory were the excuse given for his arrest in Italy in 1592 and his immolation for heresy in 1600. As Yates puts it: "The art of memory . . . is at the very centre of the life and death of Bruno" (*Art* 201).

Joyce's choice of Circe as the patroness or genius of his episode of magic and transformation can be traced to the Homeric parallel that underlies *Ulysses*, but there is another Circe—Giordano Bruno's Circe—lurking behind Joyce's chapter, working magic through Joyce's mnemotechnic.[15] It is tantalizing to consider the possible connections between *Ulysses* and one of Bruno's Latin works—a treatise published in 1582 on the magical art of memory entitled the *Cantus Circaeus*, or *Incantation* of Circe—and the Nighttown episode of *Ulysses*. Joyce reviewed J. Lewis McIntyre's *Giordano Bruno* in 1903 and, in passing, dismissed Bruno's "treatises on memory" as interesting "only because they are so fantastical and middle-aged" (*CW* 133). We do not know whether Joyce later came back to these works and improved his earlier opinion, but it is clear that Joyce knew of Bruno's more obscure works on memory, such as the *Cantus Circaeus* and the *Ars Memoriae*, when he composed *Ulysses*.

Various scholars, especially Elliott B. Gose and Norman Silverstein, have noted Bruno's presence in *Ulysses* and Bruno's interest in the enchantress Circe.[16] Silverstein has identified a subtle and complex allusion to Bruno's *Ars Memoriae* (published in the same year as the *Cantus Circaeus* and reprinted in the same volume in 1886) in the early pages of "Circe" when the Bawd tells Bloom that "Sixtyseven is a bitch" (*U*15.371). Although Silverstein notes that this strange phrase suggests a reference to a policeman's badge number, it also echoes a notation in an arcane list in the *Ars Memoriae* that identifies the "Fascinatrix" Circe with the number 67.[17]

Silverstein views this allusion partly as "a parallel of Hermes' warning to Odysseus about Circe in the *Odyssey*" ("Bruno's" 278), but clearly Joyce also places the phrase "Sixtyseven is a bitch" at the beginning of "Circe" to suggest Bruno's presence in the episode and to link his own Circe with Bruno's. Another allusion to Bruno even closer to the opening of "Circe" makes this interpretation more likely. Stephen Dedalus, flourishing his ashplant as he walks drunkenly through Nighttown with Lynch, discourses erratically on the possibility of gesture as a universal language.

> STEPHEN
>
> (*Looks behind.*) So that gesture, not music not odour, would be a universal language, the gift of tongues rendering visible not the lay sense but the first entelechy, the structural rhythm.
>
> LYNCH
>
> Pornosophical philotheology. Metaphysics in Mecklenburgh street! (*U*15.104–9)

Frances Yates, in a discussion of "the growth of scientific method" in the Renaissance, claims that "one of the preoccupations of the seventeenth century was the search for a universal language." Yates relates the efforts of "seventeenth-century universal language enthusiasts" like Francis Bacon to Bruno's research into the occult use of "universal memory systems" (*Art* 378).[18] The possibility that Joyce linked the search for a universal language to Bruno's work is suggested by the direct allusion to Bruno hidden in Lynch's scoffing reply to Stephen's ramblings. According to Dorothea Waley Singer, in a number of his works "Bruno prefixes to his name the title *Philotheus*" (21). Singer adds that a speaker named "Theophilo or Philotheo, who appears in all three of the Italian philosophical works, is of course the Nolan himself" (39).

That Lynch's reply is an allusion on Joyce's part to Bruno's *Cantus Circaeus* is borne out by the fact that on the title page of that book, the author identifies himself as "Philothei Iordani Bruni Nolani" (179). Thus, while Lynch is jokingly referring to Stephen's speech as a perversion of Bruno's philosophy, Joyce is pointing the reader toward Bruno's influence on the chapter, just as he does ten pages later when the Bawd tells Bloom that "Sixtyseven is a bitch."

Bruno's *Cantus Circaeus* links what Yates describes as "the fiercely magical incantations uttered by the sorceress" (*Art* 208) with memory and transformation into bestial forms, and thus it may have served as a direct inspiration when Joyce began planning his "Circe." Circe is a powerful and usually positive figure in Bruno's pantheon—daughter of the Sun and assistant of Apollo. Yates claims that, for Bruno, "Circe is magic, very powerful she is, and her power can be used benevolently or malevolently" (*Bruno* 330), but Yates also finds "some kind of moral reform implied in Circe's magic" (*Bruno* 202). By blurring the boundaries of the mind, heightening the power of memory, and allowing form to become transformative, Joyce's "Circe" also implies the possibility of some kind of re-forming, transformation, or metempsychosis for Bloom and Stephen in *Ulysses*.

The most complete and central example of the workings of Joyce's mnemotechnic is his use in "Circe" of the puzzling "fox riddle" that Stephen poses to his class in the "Nestor" episode. Although Stephen attempts in "Nestor" to repress the riddle's repetition of his anxiety over his mother's death, these repressed feelings attach themselves to the words that make up this revealing riddle that first exhibits and then hides his fear and guilt. These riddle words break up and move through the text, reappearing not only in Stephen's thoughts but also in the world around him to draw him back, over and over, to his memory of his mother. The riddle words gain their power or symbolic resonance not only through associations gathered around them in Stephen's mind, but also through strange transfers of associations from Bloom's experience, drawing on the shared experiences of the two characters to form occult links between them and working as effectively as "triggers" to Bloom's memory as they do to Stephen's. Joyce's textual construction of the thoughts and experiences of both Stephen and Bloom carefully sets up a repository of terms that they both seem to have access to, though clearly Bloom is not aware, on any realistic level, of Stephen's riddle or the nature of his guilt.

The fact that Stephen's fox riddle seems to make little sense when it is first told in "Nestor" leads Hélène Cixous to conclude that it is symptomatic of the "proliferation of false signs, of doors crafted without keys" ("Joyce" 19) that is the Joycean "(r)use" of writing. That the riddle is unanswerable, however—that it does not provide a meaning easily accessible to the conscious mind—does not make it meaningless, for meaning may develop and function beyond the probing reach of the conscious intellect. Cixous gives up on Stephen's riddle too quickly, hearing in it only "the laughter of the perverse text" and claiming that "it is at this point that you must stop demanding meaning" and that "it is also at this point that academic discourse is brought to its limit, or its 'dismay'" ("Joyce" 21). However, the words of Stephen's riddle are far from meaningless; they are, in fact, among the most powerful, polysemous, resonant, and subtle symbols in *Ulysses*, operating as triggers to involuntary memory throughout the text. Their "meaning," however, is not to be reconstituted in a sentence, but rather depends on the psychic charge they carry. Accordingly, this meaning is unavailable to Stephen himself in any conscious way and is not immediately apparent in the novel's textual surface.

The fox riddle repeats itself throughout the chapters leading up to "Circe," insinuating parts of itself—words and phrases—into Stephen's (and Bloom's) thoughts and collecting a mnemic charge or power. Just following the initial telling of the riddle, for example, a boy named Sargent who has stayed after class asks Stephen to help him with his sums—"Numbers eleven to fifteen" in particular—and Stephen considers the power of a mother's love, moving quickly to a thought of "A poor soul gone to heaven: and on a heath beneath winking stars a fox, red reek of rapine in his fur, with merciless bright eyes scraped in the earth, listened, scraped up the earth, listened, scraped and scraped (U2.147–50). A bit later, in the "Proteus" episode when Stephen sees the cocklepickers' dog sniffing a carcass on the beach and digging in the sand, he imagines it searching for "Something he buried there, his grandmother" (U3.360–61). The riddle words—cock, bells, eleven, fox, and hollybush or bush—come to represent guilt, sin, and death for Stephen, but also, surprisingly, for Bloom.

Joyce carefully embedded Stephen's riddle words and other memory triggers into the text of "Circe," and a look at his manuscripts, page proofs, and placards for this episode shows that at each stage of revision he worked in more of these words as part of the transformative magic of the chapter, using them to set off chains of associations not only in Stephen's mind, but in Bloom's as well. These riddle words are not clear or simple symbols, but rather they act as highly suggestive, polysemous symbolic triggers to memory that operate on many levels, including personal, shared, and wider cultural or "universal" levels of memory and association.

It is not surprising that animal words such as "fox" and "cock" should appear in "Circe," since the Homeric parallel would lead the reader to expect metamorphosis into animal form, yet these particular two animal words or words closely related to them appear often in combination with other words in Stephen's riddle. For example, when J. J. O'Molloy, waxing oratorical in Bloom's fantasy, imitates the style of Seymour Bushe, he also assumes Bushe's "avine head" and "foxy moustache" (U15.1000). Even in this distant echo of Stephen's riddle we can hear other reverberations, for Seymour Bushe was the defense counsel in the Childs Murder Case, alluded to frequently in *Ulysses*, which is itself a trigger for Bloom's feelings of guilt over the death of his own child. In the "Hades" episode, for example, Bloom muses about the Childs case, thinking, "Murderer is still at large. Clues. A shoelace. The body to be exhumed. Murder will out" (U6.481-82).

"Cock" suggests sexuality, betrayal, and guilt. Joyce uses variations of cock to refer to the penis in *Ulysses*, for example, suggesting Boylan's virility in "Sirens" ("One rapped on a door, one tapped with a knock, did he knock Paul de Kock with a loud proud knocker with a cock carracarracarra cock. Cockcock" (U11.976-78). Molly's interest in the titillating writings of Paul de Kock ("Nice name he has," she says—U4.358) suggests Bloom's sexuality as well in the union of Poldy (her nickname for Bloom) and cock ("Poldy Kock"—U15.3045). Besides the obvious sexual reference of "cock," the phrase "the cock crew" may suggest Peter's betrayal of Christ (Matt. 26). Similarly, "cock" functions as an allusion to *Hamlet*, where Horatio links the disappearance of King Hamlet's ghost to the crowing of the cock ("it started like a guilty thing / Upon a fearful summons"), and Marcellus explains the role the cock's crow plays in the Christmas season, when "The bird of dawning singeth all night long, / And then, they say, no spirit dare stir abroad" (1.1.147-61). References to "Who Killed Cock Robin?" ("Who'll read the book? I, said the rook," U6.591-92, for example) and links between cocks, cuckoos, and cuckolds (e.g., U13.1289 ff. and 15.1133 ff.) continue to mix sex, death, and guilt into the suggestive power of this memory trigger. "Cock" may have deeper roots in Stephen's memory as well, for in *A Portrait of the Artist as a Young Man*, Stephen as a young boy slips deeper into feverish delirium thinking of the cold and hot water "cocks" in the lavatory at Clongowes (*P* 11).

Stephen's fossorial fox emblematizes the dark secret of death, buried or hidden in the past. Noted for slyness and subtlety, the fox, as Ad de Vries points out, is so sly in fables that "he even fools himself sometimes" (202), and as Robert Spoo notes, "When the image of the gravedigging fox reappears later in 'Nestor' and in other episodes, it is unclear whether the animal is burying a corpse or with his nails digging it up again" (95). Alan Dundes claims that Stephen's riddle is "closely related to a subtype of an international tale type" called the "Robber Bridgeroom," in which a "villainous suitor," often called Mr. Fox, "plans to do away with his betrothed and often the frightened girl, hidden in a tree, actually watches Mr. Fox digging her grave-to-be. Later at a large gathering the girl recites the riddle describing the villain's actions and thus unmasks the villain and reveals his nefarious plot" ("Study" 137–38). Here, Stephen casts himself unconsciously in both roles: Mr. Fox, the guilty villain who tries to bury his crime, and the victim, who recites the riddle in an (here unconscious) attempt to "unmask" the secret. Bloom is referred to as "Mr Fox" in "Circe," merging Stephen's riddle with one of Parnell's aliases: "He's as bad as Parnell was. Mr Fox" (*U*15.1762). Patrick McCarthy also notes that "Stephen's fox riddle is the starting point for an important motif" in *Ulysses*, linking Stephen with Christ and Shakespeare (40)—in "Scylla and Charybdis," for example, Stephen imagines Shakespeare as a "Christfox" (*U*9.337).

Bells have an ambiguous connotation, suggesting both celebration and mourning. Stephen first thinks of bells when, in response to Haines's suggestion that "It seems history is to blame" (*U*1.649): "The proud potent titles clanged over Stephen's memory the triumph of their brazen bells: *et unam sanctam catholicam et apostolicam ecclesiam*" (*U*1.650–51). Even before the "bells in heaven" ring in his riddle, then, an association is formed between bells, the Church, and Stephen's mixed fascination and resentment. Typically, Bloom's first encounter with bells in *Ulysses* is more down to earth, for he hears the "bells of George's church" tolling "Heigho!" (*U*4.544-48) as he sits on the "cuckstool" (*U*4.500) at the end of the "Calypso" episode. Bloom's mind here associates bells and death, for as he hears the third tolling of the bells, he thinks, "Poor Dignam" (*U*4.550). This association continues in the "Sirens" episode when Bloom hears Simon Dedalus mention Ringabella as he notices Dignam's name in the *Freeman's Journal* and thinks, "Dignam Patrick. Heigho! Heigho!" (*U*11.850–58). Later, in "Nausicaa," the "touching chime of . . . evening bells" causes a bat to fly "forth from the ivied belfry" (*U*13.625–26), a bat that later causes Bloom to think, "Ba. There he goes. . . . Bell scared him out, I suppose" (*U*13.1119–21). Bloom thinks of the bat as "ba" four times in "Nausicaa" (*U*13.1117, 1119, 1127, and 1143), suggesting the Egyptian idea of the *ba* as one of the parts of the soul of the deceased that takes the form of a bird (often with the head of a man) and flies out of the tomb to find sustenance. Thus, Bloom's thoughts of the bat are interspersed with thoughts of birds, and he pictures the ba "Like a little man in a cloak . . . with tiny hands" (*U*13.1130–31).[19]

Cocks, foxes, and bells—in different ways all evoke associations of death, betrayal, or guilt appropriate to the memory buried in Stephen's riddle. The most interesting of the riddle words, however—the richest in symbolic associations—is "eleven." In a discussion of the importance of number and symmetry for Augustine, Yeats, and Joyce, Hugh Kenner has argued that eleven is "Joyce's most magical of numbers" ("Lisping" 311). A complex and highly evocative symbol for both Bloom and Stephen, the number eleven draws its power from personal associations in each character's mind, from shared associations that link Stephen and Bloom, and from associations in numerological tradition.

Kenner claims that eleven is Joyce's "number of hope, of potentiality: and yet also of death, since new potential can only dislodge potential unfulfilled." He notes that the names Marion Bloom and Hugh E. Boylan are both eleven letters long, that the two meet, "offstage," in the eleventh episode of *Ulysses*, and that "Stephen's age is 22: two times 11" ("Lisping" 311). Bloom associates eleven with death, mourning, and guilt, for Rudy died when he was eleven days old, and Bloom attributes his son's death at least partly to the failure of his own sexuality. Joyce further links Rudy and the number eleven by causing both Leopold and Molly Bloom to make the same mistake in calculating the age that the child would have been on June 16, 1904, had he lived. Though Rudy was born ten-and-a-half years previous to "Bloomsday," Bloom thinks, "He would be eleven now if he had lived" (*U*4.420), and Molly recalls, "I was in mourning thats 11 years ago now yes hed be 11" (*U*18.1306–7). Bloom and Stephen are, of course, both dressed in mourning on June 16, 1904, and Bloom attends Paddy Dignam's funeral at 11 A.M. Also significant, perhaps, is the fact that the Dublin pubs close at 11 P.M., as Stephen reminds us when he thinks, "Swill till eleven. Irish nights entertainment" (*U*9.1105). At the end of "Oxen of the Sun" and close to the portals of

"Circe," we hear in the chaotic, drunken words, "Time all. There's eleven of them. Get ye gone. Forward, woozy wobblers" (U14.1561–62), a repetition of this restriction.[20]

Eleven, as one of Stephen's riddle words, is associated in his mind with his mother's death. Eleven also ties Stephen to Bloom through a complex pattern of associations that links Stephen, Bloom, and Shakespeare. As I suggested in chapter 3, while Stephen casts himself in the role of Hamlet, the image he creates of Shakespeare resembles Bloom in strange ways. Shakespeare's son Hamnet died at eleven years of age, while Bloom's son, Rudy, died after eleven days of life. Stephen was (presumably) born on February 2—the same day that Hamnet Shakespeare and Joyce were born—under Aquarius, the eleventh sign of the zodiac—and Stephen was eleven years old when Rudy Bloom was born. Eleven thus takes on a suggestive power for both Stephen and Bloom that exceeds their own awareness of the connections between them, bringing them together unconsciously through shared, but buried, associations and memories. This complex, subliminal connection of Bloom, Stephen, Hamnet, and Rudy gives the number eleven a deep symbolic resonance and makes it a highly charged "memory trigger" in "Circe," where it occurs eleven times.

We can also trace the associative power of the number eleven on a more impersonal, cultural level in *Ulysses*, or, as Yeats might put it, as a symbol in the Great Memory, where it has become associated with various "events and moods and persons," both "momentous and trivial" ("Magic" 50). Yeats's notion of symbols as the embodiments of the greatest of magical powers "whether they are used consciously by the masters of magic, or half unconsciously by their successors, the poet, the musician and the artist" ("Magic" 49), provides an apt metaphor for the power that seemingly trivial symbols such as eleven come to have in the text of *Ulysses*, where, to continue Yeats's image, they "do their work . . . by awakening in the depths of the mind where it mingles with the Great Mind, and is enlarged by the Great Memory, some curative energy, some hypnotic command" ("Magic" 50).

Eleven gains much of its power in *Ulysses* from numerological associations in medieval and Renaissance traditions that Joyce was familiar with. Eleven is not the only numerological symbol in *Ulysses*. Joyce's interest in numbers, dates, correspondences, and proportions is evident throughout his life and art, from his fascination with many numbers— from 3 to 13 to 16 to 1132—to his insistence that *Ulysses* and *Finnegans Wake* be published on his birthday and the detailed notebook he kept of Shakespeare's life, year-by-year, with careful annotations of the ages of

Shakespeare's family members (*JJA* 12: 323-48).²¹ Adolf Hoffmeister recalled that in 1930 Joyce told him:

> Number is an enigma that God deciphers. Along with Beckett, a small, red-haired Irishman and my great friend, I have discovered the importance of numbers in life and history. Dante was obsessed by the number three. He divided his poem into three parts, each with thirty-three cantos, written in terza rima. And why always the arrangement of four—four legs of a table, four legs of a horse, four seasons of the year, four provinces of Ireland? Why are there twelve tables of the law, twelve Apostles, twelve months, and twelve Napoleon's marshals? Why was the Armistice of the Great War trumpeted forth on the eleventh minute of the eleventh hour of the eleventh day of the eleventh month? (129-30)

John Gordon has pointed out some numerological features of the "Oxen of the Sun" episode, claiming that one way of "fitting" the chapter together "is with numbers" (87), and Hugh Kenner notes the importance of the number eleven in the symbolic structure of this episode: "Eleven paragraphs—Joyce's number of regeneration is always eleven—bring Bloom inside, holding his hat; eleven more, at the end of the episode, conduct the noisy crew out of the hospital and into and out of the pub. Between the elevens stand just forty paragraphs, one for each week of gestation . . ." (Kenner, *Ulysses*, 109).²²

Diane Tolomeo, in the course of her examination of the number eight in "Penelope" points out:

> Joyce was familiar with various schools of thought which ascribe a mystical significance to numbers and number systems. By the time he was writing *Work in Progress* it is evident that he knew the medieval theology of numbers, the anthropological significances given to numbers by primitive peoples, and the occult and spiritualistic readings of the Hebrew cabbala. (439)

Joyce's interest in numerology becomes even more evident in *Finnegans Wake*, where, according to James Atherton, "Numbers have a magical, not an arithmetical significance. . . . The numbers one to twelve also indicate certain characters or groups of characters. Certain numbers (e.g., 1132) have special magical properties" (53).²³

Numerology clearly presents problems for any careful interpretation of a text that uses numbers symbolically, for various numerological traditions often provide different and even contradictory values for the same number. Any attempt, therefore, to assign specific values to a given number used by a writer familiar with various Western numerological systems—as Joyce was—must take this potential ambivalence into account, allowing for a certain ambiguity in the number's meaning. As Joyce himself told Adolf Hoffmeister: "The significance of the same number varies, depending on where it occurs and what it refers to" (Hoffmeister 130). Thus, while Finn Dano's argument in "A Note on Eleven" that eleven in *Ulysses* symbolizes "renewal and the penultimate" (276) differs from my interpretation of Joyce's use of eleven, there may be some occurrences of eleven in Joyce's writings that do suggest renewal along with the other values that I see attached to the number.[24]

I want to focus on the two predominant traditional interpretations of the number eleven, both of which are relevant to Joyce's use of the number in *Ulysses*:

1. The medieval Christian interpretation derives primarily from the biblical exegesis of Augustine and others, who sought both to Christianize earlier pagan numerological systems and to explain and expand upon their perception that certain biblical passages imply a numerological basis for God's creation.[25] Augustine writes in *The City of God* that "the Law is clearly indicated by the number ten (hence the never-to-be-forgotten 'decalogue') and therefore the number eleven undoubtedly symbolizes the transgression of the Law, since it oversteps ten; and so it is a symbol of sin" (633).[26]

2. The Renaissance interpretation derives from Classical, rather than biblical, sources, and associates eleven with death and mourning. This interpretation of eleven derives from precedents in the works of Homer and Ovid, among others. In the last book of the *Iliad*, for example, Achilles grants Priam's request that the Trojans be allowed eleven days for Hector's funeral rites before the battle must begin again, and it is in Book XI of the *Odyssey* (traditionally labeled the *nekia*, referring to the rite "by which ghosts were called up and questioned"—Liddell and Scott 528) that Odysseus descends to Hades to speak with the dead—including his dead mother—and is beseeched by Elpenor to perform proper funeral rites for him (Joyce's schema for "Hades" substitutes Dignam for Elpenor, and Dignam's funeral appropriately begins at 11 A.M. in *Ulysses*). Joyce was certainly aware of Homer's use of eleven as a key to the underworld, for he took care to remind himself, in notes he took while reading Victor Bérard's *Les Phéniciens et l'Odyssée*, that in Homer's epic we find "Nekia XI canto" (Rose 36).[27]

According to Alastair Fowler, the Renaissance writer Pietro Bongo "observes that the Spartan legislator Lycurgus limited ritual mourning at funerals to the space of 11 days" ("Shepherd's" 171), and Ovid, writing in hendecasyllabic verse in the *Fasti*, observes that the *Feralia*, the Roman holiday honoring the dead, "only lasts until there remain as many days of the month as there are feet in my verses" (*Fasti* 99).

Renaissance writers such as Milton and Spenser built on their perception of a pattern in the Classical use of eleven, using it as a structural and symbolic element in elegies and in evocations of evil, sin, or death.[28] Fowler has noted that Milton's *Lycidas* is constructed in eleven stanzas, which "seems to have been considered appropriate for funeral odes: another famous instance is Henry King's 'The Exequy.' The basis of this convention lay in the ancient association of 11 with mourning and specifically with its termination" ("Shepherd's" 171).[29] Given the associations of death and mourning connected with eleven above, it seems more than coincidental that Stephen has just finished reading *Lycidas* aloud with his class in "Nestor" when he thinks of his riddle.

These traditional interpretations of eleven—transgression, sin, death, mourning, and the cessation of mourning—are compatible enough to coexist in the symbolic value of eleven in *Ulysses*. The association of eleven with sin and transgression is fully appropriate, given that the number begins its journey through the text in Stephen's fox riddle, itself a screen for the guilt he feels over the part that he believes he may have played in his mother's "beastly" death. Eleven is also appropriate as a symbol of death and mourning in *Ulysses*, for the sin and transgression that both characters sense relates to the death of loved ones. Appropriately, the anniversary of Bloom's father's death on June 27, 1886, which Bloom plans to observe, will occur eleven days after June 16. And, as noted above, Joyce was aware that the Armistice ending World War I came into effect at 11 A.M. on the eleventh day of the eleventh month of 1918—a neat conflation of the various associations of death, mourning, and new beginnings articulated above.

The words of Stephen's fox riddle become powerful, charged symbols of mourning and guilt by the "Circe" episode, combining their force with many other memory triggers that operate on the characters in "Circe." Some make their marks through simple personal associations, some are only accessible to the mind of one character, and others, like the number eleven, combine personal, shared, and collective associations to register their effects. By following Bloom and Stephen through Nighttown, we can see how Joyce, by means of his mnemotechnic—a careful positioning of loaded memory triggers in the text—allows memory itself to bring the characters into confrontations with repressed memories—complexes formed around traumatic memories embellished with related images of guilt and failure.

Bloom and Stephen frequently encounter and utter Stephen's riddle words and other memory triggers as they move through Nighttown toward Bella Cohen's brothel. Bloom, for example, sees a "glow" in the sky and says to himself: "*Aurora borealis* or a steel foundry? Ah, the brigade of course.... Big blaze. Might be his house. Beggar's bush" (U15.170-71). Here, Bloom's mind moves easily from the possibility of a "blaze" to Blazes Boylan to a riddle word—"Beggar's *bush*." While association and memory always work hand in hand, and do so throughout *Ulysses*, in Nighttown, to a greater extent than anywhere previously in the novel, the characters and the reader have entered a realm where memory, association, and the unconscious rule. The usual servants of repression—habitual routines and what Annie Besant calls "waking consciousness"—are more or less paralyzed in "Circe" by the abnormal conditions of the tired, traumatized, and—in Stephen's case—drunken characters.

Bloom's hallucinations begin early in "Circe," with his distorted perceptions of people, animals, and machines that he encounters on the streets. As he travels through Nighttown, he travels into his own past as well, like Ulysses in Hades meeting the shades of the dead. Bloom moves from one guilty, submissive encounter to the next, meeting Molly, his father and mother, and the dead Paddy Dignam, among many others, "harking back in a retrospective arrangement" (U15.442-43) and repeating the many transgressions that he perceives himself guilty of.

It is not until he meets Zoe Higgins, however, that Bloom's most intense hallucinatory sequence begins, and this central hallucinatory experience—his most direct confrontation with the complex web of guilt and self-reproach gathered around the memory of his son's death—begins and ends with a strange symbol and a simple phrase. When Zoe provocatively touches Bloom's left thigh in front of Bella Cohen's house, she is surprised to find "a hard black shrivelled potato" in his trouser pocket (U15.1309-10), which resembles the "shrivelled potato" that Ellen Bloom has dropped earlier in the episode (U15.289). Bloom has carried this strange object with him all day, thinking "Potato I have" when he leaves his house in "Calypso" (U4.73) and feeling it in his pocket as he hurries to avoid Boylan at the end of "Lestrygonians" (U8.1189). When Bloom surrenders the potato to Zoe, he calls it, "A talisman. Heirloom" (U15.1313), and after she pockets it "greedily," she says, "You'll know me the next time" (U15.1321). The potato-talisman disappears, only to reappear after Bloom has met and vanquished the Nymph.[30]

Bloom's potato, a seemingly insignificant object, gains its power as a "talisman" by virtue of "a memory attached to it," for he later tells Zoe that it is "a relic of poor mamma" (U15.3513 and 3520). The potato preserves the memory of Bloom's mother and is itself curiously preserved, as the Daughters of Erin imply in Bloom's fantasy when they invoke it: "Potato Preservative against Plague and Pestilence, pray for us" (*U*15.1952). Bloom's potato seems facetious and ridiculous, but the idea of memory working as a "preservative" (in both senses) is not. In his schema for "Circe," Joyce indicates that the potato corresponds to the *moly* given by Hermes to Odysseus in the *Odyssey* (Ellmann, *Ulysses*, Appendix). As noted, one of the correspondences that Joyce considered for *moly* in *Ulysses* was *chance*; the potato as *moly* nicely links chance and memory, suggesting involuntary memory—the seemingly spontaneous and often overwhelming evocation of the past—as Bloom's preservative against harm. *Moly*, as a gift of the gods, allows Ulysses to resist the magic of Circe, but Joyce's Ulysses, unlike Homer's, surrenders his protection as he enters Circe's palace, demonstrating his lack of resolve, but also perhaps insinuating that Circe's magic in *Ulysses* may ultimately be benign.

After Bloom gives his "*moly*" to Zoe, he begins a long sequence of degrading, humiliating hallucinations. "Circe's" magic reduces Bloom to a representation of his repressed anxieties, forcing him to repeat symbolically the habitual behaviors that he has developed in response to this repression. Most of his humiliations are appropriately connected to his sexual problems. He is briefly apotheosized, only to be deflated when Theodore Purefoy, a figure of male virility whose wife has just delivered a son, alleges that Bloom "employs a mechanical device to frustrate the sacred ends of nature" (*U*15.1741-42). He undergoes a physical examination by "Dr Malachi Mulligan, sex specialist," who concludes that Bloom is "bisexually abnormal. . . . He is prematurely bald from selfabuse, *perversely idealistic in consequence*, a reformed rake, and has metal teeth. In consequence of a family complex he has temporarily lost his memory . . ." (*U*15.1780-83; my emphasis). After Dr. Mulligan suggests that Bloom's genitals "be preserved in spirits of wine in the national teratological museum" (*U*15.1790-91), Dr. Dixon delivers his opinion that "Bloom is a finished example of the new womanly man. . . . He wears a hairshirt of pure Irish manufacture winter and summer and scourges himself every Saturday" (*U*15.1798-1808). Buried within Bloom's bizarre imaginings are self-accusations and revelations of his fears about his masculinity, sexual potency, and his ability to father a healthy son—fears that stem from Rudy's death. He has "temporarily lost his memory"—his ability to remember Rudy's death as an event uncomplicated by his own sexual failure—and must "exercise his mnemotechnic" if he is to regain it.

When Zoe hands Bloom a piece of chocolate (corresponding, perhaps, to Circe's magic potion), he tries to remember whether chocolate is an aphrodisiac, but cannot, and thinking of his grandfather's exhortation, laments, "Mnemo. Confused light confuses memory" (U15.2737). His inability to remember is here linked with his fear of what will happen if the chocolate is indeed an aphrodisiac. He worries that if he is faced with the actual prospect of "a good old thunk" (U15.2384), he will fare the same as the priest that Zoe describes who "couldn't get a connection. Only, you know, sensation. A dry rush" (U15.2561–62). "Poor man!" Bloom exclaims (U15.2564). Bloom eats the chocolate, but frets, "It is so long since I. Seems new. Aphro. That priest. Must come. Better late than never" (U15.2740–41).

The entrance of Bella Cohen, "a massive whoremistress" (U15.2742) with "a sprouting moustache" (U15.2746–47), signals the beginning of Bloom's final descent into the sexual fantasies that represent the complex set of behaviors and attitudes he has attached to his memory of Rudy's death. In a series of violent transformations Bella becomes the dominant Bello, telling Bloom, "What you longed for has come to pass. Henceforth you are unmanned and mine in earnest, a thing under the yoke.... You will shed your male garments..." (U15.2963–65). "The sins of the past" arise to testify against Bloom (U15.3027 ff.), but the recited litany of his "sins" is a list of trivial symptoms that serves as a screen for the deeper, hidden "sin" of Rudy's death that has brought Bloom to his emotional nadir. His self-respect and willpower have been stripped away, and he seems completely vulnerable to final subjugation at the hands of the Nymph, the primary representation of the most destructive symptoms gathered around his "sin."

The words of Stephen's fox riddle occur often in "Circe," sometimes separately and sometimes in combination or close succession, sometimes as "chance" words spoken by the characters and phantoms in the brothel or occurring in the italicized "stage directions," and sometimes as elements of hallucinations in Bloom's and Stephen's minds. For example, when Bloom's tailor appears and tells Bloom, "To alteration one pair trousers eleven shillings," the image of Reuben J. Dodd *bearing on his shoulders the drowned corpse of his son* appears in the text, again solidifying the association of eleven and the death of a son (U15.1910–20). When Bloom enters Bella's house, he stops to examine "the spaniel eyes of a running fox"—a stuffed animal decorating the hallway (U15.2039). As noted, at one point he is called by Parnell's alias—"Mr Fox" (U15.1762) —and at another he is accused of sexual indiscretions by a crab "in bushranger's kit" (U15.1872–73) and by a hollybush (U15.1877). When Chris

Callanan asks Bloom a question about "the parallax of the subsolar ecliptic of Aldebaran," he responds mysteriously, "K.11" (U15.1656–58), and Lipoti Virag later "claps sideways on the wall a pusyellow flybill" reading "K.11. Post No Bills. Strictly confidential. Dr Hy Franks" (U15.2633). K, the eleventh letter in the alphabet, and eleven, Stephen's riddle word, associate themselves with Bloom's sexual anxiety here by their proximity to Dr. Franks, a "quack doctor for the clap" who Bloom thinks of when he sees an advertisement for Kino's trousers in "Lestrygonians" (U8.90–98). Trousers, in their turn, evoke the memory of a tune that pops into Bloom's mind in the "Lotus-Eaters" and comes to represent his feared impotency:

O, Mairy lost the pin of her drawers
She didn't know what to do
To keep it up,
To keep it up. (U5.281–84)

The repetition of "clap" in "claps sideways on the wall" even gains significance in the pregnant text of "Circe," for it harks back to the thunderclap Stephen hears in "Oxen of the Sun," a "black crack of noise in the street" (U14.408), a "clap" in which Stephen fears the angry voice of God may be hidden (U14.435).

The riddle words and other triggers in the text, then, link up with each other in a wider and wider web of memory until the world in which Bloom and Stephen move seems a theater of memory, a *textus* the threads of which lead back into the past even as they move forward to encounter the specters that haunt them. In "Circe," Joyce conjures up Bloom's *Photo Bits* Nymph—who represents the sterile, cold, idealized image of woman that Bloom has constructed to avoid the issue of his sexuality—by a deliberate combination of Stephen's riddle words, when Bello tells Bloom, "We'll *bury* you in our *shrubbery* jakes where you'll be dead and dirty with old *Cuck* Cohen . . . and my other ten or *eleven* husbands, whatever the buggers' names were, suffocated in the one cesspool" (U15.3207–11; my emphasis). The textual evolution of this passage makes it clear that Joyce insinuated into it words suggestive of Stephen's riddle, adding "Cuck" and "eleven" at the page proof stage (JJA 26: 237). Bloom's response to the speech is appropriate: "My willpower! Memory! I have sinned!" (U15.3215).

The Nymph speaks to Bloom as a goddess to a devotee, for he has elevated her to that status, far above mortal women. As noted in chapter 2, in the "Lestrygonians" episode Bloom retreats from the involuntary memory of himself and Molly making love on Howth that has been triggered by a sip of Burgundy to a vision of "shapely goddesses" who drink electricity and are exempted from normal human digestive processes. The *Photo Bits* Nymph above Leopold and Molly's bed has become Bloom's goddess of love and as such provides an escape from the risks of sexual love. When she appears to Bloom in "Circe," she puts him in his "proper place" by addressing him as "Mortal!" (*U*15.3240 and 3245), and later she confirms her purity by telling Bloom, "We immortals, as you saw today, have not such a place and no hair there either. We are stonecold and pure. We eat electric light" (*U*15.3392–93).

Bloom accepts the Nymph's domination passively, apologizing for past indiscretions and crawling on all fours, a position he feels is "expected of me. Force of habit" (*U*15.3243). Self-righteous and disapproving, dressed finally "in nun's white habit," the Nymph represents a rejection of the physical for an abstract, idealized image of the feminine: "Tranquilla convent. . . . No more desire. (*she reclines her head, sighing*) Only the ethereal. Where dreamy creamy gull waves o'er the waters dull" (*U*15.3434–38). These lines awaken an unpleasant memory in Bloom, for they come from his own sarcastic response earlier in the day when, seeing the poet AE accompanied by his friend Lizzie Twigg, Bloom thinks, "Those literary etherial people they are all. Dreamy, cloudy, symbolistic. Esthetes they are. I wouldn't be surprised if it was that kind of food you see produces the like waves of the brain the poetical." Bloom illustrates this poetic abstraction by supplying two lines of verse: "*The dreamy cloudy gull / Waves o'er the waters dull*" (*U*8.543–50). The Nymph's words, then, have struck a chord in Bloom's memory, reminding him of his disapproval of the abstraction that she argues for. As he begins to rise out of his subservient position, his "*back trouserbutton snaps*" (*U*15.3439), an event Budgen describes as crucial in *James Joyce and the Making of "Ulysses"*:

> It will be noticed that one of Bloom's trouser buttons gives way under the spell of la Belle Cohen sans merci. Thus chance supplies the moment through which he reconquers his virility and presence of mind. The accident tickles his sense of the ridiculous, wakes him out of his masochistic trance, quickens his fastidiousness and makes his experience available for service. (237)

Budgen leaves one essential element out of this equation. Memory allows chance to have meaning, and here the chance sound ("Bip!") of Bloom's snapping button triggers a memory of the song that he thought of earlier in the day, but now with a twist that reflects his deepest fears and lays bare the threat which the Nymph poses to him:

> O, Leopold lost the pin of his drawers
> He didn't know what to do,
> To keep it up,
> To keep it up. (U15.3444-47)

This bit of song and its established association with Bloom's fear of sexual inadequacy bring him to realize the danger of the Nymph's appeal. Coldly, he says to her, "You have broken the spell. The last straw. If there were only ethereal where would you all be, postulants and novices? Shy but willing like an ass pissing" (U15.3449-51). Bloom's song is, like so many of the memory triggers in *Ulysses*, a polyvalent symbol, for it draws part of its significance from cultural associations that Bloom may not be aware of. As Alan Dundes explains in his note, "Mairymaking in *Ulysses*: A Legendary Source for a Lost Pin," the song as it first appears in the "Lotus-Eaters" episode is related to a legend in which the Virgin Mary loses the pin that fastens her cloak. Once again, Joyce combines personal and collective or cultural associations in a mnemic symbol, and in doing so he suggests not only Bloom's fear of impotence, but also the figure of the Virgin, reminding the reader (and perhaps, on some deeper level, Bloom) of the Nymph's ethereality.

Once the Nymph's spell is broken, she tries to prevent Bloom's rebellion by drawing a "poniard" from her cloak and attempting to emasculate him (U15.3460-61). As she lunges at Bloom, she shouts "Nekum!," but Bloom responds with his own magical spell—"Nebrakada!" (U15.3463). Joyce added both of these magical words at a late stage of composition (*JJA* 26: 262), presumably to underscore the magical nature of Bloom's encounter with the repressed content of his own memory. Still again, Bloom's access to Stephen's memory provides him with a potent symbol, for "Nebrakada" derives its power in the text from a shared memory. In "Wandering Rocks," as Stephen perused a book of love charms, he read: "How to win a woman's love. For me this. Say the following talisman three times with hands folded: '—*Se el yilo nebrakada femininum! Amor me solo! Sanktus! Amen*'" (U15.847-49). This phrase enters "Circe" early in the episode, when Molly (Mrs. Marion) uses it to rebuke Bloom: "Nebrakada! Femininum!" (U15.319).

Bloom follows his magic spell with an allusion to Aesop's fable of the fox and the grapes, suggesting that the Nymph is trying to castrate him because she no longer can control his sexuality. He calls her "Reynard"—alluding, as Weldon Thornton suggests, to "the central character of the medieval beast epic *Reynard the Fox*" (408-9)—and as she flees from him, defeated, "unveiled, her plaster cast cracking, a cloud of stench escaping from the cracks" (*U*15.3469-70), Bloom calls after her, "Fool someone else, not me" (*U*15.3477). Through the subconscious exercise of his mnemotechnic, through a series of reactions to "chance" symbols thrown up by the textual memory of *Ulysses*, Bloom has exposed the reality behind the Nymph's facade of purity, exposing also the sexual posture he has assumed in avoiding his memory of Rudy's death.

Turning from the fleeing Nymph, Bloom sees Bella (no longer Bello) standing in front of him, and she repeats the magic phrase that signaled the beginning of Bloom's ordeal: "You'll know me the next time" (*U*15.3481). By exactly repeating Zoe's phrase, Bella reminds Bloom of his potato talisman and, no longer "cowed" by her, Bloom tells her, "Your eyes are as vapid as the glasseyes of your stuffed fox" (*U*15.3485-86). Bloom then retrieves his potato—"a relic of poor mamma" (*U*15.3513)—from Zoe.

Having bested the Nymph and recovered his "*moly*," Bloom is able to turn his attentions toward Stephen in a fatherly attempt to protect him. Bloom does experience another set of troubling and degrading hallucinations, but these center on Molly's affair with Boylan—a problem that Bloom has yet to come to terms with—and arise out of his attempt to protect Stephen by substituting his own hand for Stephen's when Zoe's palm reading seems to be upsetting Stephen. Stephen's central hallucinatory sequence is about to begin, and from this point on his hallucinations will dominate the episode. Stephen's visions are set in motion by the repetition of memory triggers—familiar words from his riddle and from his childhood.

When Lynch, Bloom, and the women haggle over money, for example, someone (not Stephen) calls out, "the gentleman paid down like a gentleman ... drink ... it's long after eleven" (*U*15.3559-60), and Stephen answers, "What, eleven? A riddle!" (*U*15.3562-63). He then restates his riddle, but with an important change that indicates a turn from repression to evocation:

> The fox crew, the cocks flew,
> The bells in heaven
> Were striking eleven.
> 'Tis time for her poor soul
> To get out of heaven. (*U*15.3577-81)

Joyce originally wrote the last line of this version of the riddle as "To go to heaven," just as it appears in "Nestor," but changed it to "To get out of heaven" when he revised the placards for *Ulysses* (*JJA* 20: 182).

While Stephen remembers the riddle, Bloom steps in to settle the debt with Bella, preventing her from cheating him and the others. She addresses him "admiringly": "You're such a slyboots, old cocky" (*U*15.3586). Bloom then suggests that Stephen "hand over that cash to me to take care of," and as he counts Stephen's money, he twice utters a magic word: "One, seven, eleven, and five. Six. Eleven. I don't answer for what you may have lost" (*U*15.3606-7). Joyce edited these lines heavily, and his changes show that his concern centered on the need to give the correct emphasis to the word "eleven." In typescript, Joyce isolated it in parentheses: "One. Seven (eleven) and five" (*JJA* 15: 119). In the placards of the "Circe" episode, Joyce emphasizes the word "eleven" by leaving it within parentheses and italicizing it (*JJA* 20: 183). Finally, in page proof, eleven appears to be just another number in a sequence (*JJA* 26: 237). The care that Joyce took in deciding whether to clearly distinguish eleven from the other numbers on the page suggests—as does his tendency to add more of the riddle words into the text of "Circe" at each stage of his revisions—that it is not just another number, but an important symbol in the text.

Bloom's phrase strikes a predictable note in Stephen's memory, for he reacts with a direct reference to the riddle: "Why striking eleven? Proparoxyton. Moment before the next Lessing says. Thirsty fox. (*he laughs loudly*) Burying his grandmother. Probably he killed her" (*U*15.3609-11). Bloom repeats the number once more: "That is one pound six and eleven. One pound seven, say" (*U*15.3613).

At this point, other chance words begin to appear that trigger other memories. Stephen remembers that he broke his glasses—"Broke them yesterday. Sixteen years ago" (*U*15.3628-29)—reminding himself of the first time he broke his glasses, an event that led his pandybatting by Father Dolan at age six. This earlier punishment at the hands of a priest contributes to Stephen's hatred of the *dio boia*—"the lord of things as they are" (*U*9.1048)—which in turn makes up part of his confused response to his mother's death and his refusal to pray at her deathbed. Sixteen also forms part of a symmetrical arrangement with Bloom, who, pointing to his hand, says, "That weal there is an accident. Fell and cut it twentytwo years ago. I was sixteen" (*U*15.3712-13). As noted, Stephen senses this correspondence, exclaiming, "See? Moves to one great goal. I am twentytwo. Sixteen years ago he was twentytwo too. Sixteen years ago I twentytwo tumbled. Twentytwo years ago he sixteen fell off his hobbyhorse" (U15.3718–20). As Hugh Kenner notes, *Ulysses* begins with a sentence of twenty-two words, "just as Bloom has twenty-two books" (not including one library book in his temporary possession) in "Ithaca" ("Reflections" 14).

Stephen's involuntary memory of his pandybatting at Clongowe's sets off a series of reactions in his mind. In *A Portrait of the Artist as a Young Man*, Father Dolan is to Stephen's young mind a frightening combination of all-too-human anger and religious power. The pandybatting incident begins when the irascible and unreasonable prefect of studies announces his entrance into Stephen's classroom with "the loud crack of a pandybat on the last desk" (P 48). Father Dolan asks the teacher of the class, "Any boys want flogging here, Father Arnall?" Seeing a boy named Fleming kneeling in the center of the room as a punishment for slackness in his studies, he exclaims, "Hoho, Fleming! An idler of course. I can see it in your eye" (P 48). After beating Fleming's hands with the pandybat, he singles out Stephen for questioning, and, learning that Stephen has broken his glasses and therefore cannot do his work, he says, "Out here, Dedalus. Lazy little schemer. I see schemer in your face" (P 50). Stephen must hold out first one hand and then the other, and Father Dolan hits each hand once. Joyce evokes Stephen's immediate reaction in *A Portrait* with images of fire and burning—the words "livid," "scalding," "burning," "hot," and "flaming" are repeated over and over in the space of a few paragraphs.[31]

Father Dolan's unjust punishment of Stephen in *A Portrait* is, of course, a turning point in Stephen's attitudes toward authority and religion, and it lays the groundwork for much of the guilt that animates his reaction to his mother's death. Before Father Dolan's entrance in *A Portrait*, the fabric of Stephen's religious belief was untorn and pure. In his innocence, Stephen had concluded his teacher's bad temper could not be a sin: "Was that a sin for Father Arnall to be in a wax or was he allowed to get into a wax when the boys were idle. . . . It was because he was allowed because a priest would know what a sin was and would not do it" (P 48). After his beating, Stephen thinks,

> It was cruel and unfair to make him kneel in the middle of the class then. . . . it was unfair and cruel. The prefect of studies was a priest but that was cruel and unfair. And his whitegrey face and the nocoloured eyes behind the steelrimmed spectacles were cruel looking because he had steadied the hand first with his firm soft fingers and that was to hit it better and louder. (P 52)

TEXTUAL MEMORY 163

The experience festers in Stephen's mind—"he suffered time after time in memory the same humiliation until he began to wonder whether it might not really be that there was something in his face which had made him look like a schemer" (*P* 53)—and though he seeks to exorcise its effect by speaking to the rector about it, the incident with Father Dolan remains in his mind as a prototype of the unjust, cruel, and vengeful God that he rejects in refusing to pray by his mother's deathbed. The resurrection of Father Dolan in Stephen's hallucinations in "Circe" occurs through the effects of words spoken "by chance" by Zoe and Lynch, words that parallel the exact particulars of Stephen's earlier experience.

This sequence of events begins with Stephen's memory of breaking his glasses when Zoe says to Stephen, "Blue eyes beauty I'll read your hand" (*U*15.3655-56). When Zoe tells Stephen that she reads "courage" in his palm, he denies it with a shake of his head, and she insists, "I see it in your face. The eye, like that" (*U*15.3663-64). Lynch then "slaps Kitty behind twice," exclaiming, "Like that. Pandybat" (*U*15.3666). The combination of Stephen's outstretched hand, Zoe's unknowing repetition of words almost identical to Father Dolan's in *A Portrait*, the two slaps, and Lynch's "Pandybat" work their magic by re-creating the mental coordinates of the earlier experience and stimulating the involuntary memory—here in the form of an apparition—of Father Dolan: "Twice loudly a pandybat cracks, the coffin of the pianola flies open, the bald little round jack-in-the-box head of Father Dolan springs up" (*U*15.3667-69). Through the working of involuntary memory and "fate or her stepsister chance" (*SH* 168), Father Dolan is now appropriately on hand for the staging of Stephen's confrontation with his dead mother, or rather with the religious ghoul that has taken the place of his mother in his memory, for his memory of her death has become suffused with, and distorted by, the fear of God first instilled in him by Father Dolan.

Stephen's mother finally appears after Stephen recalls his dream of the night before—"Mark me. I dreamt of a watermelon" (*U*15.3922)—and asks "Where's the red carpet spread?" (*U*15.3931). A dizzying whirl of images and hallucinations follows, in which the wallpaper betrays "A stout fox, drawn from covert, brush pointed, having buried his grandmother" (*U*15.3952-53), and Mr. Deasy, the "Nestor" who presided over the birth of Stephen's riddle, appears "on a brokenwinded isabelle nag, Cock of the North" (*U*15.3980). Bits and pieces of the day insert themselves into Stephen's hallucinations, including the personified Hours from Ponchielli's "Dance of the Hours" in *La Gioconda*, which first appeared in Bloom's thoughts in "Calypso" (*U*4.526 and 533-36; *U*15.4054 ff.), followed by the sound of the bells of George's church, which end "Calypso" right after Bloom's recollection of Ponchielli's opera (*U*4.544–48; *U*15.4086). Here, two events closely related in Bloom's mind earlier in the day insert themselves into the hallucinations leading up to the appearance of Stephen's mother. That these hallucinations are at least as much Stephen's as they are Bloom's is evident in the choice of presiding spirit—Stephen's dance teacher, Professor Maginni.

When Stephen utters the phrase "Dance of death" (*U*15.4139), the "stage directions" let loose a flood of memory triggers—the "lacquey's bell," a "cockboat," "bellhorses," the Frauenzimmer-midwives, and even Blazes Boylan on his "hackney jaunt" (*U*15.4140–47) until Stephen "stops dead" (*U*15.4153–54) and watches as his mother appears, physically decayed, rambling and mad. Stephen is at first "horrorstruck" (*U*15.4175), choked "with fright, remorse and horror," and tries to avoid blame for his sin: "They say I killed you, mother. He offended your memory. Cancer did it, not I. Destiny" (*U*15.4186–87). He seeks a revelation from her—"The word known to all men" (*U*15.4192–93)—but soon senses the voice of those elements of the Church that he most hates coiled around this memory of his mother. Her words are trivial and nagging rather than powerful or revealing, and Stephen's anger builds as she becomes more and more a representative of the *dio boia*. When she threatens him with "the fire of hell" (*U*15.4212) and the green crab of cancer—"God's hand!" (*U*15.4219–21)—he replies, "*Non serviam!*" (*U*15.4228), echoing his adoption of Lucifer's cry of rebellion in *A Portrait of the Artist as a Young Man* (*P* 117 and 239).

As Stephen confronts the religious guilt entangled with his memory of his mother's death, "The Mother" begins to metamorphose into the Virgin Mary ("Inexpressible was my anguish when expiring with love, grief and agony on Mount Calvary"—*U*15.4239–40), and Stephen breaks the lamp: "Time's livid final flame leaps and, in the following darkness, ruin of all space, shattered glass and toppling masonry" (*U*15.4244–45). The image suggests not only an Apocalypse, but also the "livid," "flaming" pain of Stephen's hands after his beating by Father Dolan (*P* 50–51).

Both Bloom and Stephen, then, face female figures in "Circe" that represent something "other" which they have repressed. Through a textual mnemotechnic, a concatenation of bits and pieces of shared and personal memory, the text brings the two to these seemingly cathartic moments of confrontation with the past. Yet, as noted, Bloom regresses soon after his battle with the Nymph into a fantasy in which he submits to Boylan, watching and listening as Boylan and Molly "ride a cockhorse" together (*U*15.3804). Even though this fantasy occurs because

Bloom substitutes himself for Stephen to protect him from the effects of Zoe's palm reading, the reader cannot fail to notice that Bloom's battle with the Nymph did not fully or consciously "cure" Bloom. We must be similarly careful not to overread Stephen's breaking of the lamp and rejection of the "corpsechewer" that has supplanted his mother's memory (U15.4214), for, after all, from the viewpoint of Bella and the others, he has done no more than break a lamp in a brothel and run out the door. He reacts to his "triumph" over the ghost of the past not with self-assurance or relief, but with wild flight, and the first words we hear him speak to the soldiers on the street reveal that the memory of his mother is still very much with him: "You are my guests. Uninvited. By virtue of the fifth of George and seventh of Edward. History to blame. Fabled by mothers of memory" (U15.4370–72).

Yet there seem to be some rewards for the characters as they leave Circe's palace. In Stephen's address to the soldiers, for example, we hear an inversion of the fox riddle, in which "grandmother" was substituted for "mother," for here "mothers of memory"—the mother no longer repressed but now expressed—takes the place of Blake's "daughters of memory" (U2.7). Bloom's interest in Stephen seems to bring a new assertiveness as he prevents Bella from prosecuting Stephen by intimating that he knows about her son at Oxford. Stunned, she asks him, "Who are. Incog!" (U15.4308), and Bloom, carrying Stephen's ashplant, runs outside as "Incog Haroun Al Raschid" (U15.4325), dedicated to helping Stephen. The riddle words are almost completely absent from the text of "Circe" after the breaking of the lamp, and the episode ends pacifically as Bloom, watchfully guarding the unconscious Stephen, has a vision of his dead son, "a fairy boy of eleven, a changeling, kidnapped, dressed in an Eton suit with glass shoes and a little bronze helmet, holding a book in his hand. He reads from right to left inaudibly, smiling, kissing the page" (U15.4957–60). Puzzling as this vision may be, it nevertheless seems to be compensation for Bloom, who for nearly eleven years has felt himself incapable of fathering a son and whose only memory of his only son has hitherto been of a deformed, and then dead, infant. Rudy's age is eleven, the number associated with transgression in numerological tradition, but also with "mourning and specifically with its termination" (Fowler, "Shepherd's" 171).

"Circe's" ambiguous ending has frustrated and challenged many readers. Insinuations of residual, unresolved problems coexist with hints of catharsis and atonement. In its refusal to provide a clear resolution for the characters, to bring them to their desired goals—whether we interpret these as a substitute father-son relationship or a full working-through of buried traumas—"Circe" mirrors the larger refusal of the novel itself to provide such answers. What I have tried to demonstrate here is simply that "Circe" is the clearest example we have of Joyce's textual mnemotechnic at work. While "Circe" appears at times to be a disordered, spasmodic series of random associations and hallucinations triggered by chance, we can see that it is actually much more than this. By examining the genetic growth of the episode through Joyce's revisions in light of his interest in traditional ideas about the relationship of memory and magic—especially the tradition of the memory theater as Bruno articulated it, where a deep structural organization of powerful symbols can focus and direct powerful forces—we can understand how he designed the "Circe" episode as a theater of involuntary or spontaneous memory in which "evil memories" rise up to confront those who have pretended "that they were not or at least were otherwise."

5   Intertextual Memory

In "The Shapes of Artistic Pasts: East and West," Arthur C. Danto argues: "Since Vasari, to be an artist in the West has been to have internalized a narrative which determines the way we can be influenced by the past.... Modernism... meant the dismantling of these narratives and a reconstitution of our relationship to the past" (11). Danto contends that "modernity begins with the loss of belief in the defining narrative of one's own culture" (12), the conviction that artists must look outside their own traditions or create something completely new in order to re-situate themselves in regard to their own traditions. We can find such attempts to reorient modern thought in relation to its own past in the writings produced by the various authors we now classify as literary "modernists," such as T. S. Eliot, Ezra Pound, H. D. (Hilda Doolittle), and James Joyce. *Ulysses* provides a specific site for the investigation of one writer's response to the relation between modern literature and historical traditions, especially in the ways in which Joyce's text responds to tradition in the form of myth and memory.

Stephen Dedalus seeks to awaken not only from his own personal nightmares, but from the various historical traditions—English, Roman Catholic, and Irish—that he views as his "masters":

> —I am the servant of two masters, Stephen said, an English and an Italian....
> —And a third, Stephen said, there is who wants me for odd jobs (*U*1.638–41).

All of the major characters in *Ulysses* are embedded or enmeshed in their own personal histories, which in turn are embedded in larger historical traditions—Leopold Bloom's identity as a Jew, for example. Behind all the more or less contemporary and identifiable personal, cultural, and political histories that define the characters of *Ulysses*, Joyce spreads the larger cloth of myth and the historical traditions implied by or embedded in mythic narratives, a framework that remains for the most part hidden to the characters (though Stephen Dedalus does consider the possible meanings of his very un-Irish surname). Much speculation on Joyce's writing concerns itself with his use of mythic paradigms as the textual substrates of his works (e.g., the Daedalus myth in *Dubliners* and *A Portrait of the Artist as a Young Man*, the *Odyssey* in *Ulysses*, and the story of Finn MacCumhal in *Finnegans Wake*). Joyce's use of the past in the "Nausicaa" episode of *Ulysses* clearly demonstrates his practice of loading a text with hidden references to other texts, myths, and traditions, a practice I will label "intertextual memory."

"Never know whose thoughts you're chewing," Leopold Bloom muses as he eats his lunch in *Ulysses* (U8.717–18), and at times the reader may feel the same way about this text that incorporates, alludes to, and plays with so many other texts and traditions. Jacques Derrida has called Joyce's writing a "hypermnesiac machine," because in texts such as *Ulysses* and *Finnegans Wake*, Joyce inscribes so many of those texts and traditions—popular, literary, mythic, scientific, and otherwise—that make up the cultural consciousness of the modern Western reader (147). In fact, *Ulysses* often includes or inscribes other texts in such a way that the reader at times does not know whose thoughts she is chewing and may not even realize she is chewing them at all.

As early as November 1923, two opposing viewpoints on the significance of the book were forming, represented at that point by Richard Aldington and T. S. Eliot. In his essay, "*Ulysses*, Order, and Myth," Eliot outlines a conflict between himself and Aldington over the novel's use of a "mythical method" (178), and he takes Aldington to task for treating "Mr. Joyce as a prophet of chaos" and for viewing *Ulysses* as "an invitation to chaos" (175–76). Eliot, on the other hand, hoped to enlist *Ulysses* in his struggle to encourage a "classical" element in modern literature as a hedge against the perceived disorder and decay of master narratives that is a central topos in modernist writing. For Eliot, Joyce's use of the *Odyssey* as "a continuous parallel between contemporaneity and antiquity . . . is simply a way of controlling, of ordering, of giving a shape and a significance to the immense panorama of futility and anarchy which is contemporary history" (177). It is, Eliot claims, "a step toward making the modern world possible for art" (178), and it has "the importance of a scientific discovery" (177).

In *Ulysses*, Joyce uses the text's recollections of other texts as another technique for constituting everyday life as a deep, if not necessarily rich, palimpsest of mythic and narrative paradigms. *Ulysses* is packed with allusions, overt and covert, to other texts, to events both ancient and contemporary, and even to personal details of Joyce's life. The unparalleled level of intertextuality in *Ulysses* and *Finnegans Wake* invites readers not only to take note of the allusions themselves, but to ponder the significance of such an overwhelming density of allusion. Joyce's intertextuality, his method of layering or "seeding" the text with traces of older texts and traditions, is based on memory and the inevitable orientation of the reader within a web of texts that forms a culture or at least part of a culture.

The remarkable intertextuality of *Ulysses* is in itself a form of memory—intertextual memory—that subtly comments on the events of June 16, 1904, and on the very act of reading the book. The past is present in Joyce's textual echoes—not just echoes of Homer, of course, but also Shakespeare, Dante, Swift, the romance novelist Maria Susanna Cummins, Maeterlinck, and many more—and these intertextual resonances are often not explicit or easily recognizable by characters or, more intriguingly, by readers. Intertextuality in Joyce's works seems to acknowledge a shared memory in the form of cultural memories theoretically available to any reader of *Ulysses:* all of us are made up not only of our own experiences, but also by the shared experiences and imaginings of cultural traditions. Joyce acknowledged this aspect of his own mind when he commented to his brother Stanislaus:

> if I put down a bucket into my own soul's well, sexual department, I draw up Griffith's and Ibsen's and Skeffington's and Bernard Vaughn's and St. Aloysius' and Shelley's and Renan's water along with my own. And I am going to do that in my novel (inter alia) and plank the bucket down before the shades and substances above mentioned to see how they like it: and if they don't like it I can't help them. (*Letters* II, 191).

According to Colin MacCabe, Joyce once advised Jacques Mercanton, who was translating *Ulysses* into French, "'the fewer quotation marks the better' and that even without them the reader 'will know early in the book that S.D.'s mind is full like everyone else's of borrowed words'" (MacCabe 117). Derrida writes that to read Joyce is to be *"in memory of him,"* in the sense that the "hypermnesia" of Joyce's work *"a priori* indebts you, and in advance inscribes you in the book you are reading" (147; original emphasis).

Intertextuality, like memory, works by signifying or recalling something that is no longer present. As Michel de Certeau writes of the disruption of the text by "the quotation of voices," "A lapse insinuates itself into language. The territory of appropriation is altered by the mark of something which is not there and does not happen (like myth)" (154). In his essay on "The Intertextual Unconscious," Michael Riffaterre has argued that "intertextuality . . . is tantamount to a mimesis of repression" (374). The substrate of intertextuality, then, can function as a shadow comment on the story before us, insinuating itself into the way we read, like a troubling but elusive memory, disturbing any easy appropriation of meaning and complicating the varieties of meanings suggested by the text.

The intensity of allusion or intertextuality in *Ulysses* exceeds what we might think of as "useful" or usual, even in a modernist text. While Eliot, conscious of the density of reference in "The Waste Land," provides notes to help the reader absorb the "meaning" of his intertextual references—the "memories" of ancient myths and customs inscribed on the otherwise bleak lives of his modern urban somnambulists—and thus attempts to help the reader complete the text's meaning, Joyce does no such thing. Although the novel's title obviously alludes to the Homeric story, it does so obliquely—*Ulysses* rather than *Odysseus*[1]—and Joyce refused to make his book correspond in any exact way with his Homeric paradigm. The title's overt suggestion of an "arche-plot" behind the events of June 16, 1904, has led more to disagreement and confusion about the relationship of the *Odyssey* and *Ulysses* than to a sense of clarification or a clear echo of meaning.[2] The "parallels" between the two books provide a wealth of tantalizing suggestions, a variety of ways to think about Bloom and Stephen in relation to Odysseus and Telemachus, but they do not "settle" anything for the reader, and, in fact, they more often complicate the reader's understanding of the text.

The Homeric parallel is part of a larger, intertextual memory that provides numerous paradigms of completion "under" *Ulysses*. Joyce's book is a palimpsest, then, in which we read an ambiguous modern ending inscribed over layers of older, "closed" texts such as *Hamlet* and *The Divine Comedy*. The book contains so many other stories, even stories from Joyce's own life, that the reader cannot possibly take them all in, and the text makes no particular effort to expose its most hidden intertextual suggestions or to articulate the relevance of its more explicit ones. Yet *Ulysses* provides these subliminal suggestions, perhaps in the hope that they encode in the text memories or echoes of other stories, other texts, other endings that will resonate on some level of the reader's mind.

While most of the texts alluded to in *Ulysses* suggest closure of some sort, their possible meanings as hidden models for the book's plot vary greatly. Joyce's references to traditionally closed texts like the *Odyssey* often seem to suggest the possibility of a textual Ithaca; on the other hand, such references often seem ironic and even mocking by forcing a contrast between the closure that they suggest and the openness and self-referentiality of the modern text in which they occur. Thus, in viewing Joyce's writing as a "chaosmos," Umberto Eco reads the intertextual echoes of older, closed texts in *Ulysses* as "an example of a paradoxical equilibrium among the forms of a rejected world and the disordered substance of the new . . ." (Eco 63), and as

> the incredible image of a world that supports itself, almost by miracle, on the preserved structures of an old world which are accepted for their formal reliability but denied in their substantial value. *Ulysses* represents a moment of transition for contemporary sensitivity. It appears as the drama of a dissociated consciousness that tries to reintegrate itself, finding, at the core of dissociation, a possible recovery by directing itself in opposition to its old frames of reference. (Eco 55)

Myth, then, operates below the surface in *Ulysses*, creating a gap between itself and the surface and suggesting a variety of supplements to the possible interpretations of this surface. The interpretive difficulty lies in judging the significance of the parallels between the text of *Ulysses* and the older plots that it "remembers." For example, do the mythic parallels between *Ulysses* and the *Odyssey* redeem Joyce's characters, rescuing them from the paralysis of Dublin by infusing their lives with an archetypal richness, or do they mock the world of twentieth-century Dublin, ironically undercutting the imperfect modern counterparts of the faithful Penelope and the cunning, bold wanderer Odysseus?

I do not wish to belabor the Odyssean parallels to *Ulysses* further—I refer to them simply because they are known to all readers of the book—but to provide another example that I hope will further illustrate this dilemma in *Ulysses* and, at the same time, suggest an additional mythic substrate or subtext for the novel (specifically, for the thirteenth episode, conventionally referred to as "Nausicaa," according to the Homeric parallels that Joyce laid out in his letters and notes). In the "Nausicaa" episode of *Ulysses*, Leopold Bloom finds himself near a chapel on a beach at twilight, tired by the day's activities and anxious about his wife's adulterous affair with Blazes Boylan. In fact, Bloom has, unlike Homer's hero, deliberately delayed his return home so as not to interrupt a meeting there between Blazes and Molly. We learn later in *Ulysses* that the

Blooms have not had "complete carnal intercourse" in almost eleven years (U17. 2278-84), and, prior to the "Nausicaa" episode, Bloom has evidenced a proclivity to avoid confronting his sexual problems by engaging in provocative pseudonymous correspondence with a woman he has never met and by running from a possible encounter on the street with Boylan. Instead, as we have seen, Bloom indulges himself with fantasies of women idealized either as pure and goddesslike or imagined as lascivious whores.

On the beach in "Nausicaa," Bloom encounters Gerty MacDowell, a young woman whose view of the opposite sex, like Bloom's, has been clouded by idealized images provided, in her case, by pulp fiction. Gerty has come to the beach with two girlfriends and the two little boys they are supervising. Though she and Bloom never really meet and never speak to each other, they exchange meaningful gazes, both "painting" the other in the colors of their own fantasies. The first part of the episode is filtered through Gerty's thoughts, while we experience the remainder immersed in Bloom's stream of consciousness.

In an investigation of some of Joyce's sources, Michael Patrick Gillespie has claimed: "While the prose style of 'Nausicaa' at first appears to be an obvious parody of pulp romances, experiences with preceding chapters suggest that models for its structure come from more diverse sources" ("Sources" 334). One of these "diverse sources" that is in fact another "romance," albeit dating from the second century, is a group of myths, *The Golden Ass* by Apuleius, also known as *The Metamorphoses of Lucius*, which intersects with *Ulysses* in the "Nausicaa" episode. In this intersection or collision between "present" twentieth-century Dublin and "absent" second-century Thessaly, *The Golden Ass* serves as an intertextual "memory" for the "surface" story of "Nausicaa."

Admittedly, the existence of a correspondence between *The Golden Ass* and "Nausicaa" is not obvious or overt, as is the relationship between *Ulysses* and the *Odyssey*, yet Joyce did not hesitate to bury extremely obscure allusions in his texts, presumably with the confidence that these hidden signs would somehow function as part of the text's dynamic. As he revised, Joyce often went back through his chapters and embedded more and more of these subtle allusions, thereby increasing the text's symbolic "density" and subtlety. Joyce's revisions to "Nausicaa" imply an attempt to load the episode with hints that point toward another mythic parallel beyond the more obvious one of Bloom and Gerty as Ulysses and Nausicaa, another intertextual echo that adds more complexity to the occurrences on Sandymount beach on June 16, 1904.

The Golden Ass is a collection of myths and stories bound together by the story of Lucius. While we might argue that Bloom makes an ass of himself in "Nausicaa," Lucius has literally become an ass, since he was transformed by a witch who caught him spying on her. Dismayed by his situation, Lucius roams the world in search of a cure, meeting many adventures and hearing many stories along the way. He finally finds salvation when he lies down on a beach at twilight, depressed and tired, and is visited by a powerful goddess—Isis—who tells him that he can regain his human shape by eating roses dedicated to her if he promises to serve her for the rest of his life.

We can quickly note some immediate parallels between the "master plot" of *The Golden Ass* and "Nausicaa." Both Lucius and Bloom find themselves despondent and weary on a beach in the darkening evening. Lucius, the ass, falls into a slumber and awakens to a vision of the goddess Isis, while Bloom views a more earthly Isis—a young woman he would rather idealize than "see"—unveiling herself in the shadow of the Star of the Sea Chapel, dedicated to the Virgin Mary.

The first tension arising from a comparison of these texts results from a narratological difference regarding the possibility of closure: the earlier text provides a deus ex machina solution for its protagonist unavailable to Bloom. Just as Bloom cannot simply or literally go home to slay the suitors and reestablish his "kingdom" as Ulysses did, so he cannot transform himself back into a man by eating roses (although Gerty wonders "why you couldn't eat something poetical like violets or roses"—*U*13.229–30) or by subordinating himself to a goddess.

Other stories from *The Golden Ass* echo in "Nausicaa." For example, at the start of the episode the two young boys—Master Tommy and Master Jacky—fight over "a certain castle of sand" referred to in the text as "the apple of discord" (*U*13.40–42), which alludes to the apple of gold in the Judgment of Paris, a story retold at length in *The Golden Ass*. The Judgment of Paris concerns, appropriately, three goddesses and a man who must choose between them, mirrored in Bloom's consideration of the relative merits of the three "girl chums" who "had of course their little tiffs from time to time like the rest of mortals" (*U*13.93–94).

The most important and suggestive parallel between *The Golden Ass* and "Nausicaa," however, involves the story of Cupid and Psyche. *The Golden Ass* is our earliest source for this legend, which takes up approximately one-sixth of Apuleius' book.[3] This myth of ideal love provides an intriguing and suggestive "background" for the less-than-ideal relationship that Gerty MacDowell and Leopold Bloom develop on Sandymount Strand. Earlier in *Ulysses*, when Bloom evades Boylan on the street, he ducks into the National Museum and ends up inspecting the statues of goddesses to see whether they are "purer" than real women, whether they have the necessary equipment for digestion and excretion (U8.920–32). Bloom's sexuality is so impaired by his sense of inadequacy, his fears of impotence, and his knowledge of Molly's affair with Boylan that he has become alienated from lovemaking and has taken refuge, as mentioned, in romanticized notions of women. "Nausicaa" demonstrates some of the bad effects of these tendencies through the episode's ironic relation to the myth of Cupid and Psyche, especially the motifs of seeing and not-seeing, knowing and not-knowing.

The schematic guide to *Ulysses* that Joyce gave to Carlo Linati lists the "eye" as one of the organs of the episode, "the projected mirage" as the "sense" or "meaning" of the episode, and "painting" as the art of "Nausicaa." The "Gorman-Gilbert schema" lists the "Virgin" as the "symbol" of this episode (Ellmann, *Ulysses*, Appendix). In "Nausicaa" we see first Gerty and then Bloom projecting "mirages" of the other, "painting" idealized pictures of the opposite sex by refusing to "see" correctly. Since the narration prior to the climax of the episode originates from Gerty's perspective, we note her participation in this idealization more fully; we do not know what goes on in Bloom's mind while he masturbates, entering his point of view only after he has finished.

Fritz Senn has pointed out that "the sentence that first announces Gerty contains just two verbs in its main clause, 'knew' and 'couldn't see'" ("Nausicaa" 291), and the episode is full of references to seeing and knowing. The legend of Cupid and Psyche as told by Apuleius provides subtle reinforcement for this motif. Our modern lovers cannot see each other clearly, partly because of the deepening twilight and partly because of their tendencies to idealize each other; nor do they want to know each other. Joyce's subtle references to the Cupid and Psyche story do more than simply provide an allusion to *The Golden Ass*; they reinforce and deepen the possible meanings that the reader can draw from the pervasive visual imagery in "Nausicaa."

Gerty "sees" Bloom through the lens of romance, painting him as "the gentleman in black" (U13.349), the "foreigner, the image of the photo she had of Martin Harvey, the matinée idol" (U13.416–17). Her ideas of love and romance form themselves through the interaction of reading and imagining, readings such as the poem she copies out of the newspaper entitled *"Art thou real, my ideal?"* (U13.645–46), a poem that causes Stephen Daedalus to experience "a sharp agony in the sensitive region" when Madden reads it to him in *Stephen Hero* (83). In forming her ideal of romantic love, Gerty casts herself unknowingly as Psyche, the young princess who becomes the lover of Cupid—of Love himself—

but only on condition that she not see him. Her two jealous sisters (here played by Edy and Cissy), suspecting that she is married to a god, convince Psyche that her nocturnal husband is actually a "most cruel serpent" (Apuleius 227). Seized with a desire to know the truth, to see her lover as he really is, the luckless Psyche lights a lamp after Cupid falls asleep that night and, amazed by seeing a beautiful god in her bed, accidently pricks herself with one of his arrows, thereby falling in love with Love. She then spills oil from the lamp, burning his shoulder and awakening him. Cupid flies away, and Psyche must begin her quest to win him back.

Joyce's notes for "Nausicaa" reveal that images related to the Cupid and Psyche story formed part of his thoughts as he composed. His notes and notesheets refer to Cupid, Venus, lamps, burning, and the urge to see and know the beloved. Bloom, we learn, "dislikes to be seen in profile" and looks at Gerty "as a snake looks at its prey" (see Appendix). Joyce went back through this episode in his typescript and placard revisions, adding elements that again hint at a correlation with *The Golden Ass* and especially with the myth of Cupid and Psyche. For example, in typescript he added to a description of Gerty's face the line, "her rosebud mouth was a genuine Cupid's bow, Greekly perfect" (U13.88-89). Soon after this, Joyce describes Gerty's "butterfly bow" (U13.157), neatly combining two traditional symbols related to Psyche (often referred to as a butterfly) and Cupid (the bow). Joyce describes a withering glance that Gerty has given Edy Boardman in terms evocative of Cupid's arrows and Psyche's relations with her jealous sisters: "that shaft had struck home for her petty jealousy and they both knew that she was something aloof, apart, in another sphere, that she was not of them . . ." (U13.601-3). Again, alluding to Cupid's parents, Venus and Vulcan, we hear from Gerty's perspective: "If she saw that magic lure in his eyes there would be no holding back for her. Love laughs at locksmiths" (U13.652-53).

These references to *The Golden Ass* form only one strand in the web of motifs and allusions that Joyce weaves into "Nausicaa." References to lamps and lamplighters, for example, may have as much, or more, to do with Maria Susanna Cummins's romance novel *The Lamplighter*,[4] just as references to goddesses and gold may participate as much in evoking the Virgin Mary as they do in alluding to Psyche, Venus, or Isis. All of these allusions, taken together, form a suggestive background for our modern Cupid and Psyche, Leopold and Gerty.

What, then, does this Apuleian background contribute to our reading of "Nausicaa"? Most immediately, it supplements the ironic contrast provided by the Homeric parallel. Bloom is no Odysseus and Gerty no

Princess Nausicaa, nor are they Cupid and Psyche. We can more easily see Bloom's lame goddess as a parody of Madame Blavatsky's *Isis Unveiled* than as a parallel to Apuleius' redemptive vision of Isis. While Bloom may resemble Lucius's asininity, he is not rescued by a goddess on the beach at Sandymount, but he is left to continue his wanderings.

The Golden Ass provides a mythic substrate that underscores the presence and importance of goddesses in this episode concerned with the effects of idealizing the object of one's desire. According to Arthur Power, Joyce once told him, "What makes most people's lives unhappy is some disappointed romanticism, some unrealizable or misconceived ideal. In fact you may say that idealism is the ruin of man . . ." (98). The myth of Cupid and Psyche as a subtext for *Ulysses* accentuates the effects of idealizing the other by providing a mythic counterpart—an intertextual "memory"—in which a woman becomes a goddess through love, in which a human being falls in love with Love itself (a fitting image for the voracious reader of romances), and, more importantly, in which love must exist without true knowledge or sight of the beloved. Gerty thinks of Bloom as her "dreamhusband" (U13.431), but this ideal image can only exist in an environment veiled, as "Nausicaa" is, by myopia and deliberate obscurity. As Bloom puts it when he sees Gerty get up and realizes she is lame, "See her as she is spoil all. Must have the stage setting, the rouge, costume, position, music" (U13.855–56). Just as Cupid flies away when he realizes that Psyche has seen him and recognized him, so infatuation disappears when Bloom sees through the romantic idealizing that pervades this episode.

Joyce ironically ends his chapter of idealized love with references to the legend of Isis and Osiris when Bloom sees a bat flying about in the twilight and thinks, "Ba. What is that flying about? Swallow? Bat probably. Thinks I'm a tree, so blind. . . . Metempsychosis. They believed you could be changed into a tree from grief. Weeping willow. Ba" (U13.1117–19). The "ba" was one of the parts of the soul in Egyptian religion,[5] and in Plutarch's retelling of the myth of Isis and Osiris in the *Moralia*—which Joyce had in his Paris library[6]—a chest containing the body of the murdered Osiris comes to rest under a tree that "enfolded, embraced, and concealed the coffer within itself." In the same story, Isis, in the form of a swallow, circles around and around this tree in grief (Plutarch 13).[7]

The "Nausicaa" episode is set next to the Star of the Sea church in Sandymount, a church dedicated to "Mary, Star of the Sea" (Gifford 384). As "Nausicaa" begins, in fact, we hear "the voice of prayer to her who is in her pure radiance a beacon ever to the stormtossed heart of man,

Mary, star of the sea" (U13.7-8). Joyce would certainly have known that "Star of the Sea" or "Stella Maris" is an epithet traditionally assigned to the Virgin Mary, and Joyce's schema lists the "symbol" of this episode as the Virgin. Joyce may also have realized, through his reading of Madame Blavatsky's *Isis Unveiled* and perhaps through his familiarity with Sir James Frazer's *The Golden Bough*, that both these authors and others accused the Catholic Church of having used the imagery of the cult of Isis as a basis for the depiction of the Virgin Mary. Frazer, for example, asserts that "to Isis in her later character of patroness of mariners the Virgin Mary perhaps owes her beautiful epithet of *Stella Maris*, 'Star of the Sea,' under which she is adored by tempest-tossed sailors" (119). By juxtaposing the myth of Isis found in *The Golden Ass* with the cult of the Virgin Mary, Joyce adds yet another shade of complexity to the intertextual memories or resonances evoked by "Nausicaa." These allusions to Isis near the ending of "Nausicaa" imply that while the hero of the ancient romance can rely on the aid of a goddess and the ingestion of a bunch of roses to become a man once more, modern romance is more problematic. The goddess does not appear; the text subtly suggests her presence only to emphasize her absence.

The tempest-tossed Leopold Bloom, then, finds himself unknowingly participating in a number of different plots, intertextual memories that help to form the cultural memory that inscribes us all in the various roles we play in daily life. We find Bloom and Gerty not only ambiguously linked to the Homeric story of Odysseus and Nausicaa, but to the stories of Cupid and Psyche, Lucius and Isis, and perhaps even Isis and the Virgin Mary. Joyce has complicated the text of "Nausicaa" by supplementing the contemporary romances that dominate the language of the episode with a much older romance hidden beneath the surface. The subtle presence of Isis and Mary in the episode provides a clever frame for Bloom's reliance on idealized images of women as goddesses and, at the same time, challenges the Catholicism dominant in the Irish setting of *Ulysses* with an older religion buried within the text. By "unveiling" these stories hidden in "Nausicaa," these allusions to *The Golden Ass* lead the careful reader to "remember" other possibilities and to consider new interpretations.

The echoes of *The Golden Ass* seem clearly ironic, localized as they are within an episode in which Bloom appears at his worst. Yet we can read this mocking memory of an older text as a mockery not of what might be—unity, love, coherence—but of what *is* (e.g., Bloom's behavior in "Nausicaa"). The problems implied by such intertextual links throughout *Ulysses* are nevertheless deep, creating an ironic distance between the modern setting most immediately evident in the text and the ancient stories encoded more subtly within it. This technique, as we have seen, may strike readers either as a negative comment on the relative emptiness and absurdity of modern life in comparison to the richness of older traditions or—as Eliot would see it—as a suggestion of stability and hope under the apparent chaos and absurdity of daily life.

This layering and density of allusion—of intertextual memory—in *Ulysses* works on a deeper level than the simple mockery implied by the ironic technique of placing an older, closed plot such as the *Odyssey* on top of the plot of *Ulysses* to emphasize the fragmentation or meaninglessness of life in Ireland in 1904. Intertextuality in *Ulysses* works in much the same way as textual memory does, in that Joyce went to extremes to load his text with cultural memory triggers in the form of allusions so subtle and obscure that no reader could be expected to catch them all in one, two, three, or more readings. Joyce embedded such subtle signs into the text not only as a demonstration of his virtuosity, not only as "bait" for academics, but also as a parallel to the general pattern of memory in the novel. Just as Bloom and Stephen need not be conscious of the effects of memory triggers such as "cock" or "eleven" for these words to "work" in their psyches, so, it would seem, Joyce had faith that the reader would somehow register the effects of the various intertextual links suggested constantly in the text, even if these effects occur in passing, without the reader's conscious awareness of their presence.

In the sense outlined above, intertextuality in *Ulysses* can be interpreted as mimetic, as a model of the way(s) that memory "works" in our minds on various levels—personal as well as cultural—and perhaps on even deeper levels. Bloom is not aware that his actions fit into an Odyssean paradigm, and yet, by virtue of a broader "design" that he can grasp, this paradigm and the other models echoing throughout the text of *Ulysses* provide patterns that structure and interpret his experiences without determining them. Similarly, when Stephen outlines his myth of Shakespeare's life, he is not conscious of the extent to which it reflects the life of the man with whom he is to spend his evening.

The contrasts between the "story" of Bloom, Stephen, and Molly as it occurs in *Ulysses* and the stories buried in the text of *Ulysses* are thus both suggestive and problematic. While the relatively complete narrative structures offered by these parallel stories offer the hint or promise of closure for the characters, in the end they may simply mock the modern text or, in another light, emphasize the inappropriateness of closure and the inevitability of fragmentation in a modern text.

Joyce's manipulation of various historical traditions to create a dense and subtle subtext for *Ulysses* should finally be read as an ambivalent modern response to the realization that our lives are inevitably involved with and to some degree shaped by the various paradigms and stories that form our culture. Joyce's decision to cram the text of *Ulysses* with references not only to the popular writings of his own time (e.g., the romances Gerty reads) but also to older narratives may suggest both our intricate and often unconscious involvement in the various discourses that form our culture—that is, the inevitable presence of tradition and of narrative paradigms that give shape to our experiences—*and* the absence of any reassuring conviction that these older plots can any longer guarantee a final coherence or meaning in modern life. As Christine van Boheemen argues, Joyce's intertextuality in *Ulysses* is "ambivalent and unclear. Bloom is *both* different from *and* similar to the classical hero" (142).

The ambivalence and ambiguity of Joyce's use of tradition in *Ulysses* helps us formulate a response to the problems of modernism articulated in the introduction to this book. Joyce's response to the modernist perception that the dominant paradigms and traditions of Western culture no longer had the power to define, control, or stabilize modern life was not to attempt to begin completely anew by severing all links to the past, nor was it a capitulation to Eliot's desire to somehow secure or moor the present moment in a mythic or traditional structure behind modern art.

Van Boheemen suggests that Joyce's intertextuality deliberately foregrounds "what all texts do unconsciously. All writing predicates itself upon previous structures, meanings, or texts.... Joyce's writing strategy proves emblematic of the intertextuality of all writing" (144). Joyce's intertextuality can be understood in the context of what Perry Meisel, in *The Myth of the Modern*, calls the modernist sense of "belatedness," of responding to the sense that the literary tradition that one is working in is exhausted. In *Ulysses*, Meisel writes, we can see that Joyce's response to the accumulation of traditions and of other stories is to enter into and embrace the situation rather than to repress or avoid it: "If there is an especially appropriate Joycean gloss for the problematic of modernism at large, it lies compact in Stephen's Miltonic remark in the first chapter, 'Dead breaths I living breathe'—the sense that one's life or one's art is the echo or repetition of another's" (139).

Joyce's intertextuality, then, is a way of coping with modernity—with the modern sense of the absurdity of life and with the modernist writer's sense of being inevitably and already inscribed within a tradition of writing. In Joyce's construction of an intertextual memory—exemplified in the way that he weaves the stories contained in older texts such as the *Odyssey* and *The Golden Ass* into the fabric of *Ulysses*—we can read both an awareness of the constant presence and influence of the past in daily life and of the ironic gap between our lives and the traditional stories that supposedly give them form and meaning.

Conclusion

Always keep Ithaca fixed in your mind.
To arrive there is your ultimate goal.
But do not hurry the voyage at all.
It is better to let it last for years;
and even to anchor at the isle when you are old,
rich with all that you have gained on the way,
not expecting that Ithaca will offer you riches.
—C. P. Cavafy, "Ithaca"

Given the argument outlined in the book up to now, reading *Ulysses* as an "odyssey of memory" might lead us to expect some sort of resolution, some sort of "Ithaca" offered by the text at the end of the characters' trials. If the text works, as I have argued, to bring Stephen and Bloom to points of "confrontation" with their pasts in "Circe," to what effect do these confrontations occur? If memory serves a deeper, purposive, teleological force—whether it be destiny or the entelechic self—we would expect to see an improvement in the attitudes and conditions of the characters. We might expect that Stephen would adjust his memory of his mother and "no more turn aside and brood," and we might hope the same for Bloom in relation to his memory of Rudy. We might also hope to see some awakening of Stephen's creative powers, since in *Ulysses* we see him so clearly as the artist who does not or cannot produce art. The Homeric parallel hovers behind the events of the final chapters, always implying that Bloom and Stephen might be able to establish some sort of relationship that mimics that of father and son, for it is in Ithaca that Homer's Odysseus reveals himself as father to Telemachus. And, of course, both *The Odyssey* and *Ulysses* focus in the end on the relationship between husband and wife. Odysseus' reconciliation with Penelope suggests the possibility that Leopold Bloom will exercise his mnemotechnic properly—as Odysseus did when he demonstrated his correct memory of the construction of the bed that he and Penelope shared—and return to a relationship with Molly free from the destructive mediation of a view of woman as either goddess or whore.

We might well also expect a transformation in the characters' orientations toward the past and, specifically, toward their memories of the past. We would hope that any release or relaxation of the knotted complexes of guilt which they have constructed over time in their memories would allow both of them to proceed in life without the constant intrusion of repressed and painful memories. We might expect that Bloom and Stephen would gain easier access to a past that has been purged of at least some of its demons, and that, correspondingly, any barriers erected by habit and nostalgia would be somehow lowered by the end of *Ulysses*.

As noted in chapter 4, the ending of the "Circe" episode seems to provide a temporary but reassuring sense of closure and catharsis, as Bloom stands watchfully over the exhausted Stephen, apparently rewarded by a vision of Rudy that suggests the possibility of reconciliation, peace, and an end to Bloom's troublesome memories of Rudy's death. The reader may feel justified in reading a sense of closure into the scene, but a second glance reveals that the ending of "Circe" may in fact provide a false sense of resolution, mirroring the problem of closure in the book as a whole. From another, more realistic perspective, the events in Nighttown may seem silly, inconclusive, even banal, mocking the implications of apocalypse and atonement suggested by the end of the episode. After all, Stephen has merely broken a lamp and run into a surly representative of the state who has left him lying semiconscious on the street, where Bloom, standing over him, misinterprets everything Stephen says. Like most of what happens in "Circe," Bloom's epiphanic vision of Rudy is apparently forgotten by the text and the characters in the chapters that follow—Bloom does not mention it again, and as far as the reader knows, he does not remember it afterward.

What is left us, then, after the mere apocalypses of a snapped trouser button and a broken lamp? Stephen unconsciously anticipates his moment of apocalypse in "Circe" at the beginning of the "Nestor" episode, as he muses on the battle of Asculum and thinks: "Fabled by the daughters of memory. And yet it was in some way if not as memory fabled it. A phrase, then, of impatience, thud of Blake's wings of excess. I hear the ruin of all space, shattered glass and toppling masonry, and time one livid final flame. What's left us then?" (*U*2.7–10). What was, as Stephen suggests, did indeed happen, and yet its significance and even its continued existence is always dependent upon the "fabling," transformative, and therefore unreliable power of memory. As we have seen, subjec-

CONCLUSION 183

tive human memory differs from the impersonal, passivist Akasic memory envisioned by Theosophy, a photographic memory that impartially records "all that ever anywhere wherever was" (U7.882–83). Our memories are more often violent, unconscious, involuntary, and "fabled" by the imagination, as Stephen's memory of his mother has been fabled into the "lemur" that he encounters in "Circe." We would be mistaken to assume that Stephen and Bloom have achieved any sort of clear resolution to their problems by the time they leave Bella Cohen's brothel or even by the end of the book, or that any transformations achieved in Nighttown will translate simply or clearly into transformations in their daily lives from June 17, 1904, onward.

After the seemingly climactic contortions and catharses of "Circe," "Eumaeus" is clearly an emotional letdown. Even the narrator seems exhausted and drained, an impression strengthened by Joyce's designation, in the Gorman-Gilbert schema for *Ulysses*, of the styles or "technics" of the last three episodes as "relaxed," ("Eumaeus"), "pacified" ("Ithaca"), and "resigned" ("Penelope") (Ellmann, *Ulysses*, Appendix). There is certainly much in the last three episodes to encourage the reader who hopes for some sort of holistic conclusion to *Ulysses*. "Eumaeus" begins with hints of some occult symbolic link between Bloom and Stephen, as we read that Bloom has taken on the role of Stephen's *fidus Achates* (U16.54–55), a role earlier ascribed to Buck Mulligan by Stephen's father (U6.49). The solicitous Bloom takes Stephen under his wing, warning him about the paralyzing habits of Dublin life, including the "habitual practice" of frequenting prostitutes and "drinking habits" (U16.65–66).

The text of "Eumaeus" repeatedly suggests return, hinting at the Homeric parallel and building reader expectations. Much of this imagery of return is hidden amid talk and thoughts of sailors, appropriate both to the Homeric parallel of Ulysses returning home from the sea and to the fact that Stephen and Bloom encounter an old sailor named Murphy in the cabman's shelter. Murphy's return from the sea suggests a larger symbolic pattern of return through small details we gather as the episode proceeds. We learn, for example, that Murphy came into Dublin on "the threemaster *Rosevean*" (U16.450)—the very same "threemaster, her sails brailed up on the crosstrees," that Stephen sees "homing, upstream" at the end of "Proteus" (U3.504–5). The strangest and most suggestive of these images of return occurs when Murphy reveals the tattoo of an anchor on his chest: "on top of the timehonoured symbol of *the mariner's hope and rest* they had a full view of *the figure 16* and a young man's *sideface* looking frowningly rather" (U16.674–76; my emphasis). We learn a few sentences later that it was "a Greek" who tattooed his own face on Murphy's chest, a face now "livid" on Murphy's skin (*U*16.679 and 686). The text is still providing hints or suggestions of connectedness for the reader in the reappearance of memory triggers such as "livid," associated with Stephen's pandybatting, and the number 16, which, as we have seen, provides a noteworthy connection between Stephen and Bloom (*U*15.3718-20). The significance of the sideface of the young Greek is underscored once more in "Eumaeus" when Bloom looks "sideways in a friendly fashion at the sideface of Stephen, image of his mother" (*U*16.1803-4).

Although the reader is left out of much of the potentially significant conversation that occurs at the beginning of "Ithaca"—we learn that Stephen and Bloom discuss such important subjects as "the past day" and "Stephen's collapse" (*U*17.16-17) as they follow "parallel courses" toward Bloom's house—the narrator does reveal their respective theories on the cause of Stephen's collapse. While Bloom attributes it to a combination of hunger, drunkenness, and mental and physical exertion, Stephen explains it by "the reapparition of a matutinal cloud (perceived by both from two different points of observation, Sandycove and Dublin) at first no bigger than a woman's hand" (*U*17.37-42). This strange explanation is as close to conscious articulation as any shared mental experience in *Ulysses* gets, referring to the cloud seen simultaneously by Stephen in "Telemachus" (*U*1.248) and by Bloom in "Calypso" (*U*4.218). One possible explanation, though unlikely, is that Stephen and Bloom have discovered this coincidental experience during their discussion of "the past day." Otherwise, it indicates that Stephen is somehow aware of this strange coincidence and its significance. This web of irony and significance is complicated further by the fact that, as Weldon Thornton notes, the wording of the description of the cloud alludes to the Old Testament book of Kings, where Elijah's servant informs him of the appearance of a "little cloud out of the sea, like a man's hand" (I Kings 18.44), which Elijah recognizes as "the cloud which will break the drought he himself had brought about" (Thornton 462). Whether Stephen voices the description of the cloud or thinks it to himself, or whether the narrator makes the connections, the text here suggests again the idea of a shared thought (now a shared memory) functioning as a hint of destiny.

Another strange suggestion of continued shared memories between Stephen and Bloom occurs when Bloom tells Stephen about an advertising scheme he had contemplated that would have included "two smartly dressed girls . . . seated engaged in writing" (*U*17.609-10). Stephen's response to this is to imagine a spare scene in a "Solitary hotel in mountain pass," in which a young man reads what a young woman has written on a sheet of paper: "Queen's Hotel, Queen's Hotel, Queen's Hotel. Queen's Ho . . ." Strangely, as Bloom realizes, Stephen seems somehow to be "remembering" the scene of Bloom's father's suicide, for Bloom "reconstructs" from this suggestion the details of his father's death. Bloom attributes "this homonymity" in Stephen's imagined scene to "coincidence" (U17.635), and indeed, the "Ithaca" episode contains numerous references to accident, coincidence, and predestination that suggest a continuing tension between chance and destiny in the text.[1]

The various suggestions of union between Stephen and Bloom in "Eumaeus" and "Ithaca"—from their sharing of "the creature cocoa" (U17.369-70) to their simultaneous urination below Molly's window, "each contemplating the other in both mirrors of the reciprocal flesh of theirhisnothis fellowfaces" (U17.1183-84)—are too numerous and too fully articulated in other sources for me to go through them in great detail here. Bloom sums up the spirit of much of this strange evidence for an optimistic reading of some sort of union—implied or actual—between the two men when he recalls the curious history of "a throwaway (subsequently thrown away) advertising Elijah" (U17.331-32) that he received in "Lestrygonians." This recollection leads him to realize that he had unintentionally predicted the winner of the Gold Cup race in "Lotus-Eaters" (U5.534). As Bloom ponders "Reminiscences of coincidences, truth stranger than fiction, preindicative of the result of the Gold Cup flat handicap" (U17.323-24), he comprehends "the difficulties of interpretation" (U17.343) attendant on such seemingly significant coincidences.

There are enough "difficulties of interpretation" in the final three episodes to frustrate any attempt to bring *Ulysses* to a neat close. Stephen and Bloom certainly still have problems after their confrontations with the ghosts of the past in "Circe." Stephen, who has no place to stay and little money, will turn down Bloom's offers of assistance and lodging to wander off into the night, taking with him any promise of an "atonement" or any superficial, quotidian father-son relationship between them. Bloom exhibits a number of disturbing behaviors in the final chapters of *Ulysses*, including an apparent desire to interest Stephen in Molly's "fleshy charms" (U16.1428) and a continued tendency to avoid direct confrontation with his problems, here by cloaking them in the story of Parnell's adultery, which serves as a screen for anxieties about his sexual inadequacy and the difficulties that he will face in returning to his marriage: "simply a case of the husband not being up to scratch . . . and then a real man arriving on the scene" (U16.1380-82). Bloom apparently still longs for his ideal—the "opulent curves" of the Nymph, reminiscent of "those Grecian statues perfectly developed as works of art, in the National Museum" (U16.1448–51). The fact that he dwells on these superficial aspects of Molly—the eight-year-old photo ("Very like her then"—U16.1438–39) and "her stage presence" (U16.1459)—in "Eumaeus" suggests that Bloom retains the same tendency to idealize, distort, exaggerate, and generally make an ass of himself that we saw displayed in "Nausicaa." Although he does return home to the clearest Ithaca that the text can offer—his home and his wife—"all is changed by woman's will" (U15.3153) since his departure the previous morning. Molly/Penelope has finally and irreversibly changed their relationship by spending the day with Boylan, and she has done so convinced of Bloom's collusion in arranging his own cuckolding (e.g., U18.1007–9). Bloom's final act before falling asleep is to revert to his role as "Adorer of the adulterous rump" (U15.2839), achieving an "approximate erection" as he gets into bed with Molly and kisses "the melons of her rump" (U17.2241).

The odyssey of memory in *Ulysses* ends in some senses at the end of "Ithaca," for Molly Bloom is for the most part excluded from the sharing of mind and the intimations of destiny that link Stephen and Bloom. Joyce wrote to Harriet Shaw Weaver: "The Ithaca episode . . . is in reality the end as Penelope has no beginning, middle or end" (*Letters* I, 172). Although "Penelope" is usually remarked for its stylistic experimentation, which makes it appear closer in style to the linguistic flow of *Finnegans Wake*, Karen Lawrence insightfully notes that "however radical the monologue first appears on the page, its underlying conventionality becomes apparent," for on a narrative level "Penelope" "contributes to our sense of return and closure: even though we have never heard this voice before, we return to the sound of one mind thinking, a type of sound we heard throughout the first part of the book" (204). Thus, although John Paul Riquelme is correct in noting that the "mimesis of consciousness" in "Penelope" approaches "the unconscious or the imagination" (228), we must note that as Molly drifts unconsciously into her memories at the end of "Penelope," blurring or "unweaving" identity and incident in a manner suggestive of *Finnegans Wake*, the content of these memories and of her unconscious mind is purely personal, with one possible exception—when Molly thinks that if Stephen were to come live with them, "Id have to get a nice pair of red slippers like those Turks with the fez used to sell" (U18.1494–96), which echoes Bloom's dream of the night before (U13.1240–41 and 14.508–10), a dream that the narrator of "Oxen of the Sun" tells us "is thought by those in ken to be for a change" (U14.510).

In the course of her reading of "Penelope," Lawrence quickly outlines various critics' approaches to "The meaning of Molly's climactic assent at the end of the chapter" (205), opposing herself to those eager to find a resolution to the book in Molly's "yes" by adding that "regardless of the specifics of these interpretations, the idea of a natural resolution is precisely what is undermined in the book as a whole" (206). Molly's final "yes" echoes a "yes" delivered sixteen years ago on Howth Hill that has yet to work itself to a close. While Molly has heard the same thunderbolt that scared Stephen in "Oxen of the Sun" (U18.134), and while she also hears "Georges church bells" (U18.1231) as her day ends, her monologue does not settle the problems remaining for Stephen, Bloom, or herself at the end of the book. We learn that she intends to continue seeing Boylan and has made an appointment with him for Monday (U18.332 and 595). Molly, like Bloom in "Ithaca," thinks about leaving and not returning—"then coming back suppose I never came back" (U18.373)—and in her memories of Boylan's sexual prowess and her longing—"I wished he was here or somebody to let myself go with and come again like that" (U18.584–85)—we can read a parody of Bloom's return, a mockery in which Boylan's ability to come again (and again and again) undercuts Bloom's return.

Many readers have tried either to discover or—when discovery will not work—manufacture the atonement and closure that the Homeric parallel and the forms of traditional narrative lead us to expect. Such readers, seizing on the apparently proleptic and positive hints in the final episodes—some of which I have outlined above—inevitably run aground on the rock of the obvious in their own journey to find this textual Ithaca. The text both hints at and mocks this desire for closure, refusing finally to provide the neat ending that most readers crave.

As Richard M. Kain has shown in his comprehensive essay, "The Significance of Stephen's Meeting Bloom: A Survey of Interpretations," readers have struggled in various and often violently opposed ways with the ending of *Ulysses*.[2] Some of the most strenuous attempts to "close" the text of *Ulysses* view everything in the last three episodes as ultimately symbolic, and in doing so they ignore tensions and problems on the narrative level that undercut such a conclusion. Thus, William York Tindall in *A Reader's Guide to James Joyce* can comfortably assume that despite "several frustrations," Bloom's day has been a success (224), for in the "jocoserious" book "unlimited by middle-class decencies or habits of mind," everything stands for something else, preferably something "higher" or even transcendent. From this trusting point of view, the cocoa that Stephen and Bloom drink becomes "Eucharistic wine," and their joint urination under Molly's window is "a sign of creation" that provides Stephen with the "final enlightenment" which he needs to become a great artist: "Knowing Bloom and Molly, as every writer must, Stephen knows humanity entirely. Let him go away and write about it" (Tindall 224-25).

The desire to close the text as completely as Tindall and others do is understandable, especially in light of the novelty that *Ulysses* presented to readers and critics, but it leads to a naive and simpleminded reduction of the text that brackets out the considerable difficulties which Bloom, Stephen, and Molly still face at the end of the book. This desire for closure results in vague, reassuring visions of the three characters as a "spiritual family," or even—at its least restrained—Peter Costello's strange attempt to "complete" *Ulysses* in *Leopold Bloom: A Biography*, which follows the continuing sagas of Leopold, Molly, and Stephen after June 16, 1904: Stephen, after living for a short time as a tenant of the Blooms, goes on to become James Joyce and write *Ulysses*, Molly dies of cancer, and Bloom lives on to become a grandfather!

The ending of *Ulysses* can lead readers to the opposite extreme as well. As early as 1930, when Joyce's friend Stuart Gilbert published *James Joyce's "Ulysses,"* readers also have read the novel as a "hopeless quest" that cannot remedy the characters' "futile isolation" and "despair" (Gilbert 64). Even a reader as interested in psychoanalytic and symbolic readings as Carl Jung concluded in *"Ulysses": A Monologue* that *Ulysses* is an "infernally nugatory" book in which "nothing happens"—it "begins in the void and ends in the void" (7)—a book that represents the abstract, objectifying, empiricist worldview of "white-skinned man who believes in the object, who is cursed with the object" (20). This reading of *Ulysses* as an ultimately frustrating, even nihilistic, text finds an echo in current readings of *Ulysses* as a book concerned only with language and the slipperiness of referentiality. From this perspective, Hélène Cixous can claim that Joyce's works join that group of "writings whose subversive force is now undermining the world of western discourse" ("Joyce" 15). In her analysis of Stephen's fox riddle, in which she hears only "the laughter of the perverse text," Cixous reduces the choices open to a reader of *Ulysses* to two:

> the first trusting to the known facts about Joyce's work . . . thus prejudging the book as a "full" text, governed by "the hypostasis of the signified," a text which conceals itself but which has something to conceal, which is findable. . . . On the other hand one can imagine a reading which would accept "discouragement," . . . by seeing in that trap which confiscates signification the sign of the willed imposture which crosses and double-crosses the *whole* of Joyce's work,

making that betrayal the very breath (the breathlessness) of the subject. Nothing will have been signified save the riddle, referral of a referral beneath a letter which, besides, is not beyond the pretence of having spirit. ("Joyce" 21)

By ignoring the metafictional or postmodern elements of *Ulysses*, readers like Tindall can make a neat box of the book, rounding the text into a symbolic whole. On the other hand, by seeing only the "imposture" of the text—the ways in which it discourages traditional, holistic readings—readers as various as Jung and Cixous can view the text as merely a mockery, a series of fragments that undercut wholeness and unity.

These two opposing poles—closure and the impossibility of closure—can easily become the Scylla and Charybdis of *Ulysses* criticism, but it is possible to work toward a middle position by reading the ending of *Ulysses* as a form of mimesis that resists closure as unrealistic. By carefully examining the tensions suspended in the book, tensions between historical paradigms outlined in my introduction and implied in Cheryl Herr's "cultural unconscious" and Umberto Eco's "chaosmos," we can avoid the unnecessary dilemma of reading *Ulysses* either as a superficial and "infernally nugatory" book or as a text that depends on a obscure "mythic method" to convey its ultimately reassuring and stabilizing meaning. *Ulysses* does not come to a neat conclusion because nothing really ever does. At the same time, this failure to conclude need not drive us into the whirlpool of absolute indeterminacy, incoherence, or meaninglessness.

What, then, becomes of the holistic, teleological impulses that comprise the textual unconscious of *Ulysses*? Perhaps those who hope to find a transformation in Joyce's characters at the end of the book, a sense that the events depicted have indeed "meant" something, can best view these events in the narrative in the same way that Bloom imagines the workings of drugs in the chemist's shop in "Lotus-Eaters": "Drugs age you after mental excitement. Lethargy then. Why? Reaction. A lifetime in a night. Gradually changes your character" (U5.474–76). While the psychic confrontations and transformations that Stephen and Bloom have encountered in "Circe" have not yet manifested themselves in any clear or obvious way in the characters' lives, this does not mean that these transformations have not occurred or that they have no effects. As a complex, transitional text that holds in tension both centripetal or holistic impulses and centrifugal, postmodern, or metafictional ones, *Ulysses* cannot deliver any more than this to a reader seeking reassuring narrative resolutions.

Perhaps Karen Lawrence best describes this middle path in reading the ending of *Ulysses* when, in her discussion of "Ithaca," she argues: "Despite the representation of events in what Joyce called 'the coldest, baldest way,' a sense of possibility mitigates the alienation of the cosmic perspective." Lawrence asserts that rather than negating meaning and belief, "Ithaca"—and, by extension, *Ulysses* itself—

> imparts instead a sense of the various possibilities that exist in life. *Ulysses* is full of meaning, but this is not to say that its final meaning is the affirmation of life. It is a book that is beyond what we generally mean by affirmation or negation; it shows us all kinds of truths about life but doesn't sum it up in any one statement of meaning. (201)

Like Lawrence, I read *Ulysses* as a book that finally "presents possibilities instead of conclusions" (Lawrence 206). The text asserts the inevitability of change and possibility over closure repeatedly in "Eumaeus" and "Ithaca." Just as various critics have struggled to bring the text to "completion," we see Bloom consider "All kinds of Utopian plans" (*U*16.1652) that would establish some sort of permanent relationship between himself and Stephen, a relationship that might well lead to Italian lessons for Molly, voice lessons for Stephen, a joint singing tour, "vicarious satisfaction" for Bloom, and "disintegration of obsession" for Molly (*U*17.935–39). Such possibilities are not destined to be actualized, however, for "The irreparability of the past" and the "imprevidibility of the future" make the "realisation" of Bloom's plans for Stephen unlikely; the reader may assume that when Stephen leaves, he, like the coin that Bloom once marked and spent, will never return (*U*17.973–84). Thus, Joyce's text mirrors not only the longing for progress and completion evidenced by the neo-Lamarckian evolutionary writings in his library, but also a suspicion of such teleological impulses similar to the Darwinian view of time and evolution as clearly noncyclical—species mutate and evolve from one form to another—not back again. Gillian Beer notes that "Darwinian theory . . . excludes or suppresses certain orderings of experience. It has no place for stasis. It debars return" (11). In *Ulysses*, these warring tendencies of teleology and randomness remain in tension through the end of the book.

What, then, of the force of "destiny" in the novel? Is the destiny suggested by the text a mockery of what we usually think of as destiny—a powerful, directed force that sweeps us along to some momentous end? Destiny in *Ulysses*, like *Ulysses* itself, does not work toward a guaranteed or predetermined end but can be viewed instead as a working-out or working-through. The clearest passage on destiny in *Ulysses* is Stephen's echo of Maeterlinck in "Scylla and Charybdis," discussed in chapter 3, in which Stephen claims that Shakespeare "found in the world without as actual what was in his world within as possible" (U9.1041–42).[3] This view of destiny as an entelechic working-through of one's nature or self echoes other holistic, teleological cultural tendencies that Joyce found in his education and reading, especially, as argued above, in the counter-Darwinian evolutionary arguments of Father Maher, Samuel Butler, Henri Bergson, and various Theosophists. These progressive, holistic forces help to constitute the cultural unconscious of *Ulysses*, operating throughout the book as a counterforce to the chaotic, destabilizing, accidental forces in the text that mimic the characteristics which many of Joyce's contemporaries associated with Darwinism. The working-out of memory and destiny in *Ulysses* may be part of a gradual process of development—the development of the self, of one's nature—on a level deeper than that of consciousness.

The reader who is willing to settle for less than full closure and who cannot ignore the suggestion of something more significant than perverse laughter behind the meeting of Stephen and Bloom realizes that although neither character can control the direction of his own "destiny," their meeting has suggested and perhaps—through the mnemotechnic of "Circe"—cleared the way for possibilities in each of their futures. Correspondingly, the same episodes that deny Bloom any final control over Stephen's future literally teem with "possibilities"; out of eighty-two occurrences of variations on the word "possible" in *Ulysses*—"possibilities," "possibility," "possible," and "possibly"—forty-six occur in "Eumaeus" and "Ithaca" alone.[4] Not all possibilities are positive; the text gives no guarantee that Bloom and Stephen will proceed onward to happy endings. When Bloom, for example, considers the possibility of leaving Molly, one destination he muses on is "the Parthenon (containing statues of nude Grecian divinities)" (U17.1984–85), suggesting the continued influence of the sexual attitudes represented by the *Photo Bits* Nymph. The text can now insinuate every kind of possibility, including both the possibility that Bloom will become "Noman," wedded to "A nymph immortal, beauty, the bride of Noman" (U17.2010–11), and the possibility that Bloom will overcome his doubts and fears to regain his full relationship with Molly.

We would do well to apply to *Ulysses* Phillip F. Herring's observation in *Joyce's Uncertainty Principle*: "Where there is a strong sense of closure in *Dubliners*, usually a character's entrapment or paralysis is emphasized" (169–70). In the "gnomonic" endings of stories such as "The Dead" and "A Painful Case," Herring notes, "We are expected to be suddenly jarred into a new awareness of possible meanings overlooked in the initial perusal" (170). Herring argues: "With all its pessimism about the possibility of human growth, or change, or perfectability, *Dubliners* ends on a note of hope, at that magical moment where Gabriel Conroy experiences a kind of egotistical death and transfiguration that is foreshadowed by the ending of 'A Painful Case'" (168–69).

Similarly, any transformations that occur at the end of *Ulysses*' odyssey of memory occur on a level beyond the control of the characters and the clear grasp of the reader, in a world of possibilities rather than predestined conclusions.

This sense of possibility at the end of *Ulysses* is subtly reinforced by a quiet explosion of memory in the final three episodes, which are full of recollecting and reminiscing. When Bloom asks in "Eumaeus" whether Stephen believes in the soul, Stephen "Thus cornered . . . had to make a superhuman effort of memory to try and concentrate and remember" (U16.754–55). Yet Stephen, after exercising his mnemotechnic, does answer, and Bloom similarly finds that "he too recollected in retrospect (which was a source of keen satisfaction in itself)" (U16.1583–84). This struggle to remember repeats itself throughout "Eumaeus" and "Ithaca," as when Bloom feels irritation at not finding his key in his pocket "Because he had forgotten and because he remembered that he had reminded himself twice not to forget" (U17.77–79). At one point, Bloom is unable to recall all the words of a Zionist song in Hebrew "in consequence of a defective mnemotechnic" (U17.766), yet later he makes a deliberate effort "to exercise mnemotechnic" in order to recall the "name of a decisive battle" that he had forgotten, an effort that is successful when "after an interval of amnesia . . . he remembered by mnemotechnic the name of the military engagement, Plevna" (U17.1419–25).

The possibility of some sort of progress or development is further implied at the end of *Ulysses* by the apparent disappearance and "taming" of memories and memory triggers that, by the climax of "Circe," had accumulated great psychic force. When Stephen watches Bloom light a fire in "Ithaca," for instance, the sight recalls for him a series of "similar apparitions," including those of Brother Michael at Clongowes, Simon Dedalus, and, most remarkably, "his mother Mary, wife of Simon Dedalus, in the kitchen of number twelve North Richmond street on the morning of the feast of Saint Francis Xavier 1898" (U17.142–44). Remarkably, Stephen is able here to recall a simple, human image of his mother as a living person without any of the ghoulish, remorseful trappings that have attended her in his dreams and visions earlier in *Ulysses*. The most striking feature of this apparently calm memory of Stephen's mother is its date—December 3, 1898—which is the Saturday following the three days of retreat held in "memory of the great saint" who "has great power in heaven" (*P* 108-9), the Jesuit Francis Xavier. This recollection of a day that so powerfully joins Stephen's memory of his mother to the sermons on hell and its punishing fires that so traumatized him at the age of sixteen (again, a number that seems significant for Stephen and Bloom in *Ulysses*) does not upset Stephen—a fact that implies a change in his attitude toward his mother. Another memory apparently not evoked by observing Bloom lighting the fire is the "livid," burning sensation connected with his memory of the pandybatting. His ability to return to such a tender date and scene so peacefully suggests that the complex of religious and personal guilt which he has constructed around his memory of May Dedalus has been loosened or even dissolved. As Douglas Hewitt has noted:

> Through most of the book, and most recently in "Circe," Stephen's mother has been a fixed, raw-head-and-bloody-bones symbol of guilt and suffering; to find her here, lighting a fire six years before, caught in Stephen's memory before he has turned her into anything, is astonishingly moving; she is transformed from a symbol into a person. (161)

Similarly, when Stephen and Bloom reminisce together about "their preexisting acquaintance," remembering their first meeting "in the lilac-garden of Matthew Dillon's house . . . in 1887, in the company of Stephen's mother" (*U*17.466-68), Stephen seems able again to pass quietly over this reference to his dead mother. No longer does she come to his mind "shrouded in the piteous vesture of the past, silent, remote, reproachful" (*U*14.1354-55). It is possible that the "chance words" of "Circe" that evoked his hallucination of his mother have affected his memory in some significant way.

Even Stephen's riddle words—among the most potent memory triggers in the novel—seem to have discharged their duty and their force by the end of *Ulysses*. Considering "the infinite possibilities hitherto unexploited of the modern art of advertisement" when it presents its subjects with "magnetising efficacy to arrest involuntary attention, to interest, to convince, to decide," Bloom contemplates the example of the advertisement for Kino's trousers that he has seen earlier in the day: "K. 11. Kino's

11/- Trousers" (U17.580-86). This repetition of the eleventh letter and number here excites no involuntary series of disturbing memories, as in "Circe," but seems rather to demonstrate the equanimity of memory in "Ithaca" and perhaps even that "termination of mourning" associated with the number 11 since the funeral of Hector in the *Iliad*.

The final experience that Stephen and Bloom share as they take leave of each other in "Ithaca" appropriately involves Stephen's riddle words. As they shake hands and part, both hear "The sound of the peal of the hour of the night by the chime of the bells in the church of Saint George" (U17.1226–27), the same bells that Bloom heard tolling in the morning as he sat in the jakes at the end of "Calypso." The characters hear different "echoes" (U17.1228) in the sound of the bells, however. Stephen hears the "Ordo Commendationis Animae" (*Liliata rutilantium. Turma circumdet. Iubilantum te virginum. Chorus excipiat*"), a prayer that had earlier attended his thoughts of his mother's death, carrying his memory of guilt and fear; yet, significantly, now Stephen's mind omits the words "*te confessorum*," which were contained in two earlier occurrences of the prayer (U1.277 and 15.4164). This omission of "confessors" may again suggest that Stephen's memory of his mother is finally free from guilt. Presumably, Stephen first heard this prayer intoned at his mother's deathbed, and its meaning ("May the lilied throng of radiant confessors encompass thee; may the choir of rejoicing virgins welcome thee," Thornton 17–18) may hearken back to Stephen's riddle, suggesting in "Ithaca" the ringing of "the bells in heaven" for the soul of May Dedalus, at least in Stephen's memory, and finally implying that " 'Tis time for this poor soul / To go to heaven" (U2.106–7).

The echo that Bloom hears in the sound of George's bells is a repetition of the sound "Heigho! Heigho!," which he first heard in the morning as he thought of Dignam's death (U4.546–51). This same sound —"Heigho!"—occurs in Bloom's thoughts in "Sirens" as he scans the *Freeman's Journal* for Dignam's name (U11.857–58) and in his fantasy in "Circe" just before the apparition of the "ghouleaten" Dignam (U15.1186). The bells also sound for Stephen just before "The Mother" appears to him in "Circe," as the "bracelets of dull bells" worn by the "night hours" in the "Dance of the Hours" he imagines ring "Heigho! Heigho!" (U15.4083–86). The reader is not privy to either character's psychological response to the ringing of the bells in "Ithaca" beyond the "echoes" mentioned in the text, but the bells, the touch of Stephen's hand, and the sounds of Stephen's footsteps as he walks away cause Bloom to remember the dead, "companions now . . . defunct," including Paddy Dignam (U17.1249–55).

As Bloom awaits the dawn, he remembers a sunrise in 1887 heralded by "a matutinal distant cock" (U17.1265). Bells and cock unite here once more as Bloom and Stephen separate from each other, but any memory that they stimulate (such as Bloom remembering an earlier dawn) is more in keeping with "Ithaca's" tone of quiet reminiscence than with the violent metamorphoses of "Circe." Memory has a notably different quality after "Circe," lacking the immediate coloring of guilt and anxiety that attended it before the *nostos* began.

I have argued for a view of *Ulysses* as a model of mind in that the book creates an environment that allows us to observe the workings of memory, workings influenced as much by external variables that can be explained by either "chance" or "destiny" as by personal tensions. *Ulysses'* failure—or reluctance—to come to a neat close is then a form of mimesis in that the book refuses to imply that these processes of mind and destiny are simple, neat, or explicable. To have Stephen, Bloom, and Molly come to a tidy understanding at the end of *Ulysses* would be a betrayal of the complexities of mind, memory, and human life that Joyce so carefully wove into his text. Critics who strive to impose an ending—either implied or hypothetical—on *Ulysses* fail to recognize this mimetic character of the book as a model of mind and of life, which resists simplification and tidy endings.

John Paul Riquelme has suggested, in *Teller and Tale in Joyce's Fiction: Oscillating Perspectives*, that "Circe" and "Penelope" "taken together anticipate the *Wake* by providing a textual metaphor, a metaphor *for* textuality, in mental processes." I earlier quoted part of Riquelme's argument that for reading *Ulysses* and *Finnegans Wake*, "We require a more supple theory of mind, one that includes some recognition of the unconscious, of memory, of imagination, of what is sometimes called the imaginary than any empiricist view can muster" (150). The more supple theories of mind and memory that Joyce was working with extend themselves from *Ulysses* into *Finnegans Wake*, as Riquelme suggests when he focuses on the passage,

> What has gone? How it ends?
> Begin to forget it. It will remember itself from
> every sides, with all gestures, in each our word. . . .
> Forget, remember! (*FW* 614.20–22)

Riquelme concludes that "through memory and imagination in writing and reading the Finnegans are to awake" (150–51). Similarly, in *Ulysses*, the reader may hope that Stephen and Bloom will "awaken" to the possibilities and potentialities of the future by learning to "read" the past correctly.

If *Ulysses* is an "odyssey of memory," it is a distinctively modern odyssey, a journey that seems at times to end nowhere. The tumultuous, seemingly cathartic, and climactic events of "Circe"—Bloom's battle with the Nymph, Stephen's confrontation of his dead mother, and Bloom's vision of Rudy as he stands over the sleeping Stephen—must be read in the context of the rest of the journey—the chapters that follow "Circe"—and here any clear sense of a textual harbor or "Ithaca" disappears. Returning to Cheryl Herr's idea of a cultural unconscious, we find that those tendencies in *Ulysses* that privilege dissolution over order, art over life, and culture over nature are powerful forces at the end of the book, forces that work against teleology, closure, and a sense of destiny implied by the more holistic elements evident elsewhere in the text. *Ulysses* remains a genuine chaosmos to the end, torn between forgetting and remembering, balancing chaos and cosmos in a creative, modernist tension that refuses to allow for a clear textual Ithaca. Just as Homer's Penelope unweaves each night what she has woven that day, the increasingly self-referential style of *Ulysses* and its refusal to provide any final sense of closure seem to unravel the implications of destiny, atonement, and closure woven into the entire text by the textual memory that Joyce has created. A number of contrary tendencies operate in tension at the end of *Ulysses:* the holistic, teleological impulses outlined above as parts of the textual or cultural unconscious of the book; a sense of experiment, play, and indeterminacy that grew as Joyce composed the novel; and a realistic impulse that resisted the simple solutions of closure provided by more traditional novels. Although the operations of a textual memory or textual unconscious in *Ulysses* might seem to promise resolution if we read according to the presuppositions of Freudian psychoanalysis, Joyce was finally no Freudian, and the ending of *Ulysses* demonstrates a suspicion of and discomfort with any notion of a final or simple narrative "cure." If any approach to life is mocked in *Ulysses,* it is idealism or utopianism, the easy answer to the complex problems suggested by life, whether that idealism lie in the Citizen's facile nationalism or in Bloom's escapist fascination with nymphs and goddesses.

As I argued in the Introduction, *Ulysses* gains much of its power for readers through its position on a historical, cognitive rift between chaos and cosmos, fragmented textual surface and cultural unconscious, modernism and postmodernism. From this perspective, the text's inability or refusal to achieve a textual Ithaca is appropriate and consistent; although memory has operated as a central part of a textual and cultural unconscious in *Ulysses*, such holistic, traditional elements of the novel, which may hint at atonement, closure, and reconciliation, always remain in tension with other, more postmodern elements of the text. On the one hand, the text of *Ulysses* mirrors the ruptures, caprice, and openness that Joyce's contemporaries associated with modern developments such as Darwinism, while, on the other hand, it encourages us—through remarkable coincidences, the operation of memory, references to older, more stable plots, and even telepathically shared thoughts between characters—to desire coherence, destiny, and closure in the novel, much as some counter-Darwinian theories of evolution wanted to see these qualities in nature. Beneath the stylistic experimentation and the triviality and chaos of modern urban life, the novel still yearns nostalgically for older ordering principles, for a teleology or determining principle that will allow desire and order to play a role in the text.

Ulysses constructs itself in the liminal or transitional zone of tension between "assertion and challenge," as Cheryl Herr puts it (23), between tradition and its unraveling, between our nostalgia for order and closure and our growing embarrassment with such feelings. Moreover, once we have understood Joyce's suspicion of nostalgia as a form of memory in Dublin, how can we doubt his suspicion of the cultural nostalgia that underlies so much of modernist writing? Writing of Dickens's compulsively resolved plots, George Levine argues: "The characters cannot perceive the design, but it is really there" (270). The difference between Joyce and Dickens in this regard is that in Joyce's text, design and the urge toward telos is only a shadow, an echo, or a hint—the reader, as well as the characters, cannot be sure in the end of its significance.

The plot of *Ulysses*, then, is part of a design that excludes closure as a possibility and yet provides *possibility* as a substitute for closure and a hedge against meaninglessness and fragmentation. What is found at the end of *Ulysses* is not an Ithaca of rest and completion for Stephen Dedalus or Leopold Bloom or Molly Bloom. For Joyce, Ithaca is not a place, or a chapter, or even a moment somewhere in the future. Nor is Ithaca to be found in the past, for only nostalgia can create an Ithaca there, and such an Ithaca, as we have seen, is not the real one. Memory in *Ulysses*, then, is part of the working-out of something deeper in life, part of the relationship between one's self, other individuals, and the world that is constantly seeking progress and alignment, though not necessarily always finding them.

Joyce's design for *Ulysses* precludes a static, resolved Ithaca for his Ulysses, Telemachus, and Penelope, for like Tennyson's Ulysses, they "cannot rest from travel," but must move constantly onward into a world of change and possibility, a world refreshingly free of ideal endings and ideal humans. As Joyce himself concluded for his friend Frank Budgen:

> A point about Ulysses (Bloom). He romances about Ithaca (Oi want teh gow beck teh the Mawl Enn Rowd, s'elp me!) and when he gets back it gives him the pip. . . .
> Can you tell a poor hardworking man where is the ideal climate inhabited by the ideal humans? Address answers (enclosing 5/-P.O.) to: sincerely yours James Joyce. (*Letters* I, 152)

Appendix: "Nausicaa" and *The Golden Ass*

I. Possible References to *The Golden Ass* in the Notes,
Notesheets, Revisions, and Text of "Nausicaa"

From *Joyce's Notes and Early Drafts for "Ulysses,"* ed. Herring:
(From Joyce's Notebook V.A. 2 = Late notes for typescripts and galleys)—
p. 91 (Page 15 of notebook) = "Nausicaa":
    Line 16: "Cupid"
    Line 17: "you don't know how nice you looked"
    Line 20: "Look daggers"

From *Joyce's "Ulysses" Notesheets in the British Museum*, ed. Herring:
    126.49–50: <Leo Dillon (16) Goddess Venus with all her belongings. Innocence>
    131.48–50: Lamplighter's lintstock.
    136.32: Aphrodite, poised hips unveiled for judgment
    139.18: butterfly bow
    142.95: the lamplight falls upon a face
    142.108–14:
      lamp
      for the love of God!
      gazing far away into the distance
      downcast eyes
      I'm dying to know
      I'd give world to—
      LB dislikes to be seen in profile
    150.29–30: His eyes burned into her as though to read her through & through
    150.37–38: Maul in dark. Kiss & never tell.
    151.71: Ass knows in whose face he brays.
    153.9: wonderful eyes, but could you trust him
    153.19: stole a look at him
    154.40: soul in her eyes

158.43: brief cold blaze from her eyes
158.45: shaft strike home
158.59: as a snake looks at his prey
159.71: love laughs at locksmiths
159.80: Poor though the light was
160.125: light broke in upon him [him = her in text]

II. Echoes of *The Golden Ass* in "Nausicaa"

13.42: "The apple of discord was a certain castle of sand"
13.87–89: "her rosebud mouth was a genuine Cupid's bow, Greekly perfect." [Added in typescript].
13.93–94: "the girl chums had of course their little tiffs from time to time like the rest of mortals"
13.107: "eyes of witchery"
13.157–58: "a butterfly bow of silk to tone."
13.189: "Her very soul is in her eyes"
13.229–30: "often she wondered why you couldn't eat something poetical like violets or roses"
13.304: "scarce saw"
13.307: "never saw"
13.314–15: "when he sang *The moon hath raised* with Mr. Dignam" [Song goes: "The moon hath raised her lamp above, to light the way to thee my love." See Weldon Thornton, *Allusions in "Ulysses,"* p. 310].
13.361: "she was determined to let them see"
13.368: "she ventured a look at him"
13.411–17: "And while she gazed her heart went pitapat. Yes, it was her he was looking at, and there was meaning in his look. His eyes burned into her as though they would search her through and through, read her very soul."
13.437: "she just yearned to know all"
13.495–96: "Gerty could see without looking that he never took his eyes off of her"
13.504: "he had eyes in his head to see the difference for himself."
13.517: "He was eying her as a snake eyes its prey."
13.578: "A brief cold blaze shone from her eyes"
13.586–88: "Their eyes were probing her mercilessly but with a brave effort she sparkled back in sympathy as she glanced at her new conquest for them to see."
13.597–98: "she could give him [in this case, "Mr Reggy"] one look of measured scorn that would make him shrivel up on the spot."
13.601–3: "that shaft had struck home for her petty jealousy and they both

knew that she was something aloof, apart, in another sphere, that she was not of them"
13.631: "lighting the lamp"
13.652–53: "If she saw that magic lure in his eyes there would be no holding back for her. Love laughs at locksmiths."
13.655: "There was the allimportant question and she was dying to know"
13.688–89: "she said she could see from where she was. The eyes that were fastened upon her set her pulses tingling. She looked at him a moment, meeting his glance, and a light broke in upon her."
13.697: "there was no-one to see only him"
13.730: "she wasn't ashamed and he wasn't either to look"
13.731: "he couldn't resist the sight"
13.744–47: "A fair unsullied soul had called to him . . ."
13.751: "the hiding twilight"
13.757: "one of love's little ruses"
13.762–64: "Their souls met in a last lingering glance and the eyes that reached her heart, full of a strange shining, hung enraptured on her sweet flowerlike face."
13.794: "Peeping Tom."
13.818–19: "You're looking splendid. Sister souls. Showing their teeth at one another."
13.832–33: "Kiss in the dark and never tell. Saw something in me."
13.836: "Didn't let her see me in profile."
13.839: "carry a bunch of flowers to smell"
13.855–56: "See her as she is spoil all."
13.872–73: "O, her mouth in the dark!"
13.902–3: "Caressing the little boy too. Onlookers see most of the game."
13.910: "picture of Venus"
13.911–13: "Never see them sit on a bench marked Wet Paint. Eyes all over them. Look under the bed for what's not there."
13.936–37: "Darling, I saw, you. I saw all."
13.1009–10: "Hm. Roses, I think. She'd like scent of that kind."
13.1058: "See ourselves as others see us."
13.1076: "A star I see. Venus?"

Notes

Introduction

1 I will use the following abbreviations for frequently cited texts, followed by the relevant page numbers:
   The Critical Writings of James Joyce [CW]
   Dubliners [D]
   Exiles [E]
   Finnegans Wake [FW]
   The James Joyce Archive [JJA]
   Richard Ellmann, *James Joyce*, new and rev. ed. [JJII]
   The Letters of James Joyce [Letters]
   A Portrait of the Artist as a Young Man [P]
   Selected Letters of James Joyce [SL]
   Stephen Hero [SH]
   Ulysses (New York: Random House, 1986) [U]

2 Other writers who have recently explored issues related to memory in Joyce's works include Udaya Kumar's *The Joycean Labyrinth: Repetition, Time, and Tradition in "Ulysses"* (Oxford: Clarendon Press, 1991); Patrick Parrinder's *James Joyce* (Cambridge: Cambridge University Press, 1984); Klaus Reichert's "Joyce's Memory" (address to the Joyce Symposium, Monaco, 1990), and Adam Piette's *Remembering and the Sound of Words: Mallarmé, Proust, Joyce, Beckett* (Oxford: Clarendon Press, 1996). Lorraine Weir's *Writing Joyce: A Semiotics of the Joyce System* (Bloomington: Indiana University Press, 1989) also takes up related issues, but takes them in a different direction.

3 See Udaya Kumar's discussion of conflicting strategies of order and disruption in *The Joycean Labyrinth*, passim.

4 For a 1996 reading of *Ulysses* as a "modernist classic . . . pregnant with a nascent postmodernism" (11), see Kevin J. H. Dettmar's *The Illicit Joyce of Postmodernism: Reading Against the Grain* (Madison: University of Wisconsin Press, 1996), passim.

5 See Gabriele Schwab's *Subjects Without Selves: Transitional Texts in Modern*

Fiction (Cambridge, Mass.: Harvard University Press, 1994) for another investigation of modernist texts as sites of epistemological transition.

6 "[E]very person, place and thing in the chaosmos of Alle anyway connected with the gobblydumped turkery was moving and changing every part of the time" (*FW* 118.21–23).

7 My use of Herr's "cultural unconscious" is not meant to comment on or deny the force of Jameson's political unconscious or his sense of the necessity of finding the traces of historical struggle buried in narrative, but rather to shift the emphasis, as Herr does, toward the similar ways in which cultural contradictions and contestations can be submerged or hidden within a text, where they nonetheless exercise a vital, shaping influence on the development of the narrative. Clearly, while Herr's model preserves elements of Jameson's political unconscious, such as the notion of a repression of that which is inexpressible or contradictory or intolerable in a discursive system, she inverts and expands his term in a number of ways. For example, what are repressed, in her reading of *Ulysses*, are not the revolutionary elements of culture, but instead reactionary, nostalgic urges to find unity within a transitional culture that is dissolving the notion of the "natural" in favor of culture and the socially constructed ("art"). Both Jameson and Herr work within a modern tradition of writers who have attempted to apply Freud's ideas on repression in the individual psyche to larger social, cultural, and political models. For an earlier example, see Erich Fromm's chapter on "The Social Unconscious" in his *Beyond the Chains of Illusion: My Encounter with Marx and Freud* (New York: Simon and Schuster, 1962), 88–134. In his comparison of Freudian and Marxist conceptions of repression, Fromm developed the idea of the social unconscious to designate "those areas of repression which are common to most members of a society; these commonly repressed elements are those contents which a given society cannot permit its members to be aware of if the society with its specific contradictions is to operate successfully" (88). Jameson and Herr follow Fromm in their use of the idea of collective repression of contradictory elements within a given culture.

8 See, for example, Patrick McGee's assertion in *Paperspace: Style as Ideology in Joyce's "Ulysses"* (Lincoln: University of Nebraska Press, 1988) that "Joyce has complicated the interpretation of his book by constructing frames of reference whose status is unstable. He deposits these outlines—the schemata with titles, symbols, organs, and so on—in a space proper neither to the author nor to the text. By doing so he calls the authority of his intentions and the finality of his signature into question" (3).

9 See, for example, Cheryl Herr's *Joyce's Anatomy of Culture* (Urbana: University of Illinois Press, 1986), R. B. Kershner's *Joyce, Bakhtin, and Popular Literature* (Chapel Hill: University of North Carolina Press, 1989), and Stephen Watt's *Joyce, O'Casey, and the Irish Popular Theater* (Syracuse, N.Y.: Syracuse University Press, 1991) for three important studies of Joyce and popular culture.

10 In my examination of the "intertextual memory" of *Ulysses*, I seek, in Julia Kristeva's words, to read Joyce's texts in the Bakhtinian sense of *"dialogue and ambivalence"* in which "any text is constructed as a mosaic of quotations; any text is the absorption and transformation of another" (Kristeva, *Desire in Language: A Semiotic Approach to Literature and Art* [New York: Columbia University Press, 1980], 66). At the same time, I seek in my use of this much-used and abused term *intertextuality* the sort of flexibility outlined by Susan Stanford Friedman in her argument for a concept of intertextuality that does not exclude the sense of agency and historical position involved in the study of influence. Friedman's thorough critique of the recent history of intertextuality makes the case that "the discourses of influence and intertextuality have not been and cannot be kept pure, untainted by each other" (154). See Friedman's "Weavings: Intertextuality and the (Re)birth of the Author," in *Influence and Intertextuality in Literary History* (Madison: University of Wisconsin Press, 1991), 146–80.

11 Parenthetical references to Freud's works are to volume and page numbers in the Standard Edition.

12 See, for example, Freud's 1937 essay, "Constructions in Analysis" (23:258–59). Peter Brooks discusses the implications of Freud's essay for narrative in "The Idea of a Psychoanalytic Criticism" and "Changes in the Margins: Construction, Transference, and Narrative" in his *Psychoanalysis and Storytelling* (Cambridge, Mass.: Blackwell, 1994), 20–75.

13 One useful scheme for viewing the difference between passivist and activist modes of memory is the distinction between *mneme* (μνήμη) and *hypomnesis* (ὑπόμνησις) developed by Socrates in the *Phaedrus*, where he attacks writing as a mere recording of information useful only as a note or reminder (274d–76d). Writing is a form of "low-memory" (ὑπόμνηματα) that threatens true memory (μνήμη), which seeks truth through a dialectic exchange between two souls.

14 See Michael Riffaterre, "The Intertextual Unconscious," *Critical Inquiry* 13 (Winter 1987): 371–85, and Jonathan Culler, "Textual Self-Consciousness and the Textual Unconscious," *Style* 18 (Summer 1984): 369–76, for different uses of the term "textual unconscious."

15 Parrinder and Udaya Kumar also use this term. In his reading of *A Portrait* in *James Joyce* (Cambridge: Cambridge University Press, 1984), Parrinder identifies "an 'unconscious' textual memory or series of repetitions, which are most easily traced at the level of imagery" (80). Udaya Kumar uses the term in a slightly different manner than I do. Generally, Kumar employs it as a way to explain Joyce's deliberate violations of narrative boundaries in the novel, while I focus more on Joyce's compositional method as a model of mind. Joseph A. Boone employs a similar term when he claims that "the words that compose 'Circe' well up from the text's entire repertoire of figures and images—from, if you will, the *dreaming unconscious* of *Ulysses* itself" (194; my emphasis). See Boone, "Staging Sexuality: Repression, Representation, and 'Interior' States in *Ulysses*," in *Joyce: The Return of the Repressed*, ed.

Susan Stanford Friedman (Ithaca, N.Y.: Cornell University Press, 1993). Karen Lawrence, in *The Odyssey of Style in "Ulysses"* (Princeton, N.J.: Princeton University Press, 1981), also speaks of "the dream of the text," claiming that "the narrative memory of the book provides the resources for this extraordinary drama, often in violation of the actual memories and associations of the characters" (151–52; quoted in Boone, "Staging Sexuality," 194, n. 9). See also Adam Piette's *Remembering and the Sound of Words: Mallarmé, Proust, Joyce, Beckett* (Oxford: Clarendon Press, 1996), 178–84.

16   Although I plan to use these terms idiosyncratically, hoping their meanings for my work will become clearer as the argument develops, the reader who seeks further discussion can refer to Gérard Genette's use of prolepsis in *Narrative Discourse: An Essay in Method* (Ithaca, N.Y.: Cornell University Press, 1980) and to Roland Barthes' use of "hermeneutic" as a narratological term in *S/Z* (New York: Hill and Wang, 1974) (e.g., 19). Peter Brooks elaborates on Barthes's use of the term in *Reading for the Plot: Design and Intervention in Narrative* (New York: Random House, 1984) (e.g., 18). Although Genette opposes analepsis to prolepsis in his catalogue of narrative forces, I will use the term hermeneutic memory to designate those forms of memory that attempt to probe and investigate the past willfully and deliberately. I prefer hermeneutic to analeptic because the former carries a clearer sense of volition, of an individual seeking, like a detective, to find "clues," to solve a mystery in the past.

17   See Lawrence, *The Odyssey of Style in "Ulysses,"* and Daniel R. Schwarz, *Reading Joyce's "Ulysses"* (New York: St. Martin's Press, 1987).

18   I do not wish to suggest that all readers read *Ulysses* as a traditional novel. Certainly many readers come to see *Ulysses* as a challenge to traditional narrative and traditional forms of narrative resolution and, beyond that, to traditional notions of subjectivity and character. I do believe, however, that at one point or another, most readers of *Ulysses* will consider the problems faced by the principal characters within a traditional narrative framework, even if they then move beyond that perspective.

1   Personal Memory and the Construction of the Self

1   See also Judith Ryan's investigation of the relationships between modernist writing and the empiricist philosophy of the period in *The Vanishing Subject: Early Modern Psychology and Literary Modernism* (Chicago: University of Chicago Press, 1991), esp. 138–49. Ryan effectively identifies a number of important and neglected sources for the challenge to unified subjectivity in the early twentieth century.

2   For example, Richard Ellmann in *James Joyce* (New York: Oxford University Press, 1982) notes that "the atmosphere of literary experimentation braced Joyce for *Ulysses*. In 1915 at the Café Voltaire in the old city, the surrealist movement was fomented by Tristan Tzara, Hans Arp, and others, and this

group, with which Joyce was sometimes mistakenly identified, was to move on like him to Paris after the war" (*JJ* 409). Tom Stoppard's play *Travesties* presents a wonderful imaginary collision between three avatars of modern revolution and instability (Joyce, Tzara, and Lenin) and the hapless British official, Henry Carr, in Zurich in 1917.

3 Brandon Kershner's edition of *A Portrait of the Artist as a Young Man* incorporates Chester Anderson's textual revisions, in which "green" is appropriately changed to "geen" in Stephen's infant rendition of the song (19).

4 See Marguerite Harkness, *"A Portrait of the Artist as a Young Man": Voices of the Text*, esp. 21–35.

5 Joyce recycles these ideas in *Stephen Hero*, where he describes Stephen Daedalus using crude and bold expressions in his writing "as sudden defence works while he was busy constructing the enigma of a manner" (27). The phrase, "shocks had driven him from breathless flights of zeal shamefully inwards," is repeated in *Stephen Hero*, 29.

6 Lawrence's *The Odyssey of Style in "Ulysses"* provides the most thorough examination of this "initial style" or narrative norm and the subsequent challenges posed to it. See esp. chap. 2, "The Narrative Norm," 38–54. Lawrence wants to isolate one strain of the narrative in the earlier episodes that serves as "the nonparodic style that establishes the decorum of the novel" (43), "a certain contract that is subverted" (53). She argues that "The opening section of the book was left as a kind of testimony to an older order, a norm for the reader at the same time as it is an anachronism in terms of the book as a whole" (53).

7 Michael Patrick Gillespie in *James Joyce's Trieste Library* (Austin, Tex.: Harry Ransom Humanities Research Center, 1986) notes that Joyce possessed a copy of Hume's *Essays* in his Trieste library and reminds us that "In his notes for *Exiles*, Joyce includes Hume in a group of philosophers 'inclined towards incertitude or scepticism' " (*Trieste* 123). Joyce's copy of Michael Maher's *Psychology*, which may have been a textbook at Belvedere College (see Gillespie, *Trieste* 159), contains many refutations of Hume's philosophy from a Jesuit perspective (see below).

8 Weldon Thornton in *Allusions in "Ulysses"* (Chapel Hill: University of North Carolina Press, 1968) points out: "Although Locke would have disagreed with Mulligan's saying he remembers sensations (since, strictly speaking, only ideas are the objects of memory), this is apparently an allusion to Locke's theory of knowledge.... This allusion links Mulligan with the sense-data empiricism of Locke's philosophy; there are numerous allusions later in *Ulysses* linking Stephen with Bishop Berkeley, the idealist who argued against Locke and Hume" (15–16).

Don Gifford and Robert J. Seidman in *Joyce Annotated: Notes for James Joyce's "Ulysses"* (Berkeley: University of California Press, 1988) note the similarity between Mulligan's assertion and "the essentially mechanistic concept of the human psyche developed by the English philosopher David Hartley

(1705–57) and derived from the work of John Locke (1632–1704) and Sir Isaac Newton (1642–1727)" (17).

9   Gillespie speculates that Joyce may have used this book as a student at Belvedere College (*Trieste* 158–59). I am grateful to the Harry Ransom Humanities Research Center for the opportunity to inspect Joyce's copy of this volume.

10 We may hear an echo of Maher's warnings to the young Catholic's mind in *Stephen Hero* when Stephen imagines a long argument in which "an embassy of nimble pleaders" (204) from the Church attempt to win his mind back. As part of their plea, these voices argue, "Catholicism is in your blood. Living in an age which professes to have discovered evolution, can you be fatuous enough to think that simply by being wrong-headed you can recreate entirely your mind and temper or can clear your blood of what you may call the Catholic infection?" (206).

11 This comparison of the self to a "bucket of water" sets up a curious echo with Joyce's later image of his soul as a well composed of many "parts"—an image contrary to Maher's beliefs but nonetheless suggested in the negative analogy above. In a letter to Stanislaus Joyce, he wrote, "if I put down a bucket into my own soul's well, sexual department, I draw up Griffith's and Ibsen's and Skeffington's and Bernard Vaughn's and St. Aloysius's and Shelley's and Renan's water along with my own" (*Letters* II, 191).

12 For example, Aristotle calls the soul "the entelechy of the body" in *De Anima* (2.1.412a21). For an extended discussion of the entelechy as a force in Joyce's texts, see Fritz Senn's "In Quest of a *Nisus Formativus Joyceanus*," in *Inductive Scrutinies: Focus on Joyce*, ed. Christine O'Neill (Baltimore: Johns Hopkins University Press, 1995), 59–74.

13 See Shiv K. Kumar's *Bergson and the Stream of Consciousness Novel* (New York: New York University Press, 1963) for a detailed and perceptive discussion of Joyce and Bergson (see esp. "Bergson's Theory of the Novel," 17–35, and "James Joyce," 103–38). Udaya Kumar also discusses Bergson and Joyce at length in *The Joycean Labyrinth*, passim. See also Robert Klawitter, "Henri Bergson and James Joyce's Fictional World," *Comparative Literature Studies* 3 (1966): 429–37.

14 Joyce had a copy of Joseph Solomon's *Bergson* in his Trieste library (Gillespie, *Trieste* 221).

15 Joyce may well have come across a connection between Heraclitus and Bergson's notion of duration as a flow in Solomon's *Bergson* (27), where Solomon asserts: "Heraclitus expressed in vivid metaphors and dark riddling language that at once stimulated and mystified his successors the central idea of the present chapter—that the world was a universal flux, that existence was a perpetual change, to which our language with its words of definite meaning could never do justice. We name a thing, and straightaway the name becomes inapplicable, for the thing has become different; 'we cannot step twice into

the same river.' " Solomon goes on to claim that "Bergson is the modern Heraclitus, insisting that existence is a perpetual change . . ." (28).

16 Bergson generally avoided using the word "entelechy" because it had been appropriated by the vitalist Hans Driesch. Bergson felt that Driesch's entelechy was too reductive and "finalistic"—too mechanical and teleological—to be equated with his élan vital. See *Creative Evolution,* 48, n. 1.

17 In the "Lotus-Eaters" episode of *Ulysses,* Bloom thinks, "Poisons the only cures. Remedy where you least expect it. Clever of nature" (*U*5.483–84).

18 Djuna Barnes, for example, claimed in a 1922 *Vanity Fair* article that Joyce told her he had populated *Ulysses* with "the great talkers . . . them and the things they forgot. In *Ulysses* I have recorded, simultaneously, what a man says, sees, thinks, and what such seeing, thinking, saying does, to what you Freudians call the subconscious,—but as for psychoanalysis," he broke off, "it's neither more nor less than blackmail" (65).

The question of Joyce's familiarity with Freud's writing has been much debated. His possession of a copy of *The Psychopathology of Everyday Life,* especially, would have allowed him to learn something of Freud's theories of repression and recollection. Chester Anderson has made an interesting case for Joyce's acquaintance with Freud's *Zur Auffassung der Aphasien* ("Introduction" 54–55), and in "Leopold Bloom as Dr. Sigmund Freud," Anderson argued that Joyce indeed did refer to *The Psychopathology of Everyday Life* while composing *Ulysses.* See Anderson, "Introduction: Joyce and Freud," in *The Seventh of Joyce,* ed. Bernard Benstock (Bloomington: Indiana University Press, 1982), 53–56. Ellmann claimed that, "in later life, no matter how diligently the critics worked to demonstrate that he had borrowed the interior monologue from Freud, Joyce always made it a point of honor that he had it from Dujardin" (*JJII* 126). On the relationship between Joyce and Freud's work, see also, for example, Jean Kimball's "Freud, Leonardo, and Joyce: The Dimensions of a Childhood Memory," *James Joyce Quarterly* 17 (Winter 1980): 165–82; Mark Shechner's *Joyce in Nighttown, A Psychoanalytic Inquiry into "Ulysses"* (Berkeley: University of California Press, 1974); and Sheldon Brivic's *Joyce Between Freud and Jung* (Port Washington, N.Y.: Kennikat Press, 1980).

19 In "Joyce in Language," Stephen Heath provides a relevant caution for those who strain to find direct relationships between Joyce and Freud in *Finnegans Wake:* "What is finally interesting is not the question of immediate influence (references to Freud and Freudian terms and ideas, though these abound) but the way in which Joyce's practice of writing in the *Wake* finds the same concerns and occupies the same terrain as psychoanalysis. . ." (142–43).

20 For additional discussion of Rudy's possible deformity, see John Z. Bennett, "Unposted Letter: Joyce's Leopold Bloom," *Bucknell Review* 14, no. 1 (1966): 9–13.

21 Many critics have commented on the so-called madonna-whore dichotomy in Joyce's writings. See, for example, Hugh Kenner's comments on "The

Double Female" in his essay, "The *Portrait* in Perspective," where he writes of physical love in *A Portrait:* "The poles between which this affection moves are those of St. Augustine and St. John: the Whore of Babylon and the Bride of Christ. The relation between the two is far from simple, and Stephen moves in a constant tension between the two" (46). Suzette Henke provides a thorough examination of this virgin-whore dichotomy in *A Portrait* in her "Stephen Dedalus and Women: A Feminist Reading of *Portrait*," in *A Portrait of the Artist as a Young Man*, ed. R. B. Kershner (Boston: Bedford Books, 1993), esp. 311–17. Most recently, Christine Froula's *Modernism's Body: Sex, Culture, and Joyce* (New York: Columbia University Press, 1996) examines the workings of this *"putana madonna"* (170) opposition in *Stephen Hero*, *A Portrait of the Artist as a Young Man*, and *Ulysses*.

22 Gifford and Seidman, *Joyce Annotated*, argue that "if the period between her death and burial was the traditional three days, she must have died on 23 June 1903, and Stephen would be free to go into 'second mourning' (gray would be acceptable) on 24 June 1904, or in eight days" (15).

2 The Past as Obstruction

1 Hélène Cixous makes a similar point based on very different assumptions, in her essay "Joyce: The (R)use of Writing," in *Post-Structuralist Joyce: Essays from the French*, ed. Derek Attridge and Daniel Ferrer (Cambridge: Cambridge University Press, 1984), 15–30.

2 For example, Thornton, *Allusions in "Ulysses,"* cites one of the "other things he alludes to" and then suppresses as Stephen's reference to another riddle, this time as told by Guido Cavalcanti in the *Decameron:* "the story of Guido's walking in the Orto San Michele is told in the *Decameron*, the ninth story of the sixth day. While he was in a cemetery his friends came to mock him about his pensiveness. He told them that they could say to him what they pleased since they were in their own house. One of them realized he meant they were in the house of Death" (60). When Stephen thinks of this story in *Ulysses*, he once again tells a riddle without an answer, for he leaves the last word off: "the courtiers who mocked Guido in Or san Michele were in their own house. House of . . ." (*U*3.318–19). Thornton points out that Stephen suppresses the word "Death" here (59–60).

3 Again, see Cixous, "Joyce: The (R)use of Writing," 19–21. As I will demonstrate, Cixous errs in taking the riddle at face value and in seeing it as an emblem of absolute meaninglessness. She is correct in arguing that the riddle has no solution, but wrong in assuming that this means the riddle itself is meaningless. Robert Spoo, on the other hand, argues that the fox riddle "can be read as a rich, roundabout image, a sort of macabre kenning, for that nightmare of history Stephen complains of to the headmaster Garrett Deasy and would bury if he could, a nightmare associated with the memory of

his dying mother" (17). See Spoo, *James Joyce and the Language of History: Daedalus's Nightmare* (New York: Oxford University Press, 1994). I also address this riddle in my essay "Stephen Dedalus Among School Children: The Schoolroom and the Riddle of Authority in *Ulysses*," *Studies in the Literary Imagination* 30 (Fall 1997): 17-36.

4 *U* 7.83; 11.805 and 11.1036.

5 In a letter to Frank Budgen dated October 24, 1920, Joyce admits to having read "some pages of his [i.e., Proust's]," adding, "I cannot see any special talent but I am a bad critic" (*Selected Letters* 273). According to Richard Ellmann, Joyce told Sylvia Beach in October 1922 that he had "read the first two volumes" of Proust's masterpiece (*JJII* 508n.). Joyce met Proust at a dinner party on May 18, 1922, and attended the French writer's funeral in November 1922. For more information on the relationship between Joyce and Proust, see *JJII* 488 and 508-9; Willard Potts, ed., *Portrait of the Artist in Exile: Recollections of James Joyce by Europeans* (Seattle: University of Washington Press, 1979), 129 and 227; and George D. Painter, *Marcel Proust: A Biography* (New York: Random House, 1959), vol. 2, 340-42.

6 For the details of Beckett's authorship of *Proust*, see Deirdre Bair, *Samuel Beckett: A Biography* (New York: Harcourt Brace Jovanovich, 1978), esp. 508-9. Joyce made numerous allusions to Proust and his writings in *Finnegans Wake* (see Painter, *Marcel Proust*, vol. 2, 342 n.).

7 See A. E. Pilkington's chapter on Proust in *Bergson and His Influence: A Reassessment* (Cambridge: Cambridge University Press, 1976), 146-77, for a careful distinction between the two writers' ideas on memory.

8 Pour moi, la mémoire volontaire, qui est surtout une mémoire de l'intelligence et des yeux, ne nous donne du passé que des faces san vérité; mais qu'une odeur, une saveur retrouvées, dans des circonstances toutes différentes, réveille en nous, malgré nous, le passé, nous sentons combien ce passé était différent de ce que nous croyions nous rappeler, et que notre mémoire volontaire peignait, comme les mauvais peintres, avec des couleurs sans vérité.

9 This tendency to break memory into two very different forms can be traced back to Plato's *Phaedrus*, when Socrates distinguishes between *mneme* (the true memory of the ideal) and *upomnemata*, or low memory—the memory of reminders, address books, and the other cluttered details of everyday life.

10 A good example is Marcel's feeling of absolute happiness when he sees the milk girl in Balbec: "on this morning of travel, the interruption of the routine of my existence, the unfamiliar place and time, had made their presence indispensable. My habits, which were sedentary and not matutinal, for once were missing, and all my faculties came hurrying to take their place, vying with one another in their zeal, rising, each of them, like waves, to the same unaccustomed level . . ." (1:706).

11 I use the *Oxford English Dictionary*'s etymology here; *Webster's New Colle-*

giate Dictionary argues for nostos + algia (from the Latin, "akin to OE *genesan* to survive, Skt *nasate* he approaches"). The OED's etymology seems more satisfying and sensible.

12 Richard Ellmann reprints, translates, and compares the various schemas in the appendix to *Ulysses on the Liffey* (New York: Oxford University Press, 1972), 186 ff.

13 Appropriately, Liddell and Scott's *Greek-English Lexicon* notes that the Symplegades were also referred to as the Κυανεαι νμσοι or "dark islands" (454 and 763).

14 In *Ulysses on the Liffey*, 93 ff., Ellmann argues that "Wandering Rocks" is a tribute to Hume's skepticism, claiming that "against Stephen's theory of persons and things having each its own signature, Hume refuses to concede uninterrupted identity" (95), and that "the dominant mood from the 'Wandering Rocks' through 'Circe' is scepticism, Bloom's day but also, for the nine hours from three to midnight, Hume's day" (96).

15 *U*10.294-97; 10.752-54; and 10.1096-99.

16 See, for example, *Ulysses on the Liffey*, 33-36.

17 Weldon Thornton, *Allusions in "Ulysses,"* has noted that Bloom's mnemotechnic is defective here in that "Rip's home town is never named; Sleepy Hollow—though it sounds appropriate enough to the story—is the setting of the story of Ichabod Crane and the Headless Horseman, 'The Legend of Sleepy Hollow'" (319).

18 Significantly, this image of being "stuck" appears repeatedly in the "Nausicaa" episode, once in direct connection with Bloom's masturbation. See *U*13.864, 13.979, 13.1182, 13.1211, and 13.1270.

3 Memory, Destiny, and the Limits of the Self

1 A number of observers have concluded that the mysterious and forlorn M'Intosh in *Ulysses* is James Duffy. See Phillip Herring, *Joyce's Uncertainty Principle* (Princeton, N.J.: Princeton University Press, 1987), 108-17, for a review of the various theories on M'Intosh's identity and a convincing argument for accepting indeterminacy as the only "solution" to the identity of "Joyce's Raincoat Phantom."

2 Freud did confess to a belief in "the inheritance of memory-traces of the experience of our ancestors, independently of direct communication and of the influence of education" in his late work *Moses and Monotheism* (23:99-100). His unpublished collaboration with Sandor Ferenczi (*A Phylogenetic Fantasy: Overview of the Transference Neuroses;* see discussion in chap. 4) takes an even more openly and radically Lamarckian approach to memory.

3 Weldon Thornton notes that Stephen here misquotes the Ghost's speech by adding Hamlet's name to the Ghost's "I am thy father's spirit." Bloom makes exactly the same error in "Lestrygonians" (*U*8.67). See Thornton, *Allusions in "Ulysses,"* 163.

4 The fact that Hamnet Shakespeare died at age eleven is never explicitly mentioned in *Ulysses*. However, Joyce kept a year-by-year notebook of dates in Shakespeare's life that included the ages of the members of Shakespeare's family for each year. Joyce's entry for 1596 notes, "9 August: Hamnet (son) dies," and in the list of family members' ages for this year he writes "H.S. 11" (*JJA* 12: 328). A compelling extratextual correspondence that Joyce was almost certainly aware of is the fact that he and Hamnet shared the same birthday. According to George Brandes's book *William Shakespeare: A Critical Study* (London: Heinemann, 1902), which Joyce owned and admired and to which Stephen Dedalus refers in the "Scylla and Charybdis" episode,

> Shakespeare's only son was born on the 2nd of February 1585; he was thus only eleven and a half when he died.
>
> We cannot doubt that this loss was a grievous one to a man of Shakespeare's deep feeling; doubly grievous, it would seem, because it was his constant ambition to restore the fallen fortunes of his family, and he was now left without an heir to his name. (140)

Brandes goes on to suggest some possible reflections of Shakespeare's anguish over the death of his son in *King John* and makes similar suggestions about *Hamlet* and *A Winter's Tale* (324, 341, and 637).

5 The allusion is to Ophelia's song in *Hamlet*, 4.5.26–26. David Bevington explains "Cockle hat" in *Hamlet* as a reference to a "hat with cockleshell stuck in it as a sign that the wearer had been a pilgrim to the shrine of St. James of Compostella in Spain" (Shakespeare 1107 n). Strangely, the "petite madeleine" that triggers the first shattering involuntary memory in Proust's *Du côté de chez Swann* is described as "the little scallop-shell of pastry, so richly sensual under its severe, religious folds" (I, 50).

6 In the complex and often confused Theosophical lore about the fate of the various parts of the human self after death, the term *shell* designates an "astral corpse" (Besant, *Ancient* 115), a sort of empty spiritual shell or husk left behind after the Higher Self has departed the dead body. According to Madame Blavatsky, this psychic shell remains temporarily in "*Hades*, which we call the *Kamaloka*" (*Key* 190–91), or "The *semi*-material plane, to us subjective and invisible, where the disembodied 'personalities' . . . remain until they fade out from it by the complete exhaustion of the effects of the mental impulses that created these *eidolons* of the lower animal passions and desires" (*Key* 340). These psychic shells, Blavatsky argues, often endure long enough to be contacted by spiritualists, who may mistakenly think they have actually contacted the Higher Self of the departed: "And you may be sure of it, it is not they who incarnate; and, therefore, so few of these 'dear departed ones' know anything of re-incarnation, misleading thereby the Spiritualists" (*Key* 191). This Theosophical concept works not only as one context for the "shells" in the midwife's bag, but also as a background for the apparitions in *Ulysses*, especially the parodied seance in "Cyclops" in which Paddy Dignam appears (*U*12.338–73).

7   The reader can find thorough investigations of the relationship between Joyce and Shakespeare in Vincent Cheng's *Shakespeare and Joyce: A Study of "Finnegans Wake"* (University Park: Pennsylvania State University Press, 1984) and William Schutte's *Joyce and Shakespeare: A Study in the Meaning of "Ulysses"* (New Haven, Conn.: Yale University Press, 1957).
8   See Schutte, *Joyce and Shakespeare*, 24.
9   Brandes, *William Shakespeare*, comments repeatedly on the extent to which Hamnet's death "haunted" Shakespeare (324), and certainly Joyce knew Brandes's work well. See Brandes, 341 and 677.
10 See Schutte, *Joyce and Shakespeare*, 127–35, for a thorough discussion of the similarities between Bloom and the Bard.
11 See Thornton, *Allusions in "Ulysses,"* 73, for a guide to these references.
12 The "pard" is associated with Bloom later on in the novel; e.g., U9.1214 and 15.4326.
13 This line reads, "Who are you incog?" in the first edition, the 1932 Odyssey Press edition, and the 1961 Random House edition.
14 For Plato's use of this term, see *Meno* 81d.5, 81e.4, and 98a.4; *Phaedo* 72e.5, 73b.5, 73d.8, 73e.1, and 76a.7; and *Phaedrus* 249c, where Socrates develops the idea that objects we perceive through our senses can "remind" us of Forms we encountered previous to our current incarnation: "this is a recollection [ἀνάμνησις] of those things which our soul once beheld, when it journeyed with God and, lifting its vision above the things which we now say exist, rose up into real being."
15 James S. Atherton's *The Books at the Wake: A Study of Literary Allusions in James Joyce's "Finnegans Wake"* (Mamaroneck, N.Y.: Appel, 1974), 140–43, notes allusions to Augustine in *Finnegans Wake* and points out several parodies of the Tenth Book of the *Confessions* in *Finnegans Wake*.
16 Fritz Senn uses this explanation of metempsychosis as a stimulus to consider the many varieties of memory operating in *Ulysses*: "The soul in its wanderings does not remember its previous innings, as Bloom well knows, and so he expands: 'They say we have forgotten it. Some say they remember their past lives' (U4.364–65). Remembering, memory—and conversely oblivion (the next episode, 'Lotus Eaters,' will ring changes on that theme)—are basic principles. *Ulysses* celebrates memory and recalls and elaborates on manifold distortions. Its readers depend on *their* memories" (110). See "Met Whom What?" *James Joyce Quarterly* 30 (Fall 1992): 109–13.
17 For the essay on Mangan, see esp. *CW* 82–83, where Joyce mentions "the ancient gods, who are visions of the divine names . . . ," a passage that Ellsworth Mason and Richard Ellmann label "orthodox Theosophy."
18 Evidence for Joyce's interest in Maeterlinck exists as early as *Stephen Hero*, where we learn that Stephen's interest in Maeterlinck is one of the things "he held so dear at heart" (*SH* 39–40). In a letter to Stanislaus dated February 11, 1907, Joyce refers to Maeterlinck as "the most Belgian of Shakespeares" (*SL* 147).

19 Stephen notes that the ghost in *Hamlet* must have learned of the manner of his death through the memory of God: "those who are done to death in sleep cannot know the manner of their quell unless their Creator endow their souls with that knowledge in the life to come. The poisoning and the beast with two backs that urged it King Hamlet's ghost could not know of were he not endowed with knowledge by his creator. That is why the speech . . . is always turned elsewhere, backward" (*U*9.467–72; see also *U*7.750–52).

20 Joyce owned a copy of *Ideas of Good and Evil*, in which this essay first appeared (Gillespie, *Trieste* 264).

21 Gillespie notes that Joyce had Besant's *Une introduction à la théosophie* and *The Path of Discipleship* in his Trieste library. Gifford and Seidman suggest a number of connections to Besant's *Ancient Wisdom* and *Esoteric Christianity* in *Ulysses* (see, e.g., 173 and 196–97).

22 E.g., *U*17.850–57.

23 James suggests that Samuel Butler argued for a similar view of the persistence of one's actions in the physical "memory" of the universe, quoting a 1908 essay of Butler's as follows: "It is Handel's work, not the body with which he did the work, that pulls us half over London. There is not an action of a muscle in a horse's leg upon a winter's night as it drags a carriage to the Albert Hall but is in connection with, and part outcome of, the force generated when Handel sat in his room at Gopsall and wrote the Messiah. . . . This is the true Handel, who is more a living power among us one hundred and twenty-two years after his death than during the time he was amongst us in the body" (Butler, *Notebooks* 22; quoted in James, *Essays* 358 n.).

24 In my note, "Chiromancy in *Ulysses*," I suggest that the source for the palm reading lore incorporated into "Circe" is *The Book of Charms and Ceremonies: Whereby All May Have the Opportunity of Obtaining Any Object They Desire*, by "Merlin" (catalogued in Gillespie, *Trieste* 163–64).

25 Madame Blavatsky's "mudhen republican name" (*FW* 393.23), or maiden name, was Hahn (German for "cock"), as we learn in *Finnegans Wake* 66.23–24, where Blavatsky becomes a hen married to Roger Cox, Jonathan Swift's clerk: "Cox's wife, twice Mrs. Hahn, pokes her beak into the matter." See Atherton, *The Books of the Wake*, 237, and Roland McHugh, *Annotations to "Finnegans Wake"* (Baltimore: Johns Hopkins University Press, 1980), 66.

26 For other instances of this motif in the minds of both Bloom and Stephen, see *U*4.91–92; 9.579–80; 9.1199–1201; 13.828–29; 13.1109–11; and 15.2117–21.

27 In an essay entitled "Darwinism—(Then Furthermore)," which Joyce owned in his Trieste library, Whitman embraces Darwinian evolution as a radical attack on old superstitions ("It has so much in it, and is so needed as a counterpoise to yet widely prevailing and unspeakably tenacious, enfeebling superstitions") and simultaneously holds it at a distance, arguing: "In due time the Evolution theory will have to abate its vehemence, cannot be allow'd to dominate everything else, and will have to take its place as a segment of the circle, the cluster—as but one of many theories, many thoughts, of profound-

est value—and readjusting and differentiating much, yet leaving the divine secrets just as inexplicable and unreachable as before—maybe more so" (164-65). In Joyce's copy of *Democratic Vistas and Other Papers*, the title of this essay is marked with a penciled check (163; see Gillespie, *Trieste* 257).

4 Joyce's Mnemotechnic: Textual Memory in *Ulysses*

1   Spoo in *James Joyce and the Language of History* investigates Joyce's responses to the Aristotelian idea of entelechy, to the providential teleology embraced by Mr. Deasy, and to counterteleological impulses as well. See esp. his discussion of "W. E. H. Lecky and Moral History," 22–27, and his chapter "Teleology, Monocausality, and Marriage in *Ulysses*," 66–88, in which he examines the ways in which *Ulysses* examines "teleological assumptions of all kinds" (66). Spoo's discussion is especially valuable in demonstrating Joyce's resistance to teleological views of history, while at the same time Spoo acknowledges Joyce's interest in teleological notions such as entelechy, reminding us again that Joyce's texts reflect a tension in his time and in his education between conflicting paradigms.

2   See especially Gillian Beer's *Darwin's Plots: Evolutionary Narrative in Darwin, George Eliot, and Nineteenth-Century Fiction* (London: Routledge and Kegan Paul, 1983) and George Lewis Levine's *Darwin and the Novelists: Patterns of Science in Victorian Fiction* (Cambridge, Mass.: Harvard University Press, 1988). Daniel C. Dennett's *Darwin's Dangerous Idea: Evolution and the Meanings of Life* (New York: Simon and Schuster, 1995) provides a thorough and thoughtful consideration of the general cultural and philosophical impact of Darwinism.

3   While Joyce's library included many books with a counter-Darwinian bias, as far as I have been able to discern he owned only one explicitly Darwinian text —Thomas Huxley's *Twelve Lectures and Essays* (see Gillespie, *Trieste* 124).

4   Note also that when Stephen's mother comes to him in a dream, she comes "silently" and is "mute, reproachful" (*U* 1.102–5 and 1.270–72).

5   For other occurrences of the "corpsechewing" motif, see *U* 3.476–77; 5.350–52; 6.980–82; 8.745; 11.805–6; 15.4214; 15.4703; and 16.1211. Appropriately, many of these references occur in Bloom's thoughts, underscoring the sharing of memory discussed above.

6   Labels such as "neo-Lamarckian" are always problematic. I do not intend to reduce the work of these writers to one restricted position by implying that neo-Lamarckism was the center of their thinking, though this may be near the mark in Butler's case. Bergson was not strictly a neo-Lamarckian, but he found that "Neo-Lamarckism is . . . of all the later forms of evolutionism, the only one capable of admitting an internal and psychological principle of development, although it is not bound to do so" (*Creative Evolution* 86). Neo-Lamarckism's willingness to allow a vitalist impulse behind the evolutionary process (as in Hans Driesch's adaptation of Aristotelian entelechy)

gave Bergson a scientific vehicle for his notion of his dynamic élan vital. For a concise synopsis of Bergson's relation to, and importance in, French evolutionary theory, see Madeleine Barthélemy-Madaule, *Lamarck the Mythical Precursor: A Study of the Relations Between Science and Ideology* (Cambridge, Mass.: MIT Press, 1982), 137–39.

7 Joyce owned a copy of *The Humour of Homer and Other Essays*, in which "The Deadlock in Darwinism"—a long essay in three parts—is included. As Gillespie notes, one of the two pencil marks found in the margins of Joyce's copy of this book occurs on a page devoted to an exposition of Butler's "neo-Lamarckian" ideas on heredity as a function of habit and unconscious memory (Butler, *Humour* 304; Gillespie, *Trieste* 63).

8 See Gillespie, *Trieste* 210–15.

9 See Martha Fodaski Black's *Shaw and Joyce: "The Last Word in Stolentelling"* (Gainesville: University Press of Florida, 1995), passim, for a detailed discussion of Joyce's interest in Shaw's evolutionary beliefs. Black notes that Joyce read Shaw while completing *A Portrait* in 1913 and 1914, purchasing "copies of *Major Barbara* and *The Devil's Disciple* as well as Henri Bergson's *Creative Evolution* . . . perhaps in an effort to understand the philosophy for which Shaw had made himself spokesperson" (44).

10 Note the remarkable, coincidental echo of this phrase in the "Circe" episode of *Ulysses*, where Bloom tells Virag "It has been an unusually fatiguing day, a chapter of accidents" (*U*15.2380).

11 Stuart Gilbert has argued that Joyce considered this phrase "a variant of the kabbalistic axiom of metempsychosis," which Gilbert cites as " 'a stone becomes a plant, a plant an animal, an animal a man, a man a spirit, and a spirit a god' " (128). Gilbert provides no source for this citation, which in fact originates in Madame Blavatsky's *Isis Unveiled*, where she ties the processes of human gestation to "the Pythagorean esoteric doctrine of metempsychosis, so erroneously interpreted by critics" and embodied in "the kabbalistic axiom: 'A stone becomes a plant; a plant a beast; a beast a man, etc.' " (1: 388).

12 Ellmann unfortunately provides no reference for this remark.

13 Klaus Reichert has also discussed Joyce's relation to the memory theater tradition and called attention to some of the same passages in a lecture on "Joyce's Memory" presented to the Monaco Joyce Symposium in 1990.

14 Stephen Heath argues that Joyce's diagram for the "Oxen of the Sun" episode "is also and importantly a memory system, a 'memory theatre' very much like those Frances Yates describes." Heath goes on to claim that "*Ulysses* itself is written and works anyway as a gigantic memory theatre, with its encyclopedism, its chapter by chapter correspondence (each with its organ, art, technic, symbol, colour and so on), everything that Pound refers to as the result of Joyce's 'medievalism' " (133). See Heath, "Joyce in Language," in *James Joyce: New Perspectives*, ed. Colin MacCabe (Bloomington: Indiana University Press), 129–48.

15 The following material on Joyce and Bruno has appeared in slightly different

form in my note, "Philotheology in Mecklenburg Street," published in the *James Joyce Quarterly*, 23 (Fall 1985): 80–82.

16 See, for example, Elliott B. Gose's *The Transformation Process in Joyce's "Ulysses"* (Toronto: University of Toronto Press, 1980) for a thorough investigation of Joyce's debt to Bruno.

17 See Silverstein's "Bruno's Particles of Reminiscence," *JJQ* 2 (Summer 1965): 271–80, and his unpublished dissertation, "Joyce's 'Circe' Episode: Approaches to *Ulysses* Through a Textual and Interpretative Study of Joyce's Fifteenth Chapter," pp. 227–45. Bruno's label of "Fascinatrix" for Circe echoes Bérard's discussion of the sirens as "fascinators" (see above, chapter 2). For Silverstein's interesting speculation that the number 67 also links up Circe with Ann Hathaway, who died, as Stephen tells us, "sixtyseven years after she was born" (*U*9.217), see 236 and 245. Bruno's list in the *Ars Memoriae* appears in *Opera Latine Conscripta*, vol. 2, 126.

18 Stephen Heath's "Joyce in Language" also argues convincingly for a link with the Abbé Marcel Jousse's ideas on gesture as the basis of language.

19 More evidence for this correspondence between Bloom's "ba" and the Egyptian *ba* is provided in my note, "Isis on Sandymount," *James Joyce Quarterly* 20 (Spring 1983): 356–58 and in chap. 5 of this book.

20 Kenner adds in his *Ulysses* that the public transport in Dublin also closes at 11 P.M. (115).

21 See Ellmann, *Ulysses on the Liffey*, e.g., on three as "the determining element of structure" in Joyce's work (2) and on 16 as a "token of homosexuality" in "Eumaeus" (155).

22 Kenner has noted that typographical changes in the Gabler edition of *Ulysses* have "blurred" this feature of "Oxen of the Sun" ("Reflections" 17).

23 See also Clive Hart's *Structure and Motif in "Finnegans Wake"* (Evanston, Ill.: Northwestern University Press, 1962), 186–88, and Roland McHugh's discussion of 1132 and *Finnegans Wake* in *The Sigla of "Finnegans Wake"* (Austin: University of Texas Press, 1976), 47.

24 In his *Ulysses*, Kenner points out that at the end of *A Portrait*, "Ascension Day is eleven days off" (12), noting that "to let Stephen commence his flight on Ascension Day of whatever year would have been heavy-handed, but the connection asked to be made and while he was considering 1902 'eleven' would have seemed a good way to make it. Eleven is a recurrent Joycenumber. Bloom's son in *Ulysses* lived 11 days and would be in his eleventh year if he were alive on Bloomsday. The last phrase in *Finnegans Wake* has 11 words, and the text encodes variations on 11 throughout. By one gloss, 11 signifies renewal by inaugurating a new decade, and Joyce may have noticed that 1881, the year of his conception, is divisible by 11" (18). In his book *The Economy of "Ulysses": Making Both Ends Meet* (Syracuse, N.Y.: Syracuse University Press, 1995), Mark Osteen notes that Bloom's "gift" to Stephen in the "Circe" episode amounts to eleven shillings. He sees the moment when Bloom spends the eleventh shilling (*U*15.4312) as a point of "fusion," arguing

that "since eleven is the number of rebirth in *Ulysses*, this sum indicates the regeneration of life out of death. . . . In short, eleven shillings means that both ends meet" (347).

25 See, for example, *Wisdom of Solomon* 11:20; Isa. 11.26; and Matt. 10.30.
26 Kenner also notes Augustine's thoughts on eleven ("Lisping" 312).
27 Bérard writes, "cette *Nekyia* est une sorte de monstre démesuré, qui dépare l'agencement général du poème. La *Nekyia* occupe tout le chant XI" (II, 311). Nowhere else in his notes on *Les Phéniciens et l'Odyssée* does Joyce take note of numbers or their significance in the *Odyssey*.
28 For example, in *Spenser and the Numbers of Time* (New York: Barnes and Noble, 1964), Fowler suggests that in the *Faerie Queene* "in every book except IV an elaborately described image of evil is assigned to the eleventh canto" (54). H. Neville Davies notes: "Colin's lament for Dido in *The Shepheardes Calender* is appropriately placed in the November eclogue, November being the eleventh month and eleven being associated with death. The lament itself has eleven stanzas with a doleful refrain mourning the death of Dido, followed by four stanzas with joyful refrains celebrating Dido's new life in Elysian fields" (94). See Davies, "Laid Artfully Together: Stanzaic Design in Milton's 'On the Morning of Christ's Nativity,'" in *Fair Forms: Essays in English Literature from Spenser to Jane Austen*, ed. Mareo-Sofie Rostvig (Cambridge: D. S. Brewer, 1975), 85–117. See also Vincent Foster Hopper, *Medieval Number Symbolism: Its Sources, Meaning, and Influence on Thought and Expression* (New York: Columbia University Press, 1938), 152, on Dante's use of eleven as a structural element for the ninth and tenth *bolgia* of his *Inferno*.
29 Milton's early funereal poem "On the Death of a Fair Infant Dying of a Cough" is also written in eleven stanzas.
30 Kenner provides a thorough catalogue of the potato's appearances in his *Ulysses*, 79.
31 For a thorough study of Joyce's development of patterns of imagery in *A Portrait of the Artist as a Young Man*, see John B. Smith's *Imagery and the Mind of Stephen Dedalus: A Computer-Assisted Study of Joyce's "A Portrait of the Artist as a Young Man"* (Lewisburg, Pa.: Bucknell University Press, 1980), esp. 75–79, which carefully outlines the images associated with the pandybatting. Smith shows how carefully images of burning, scalding, etc., discussed above, are integrated with other groups of images in chapter 1 of *A Portrait*, so that "there is the convergence and fusion of virtually every major theme of the chapter in the blinding, burning pain of the pandybat" (75). I discuss Stephen's pandybatting in greater detail in my essay "Stephen Dedalus Among School Children: The Schoolroom and the Riddle of Authority in *Ulysses*."

5   Intertextual Memory

This chapter has appeared in slightly different form as "Tradition and Intertextual Memory in James Joyce's *Ulysses*," in *Philosophical Imagination and Cultural Memory: Appropriating Historical Traditions,* ed. Patricia Cook (Durham, N.C.: Duke University Press, 1993).

1. Perry Meisel argues that "by virtue of a Latin rather than properly Greek title, the novel gives us a graphic clue for its programmatic failure to complete Eliot's 'parallel' even on its face. If *Ulysses*, as Eliot claims, is a mythic replication of the *Odyssey*, why, then, is the book not called *Odysseus!*" (145). In *The Novel as Family Romance: Language, Gender, and Authority from Fielding to Joyce* (Ithaca, N.Y.: Cornell University Press, 1987), Christine van Boheemen also takes up this issue, arguing for the "ambivalent" nature of *Ulysses'* reference to the *Odyssey:* "Thus, this title, which points to the epic, also marks the text's revisionary difference from the classic narrative. The title as sign functions as an epitaph, marking the last remains of the *Odyssey*. In giving his novel the title *Ulysses*, Joyce incorporated Homer into his fiction as the paradoxical presence of a defunct absence" (145). See Meisel, *The Myth of the Modern: A Study in British Literature and Criticism After 1850* (New Haven, Conn.: Yale University Press, 1987).
2. One anonymous reviewer in 1922 wrote that *Ulysses* "has nothing at all to do with Homer" (Deming 194), while Shane Leslie wrote in the *Quarterly Review:* "The great name of Ulysses is horribly profaned. We have only an Odyssey of the sewer" (Deming 207). Valéry Larbaud, on the other hand, claimed in 1922 that "the reader who approaches this book without the *Odyssey* clearly in mind will be thrown into dismay" (Deming 258).
3. Joyce owned an Italian version of this story excerpted from *The Golden Ass*. See Gillespie, *Trieste* 33.
4. See Thornton, *Allusions in "Ulysses,"* 313–14.
5. See, for example, James Henry Breasted, *Development of Religion and Thought in Ancient Egypt* (London: Hodder and Staughton, 1912), 55–56. The *ba* appears in *Finnegans Wake* as well ("Ba's berial nether," *FW* 415).
6. See Richard Ellmann, *The Consciousness of Joyce* (New York: Oxford University Press, 1977), 123.
7. For more detail on the relation of this myth to "Nausicaa," see Rickard, "Isis on Sandymount."

Conclusion

1. For example, the narrator tells us that Bloom asks Stephen if he "had known the late Mrs Emily Sinico, accidentally killed at Sydney Parade railway station" (U17.947–48), and he informs us that Bloom sees in Stephen's "quick young familiar form the predestination of a future" (U17.780). Most curiously, Stephen interprets the song he sings about Little Harry Hughes and the Jew's daughter as a puzzling admixture of predestination and choice: "One of all, the least of all, is the victim predestined. Once by inadvertence, twice by design he challenges his destiny. It comes when he is abandoned and challenges him reluctant and, as an apparition of hope and youth, holds him unresist-

ing. It leads him to a strange habitation, to a secret infidel apartment, and there, implacable, immolates him, consenting" (U17.833–37).

2. In his review of the many types of critical responses to the ending of *Ulysses*, Kain outlines eight "theories" of how to interpret the relationship achieved by Bloom and Stephen at the end of *Ulysses*, ranging from "isolation," which reads the meeting as "fortuitous and unimportant, a demonstration of modern keylessness or of the existential position of man" to "creativity," in which "Stephen becomes a discoverer of mankind, through communion with Bloom" (159).

3. Maeterlinck's passage on Socrates, Judas, and destiny in *Wisdom and Destiny* appears a few pages after a discussion of the death of Antoninus Pius that may have provided Joyce with a model for the puzzling and at times disturbing "equanimity" that Bloom reaches at the end of "Ithaca": "Antoninus Pius—who was perhaps truly the best and most perfect man this world has known, better even than Marcus Aurelius. . . . lay on his bed, awaiting the summons of death, his eyes dim with unbidden tears, his limbs moist with the pale sweat of agony. At that moment there entered the captain of the guard, come to demand the watchword, such being the custom. *Aequanimitas—evenness of mind*, he replied, as he turned his head to the eternal shadow" (23–24; original emphasis). Joyce's continuing interest in Maeterlinck's ideas is indicated by Ellmann's claim that Maria Jolas discovered Joyce "reading Maeterlinck on life after death" soon after his father's death in 1931 (*JJII* 645).

4. Also interesting is the fact that "impossible" and its variants occur only twelve times in the whole novel. Spoo in *James Joyce and the Language of History* has also noticed the fact that "In 'Ithaca' we are as often in the realm of the potential as that of the actual. The words 'possible,' 'possibility,' and 'potential' proliferate in this episode." However, Spoo also argues that the "Ithaca" episode "tempers the possible with the *im*possible, human perfectibility with limitation" (159), a reading in keeping with my sense that the final episodes of *Ulysses* maintain a delicate, chaosmic balance.

Bibliography

"Anamnesis." *New Catholic Encyclopedia*. 15 vols. New York: McGraw-Hill, 1967.
Anderson, Chester G. "Introduction: Joyce and Freud." In *The Seventh of Joyce*. Ed. Bernard Benstock. Bloomington: Indiana University Press, 1982. 53–56.
———. "Leopold Bloom as Dr. Sigmund Freud." *Mosaic* 6 (Fall 1972): 23–43.
Apuleius. *The Golden Ass: Being the Metamorphoses of Lucius Apuleius*. Trans. W. Adlington (1566). Loeb Classical Library. Rev. by S. Gaselee. Cambridge, Mass.: Harvard University Press, 1977.
Atherton, James S. *The Books at the Wake: A Study of Literary Allusions in James Joyce's "Finnegans Wake."* Expanded and corrected ed. Mamaroneck, N.Y.: Appel, 1974.
Augustine, Saint. *Concerning the City of God Against the Pagans*. Trans. Henry Bettenson. Harmondsworth, Eng.: Penguin Books, 1972.
———. *Confessions*. Trans. R. S. Pine-Coffin. Harmondsworth, Eng.: Penguin Books, 1961.
Bair, Deirdre. *Samuel Beckett: A Biography*. New York: Harcourt Brace Jovanovich, 1978.
Barnes, Djuna. "James Joyce: A Portrait of the Man Who Is, at Present, One of the More Significant Figures in Literature." *Vanity Fair* 18 (April 1922): 65 and 104.
Barthélemy-Madaule, Madeleine. *Lamarck the Mythical Precursor: A Study of the Relations Between Science and Ideology*. Trans. M. H. Shank. Cambridge, Mass.: MIT Press, 1982.
Barthes, Roland. *S/Z*. Trans. Richard Miller. New York: Hill and Wang, 1974.
Beach, Sylvia. *Shakespeare and Company*. Lincoln: University of Nebraska Press, 1959.
Beckett, Samuel. *Proust*. New York: Grove Press, 1931.
Beer, Gillian. *Darwin's Plots: Evolutionary Narrative in Darwin, George Eliot, and Nineteenth-Century Fiction*. London: Routledge and Kegan Paul, 1983.
Bennett, John Z. "Unposted Letter: Joyce's Leopold Bloom." *Bucknell Review* 14, no. 1 (1966): 1–13.
Bérard, Victor. *Did Homer Live?* Trans. Brian Rhys. New York: E. P. Dutton, 1931.
———. *Les Phéniciens et l'Odyssée*. 2 vols. Paris: Librairie Armand Colin, 1902.

Bergson, Henri. *Creative Evolution*. Trans. Arthur Mitchell. New York: Modern Library, 1944.
———. *Matter and Memory*. Trans. Nancy Margaret Paul and W. Scott Palmer. London: George Allen, 1912.
Besant, Annie. *The Ancient Wisdom: An Outline of Theosophical Teachings*. 1897. Adyar, India: Theosophical Publishing House, 1939.
Black, Martha Fodaski. *Shaw and Joyce: "The Last Word in Stolentelling."* Gainesville: University Press of Florida, 1995.
Blavatsky, Helena Petrovna. *Isis Unveiled: A Master-Key to the Mysteries of Ancient and Modern Science and Theology*. 2 vols. New York: J. W. Bouton, 1886.
———. *The Key to Theosophy*. 1889. Pasadena, Calif.: Theosophical Publishing House, 1972.
Boheemen, Christine van. *The Novel as Family Romance: Language, Gender, and Authority from Fielding to Joyce*. Ithaca, N.Y.: Cornell University Press, 1987.
Boone, Joseph A. "Staging Sexuality: Repression, Representation, and 'Interior' States in *Ulysses*." In *Joyce: The Return of the Repressed*. Ed. Susan Stanford Friedman. Ithaca, N.Y.: Cornell University Press, 1993. 190–221.
Brandes, George. *William Shakespeare: A Critical Study*. London: Heinemann, 1902.
Breasted, James Henry. *Development of Religion and Thought in Ancient Egypt*. London: Hodder and Stoughton, 1912.
Brivic, Sheldon. *Joyce Between Freud and Jung*. Port Washington, N.Y.: Kennikat Press, 1980.
Brooks, Peter. *Psychoanalysis and Storytelling*. Cambridge, Mass.: Blackwell, 1994.
———. *Reading for the Plot: Design and Intention in Narrative*. New York: Random House, 1984.
Brown, Dennis. *The Modernist Self in Twentieth-Century English Literature: A Study in Self-Fragmentation*. New York: St. Martin's Press, 1989.
Bruno, Giordano. *Opera Latine Conscripta*. Vol. 2, pt. 1. 1886. Stuttgart-Bad Canstatt: F. Frommann-G. Holzboog, 1961.
Budgen, Frank. *Further Recollections of James Joyce*. London: Shenval Press, 1955.
———. *James Joyce and the Making of "Ulysses" and Other Writings*. Oxford: Oxford University Press, 1972.
———. *Myselves When Young*. New York: Oxford University Press, 1970.
Butler, Samuel. "The Deadlock in Darwinism." In *The Humour of Homer and Other Essays*. Ed. R. A. Streatfeild. London: A. C. Fifield, 1913. 245–313.
———. *Life and Habit*. New York: E. P. Dutton, 1923.
———. *The Notebooks of Samuel Butler*. Ed. Henry Festing Jones. London: A. C. Fifield, 1912.
———. *Unconscious Memory*. New York: E. P. Dutton, 1924.
Buttigieg, Joseph. *A Portrait of the Artist in Different Perspective*. Athens: Ohio University Press, 1987.
Casey, Edward S. *Remembering: A Phenomenological Study*. Bloomington: Indiana University Press, 1987.

Certeau, Michel de. *The Practice of Everyday Life.* Trans. Stephen Rendall. Berkeley: University of California Press, 1984.
Cheng, Vincent. *Shakespeare and Joyce: A Study of "Finnegans Wake."* University Park: Pennsylvania State University Press, 1984.
Cixous, Hélène. "At Circe's, or the Self-Opener." *Boundary 2,* 3 (Winter 1975): 387–97.
———. "Joyce: The (R)use of Writing." In *Post-Structuralist Joyce: Essays from the French.* Ed. Derek Attridge and Daniel Ferrer. Cambridge: Cambridge University Press, 1984. 15–30.
Clayton, Jay, and Eric Rothstein, eds. *Influence and Intertextuality in Literary History.* Madison: University of Wisconsin Press, 1991.
Clément, Catharine. *The Weary Sons of Freud.* Trans. Nicole Ball. New York: Verso, 1987.
Cornford, Francis M. *Plato's Theory of Knowledge: The "Theaetetus" and the "Sophist" of Plato Translated.* . . . New York: Harcourt Brace, 1935.
Costello, Peter. *Leopold Bloom: A Biography.* Dublin: Gill and Macmillan, 1981.
Culler, Jonathan. "Textual Self-Consciousness and the Textual Unconscious." *Style* 18 (Summer 1984): 369–76.
Dano, Finn. "A Note on Eleven." *James Joyce Quarterly* 5 (Spring 1968): 275–76.
Danto, Arthur C. "The Shape of Artistic Pasts: East and West." In *Philosophical Imagination and Cultural Memory: Appropriating Historical Traditions.* Ed. Patricia Cook. Durham, N.C.: Duke University Press, 1993. 125–38.
Davies, H. Neville. "Laid Artfully Together: Stanzaic Design in Milton's 'On the Morning of Christ's Nativity.'" In *Fair Forms: Essays in English Literature from Spenser to Jane Austen.* Ed. Maren-Sofie Rostvig. Cambridge: D. S. Brewer, 1975. 85–117.
Deming, Robert H., ed. *James Joyce: The Critical Heritage.* Vol. 1, *1907–1927.* London: Routledge and Kegan Paul, 1970.
Dennett, Daniel C. *Darwin's Dangerous Idea: Evolution and the Meanings of Life.* New York: Simon and Schuster, 1995.
Derrida, Jacques. "Two Words for Joyce." Trans. Geoff Bennington. In *Post-Structuralist Joyce: Essays from the French.* Ed. Derek Attridge and Daniel Ferrer. Cambridge: Cambridge University Press, 1984. 145–59.
Dettmar, Kevin J. H. *The Illicit Joyce of Postmodernism: Reading Against the Grain.* Madison: University of Wisconsin Press, 1996.
Dundes, Alan. "Mairymaking in *Ulysses:* A Legendary Source for a Lost Pin." *Cahiers du Centre d'Etudes Irlandaises* 3 (1978): 69–73.
———. "The Study of Folklore in Literature and Culture: Identification and Interpretation." *Journal of American Folklore* 78 (1965): 136–42.
Eco, Umberto. *The Aesthetics of Chaosmos: The Middle Ages of James Joyce.* Trans. Ellen Esrock. University of Tulsa Monograph Series, no. 18. Tulsa: University of Oklahoma, 1982.
Eliot, T. S. "*Ulysses,* Order and Myth." In *Selected Prose of T. S. Eliot.* Ed. Frank Kermode. New York: Harcourt Brace Jovanovich, 1975. 175–78.

Ellmann, Maud. "Disremembering Dedalus: 'A Portrait of the Artist as a Young Man.'" In *Untying the Text: A Poststructuralist Reader*. Ed. Robert Young. New York: Routledge, 1981. 189–206.

Ellmann, Richard. *The Consciousness of Joyce*. New York: Oxford University Press, 1977.

———. *Four Dubliners: Wilde, Yeats, Joyce, and Beckett*. New York: George Braziller, 1988.

———. *James Joyce*. New and rev. ed. New York: Oxford University Press, 1982.

———. *Ulysses on the Liffey*. New York: Oxford University Press, 1972.

Ferrer, Daniel. "Circe, regret and regression." Trans. Gilly Lehmann. In *Post-Structuralist Joyce: Essays from the French*. Ed. Derek Attridge and Daniel Ferrer. Cambridge: Cambridge University Press, 1984. 127–44.

Fowler, Alastair. *Spenser and the Numbers of Time*. New York: Barnes and Noble, 1964.

———. "'To Shepherd's Ear': The Form of Milton's 'Lycidas.'" In *Silent Poetry: Essays in Numerological Analysis*. Ed. Alastair Fowler. London: Routledge and Kegan Paul, 1970. 170–84.

Frazer, James G. *Adonis, Attis, Osiris: Studies in the History of Oriental Religion*. Part 4, vol. 2 of *The Golden Bough: A Study of Magic and Religion*. 3rd ed. 1913. London: Macmillan, 1980.

Freud, Sigmund. *A Phylogenetic Fantasy: Overview of the Transference Neuroses*. Ed. Ilse Grubrich-Simitis. Trans. Axel Hoffer and Peter T. Hoffer. Cambridge, Mass.: Belknap Press of Harvard University Press, 1987.

———. *Standard Edition of the Complete Psychological Works of Sigmund Freud*. Ed. James Strachey. London: Hogarth, 1953–72.

Friedman, Susan Stanford. "Weavings: Intertextuality and the (Re)Birth of the Author." In *Influence and Intertextuality in Literary History*. Madison: University of Wisconsin Press, 1991. 146–80.

Fromm, Erich. *Beyond the Chains of Illusion: My Encounter with Marx and Freud*. New York: Simon and Schuster, 1962.

Froula, Christine. *Modernism's Body: Sex, Culture, and Joyce*. New York: Columbia University Press, 1996.

Genette, Gérard. *Narrative Discourse: An Essay in Method*. Trans. Jane E. Lewin. Ithaca, N.Y.: Cornell University Press, 1980.

Gifford, Don, with Robert J. Seidman. *Joyce Annotated: Notes for James Joyce's "Ulysses."* Rev. and expanded ed. Berkeley: University of California Press, 1988.

Gilbert, Stuart. *James Joyce's "Ulysses": A Study*. New York: Vintage Books, 1952.

Gillespie, Michael Patrick. *James Joyce's Trieste Library: A Catalogue of Materials at the Harry Ransom Humanities Research Center, The University of Texas at Austin*. Austin, Tex.: Harry Ransom Humanities Research Center, 1986.

———. "Sources and the Independent Artist." *James Joyce Quarterly* 20 (Spring 1983): 325–36.

Glasheen, Adaline. "Calypso." In *James Joyce's "Ulysses": Critical Essays*. Ed. Clive

Hart and David Hayman. Berkeley: University of California Press, 1974. 51–70.
Goldman, Arnold. *The Joyce Paradox: Form and Freedom in His Fiction.* Evanston, Ill.: Northwestern University Press, 1966.
Gordon, John. *James Joyce's Metamorphoses.* Dublin: Gill and Macmillan, 1981.
Gose, Elliott B. *The Transformation Process in Joyce's "Ulysses."* Toronto: University of Toronto Press, 1980.
Groden, Michael. *"Ulysses" in Progress.* Princeton, N.J.: Princeton University Press, 1977.
Harkness, Marguerite. *"A Portrait of the Artist as a Young Man": Voices of the Text.* Boston: Twayne, 1990.
Hart, Clive. *Structure and Motif in "Finnegans Wake".* Evanston, Ill.: Northwestern University Press, 1962.
———. "Wandering Rocks." In *James Joyce's "Ulysses": Critical Essays.* Ed. Clive Hart and David Hayman. Berkeley: University of California Press, 1974. 181–216.
Heath, Stephen. "Joyce in Language." In *James Joyce: New Perspectives.* Ed. Colin MacCabe. Bloomington: Indiana University Press, 1982. 129–48.
Henke, Suzette. "Stephen Dedalus and Women: A Feminist Reading of *Portrait.*" In *A Portrait of the Artist as a Young Man.* Ed. R. B. Kershner. Boston: Bedford Books, 1993. 307–25.
Herr, Cheryl. "Art and Life, Nature and Culture, *Ulysses.*" In *Joyce's "Ulysses": The Larger Perspective.* Ed. Robert D. Newman and Weldon Thornton. Newark: University of Delaware Press, 1987. 19–38.
———. *Joyce's Anatomy of Culture.* Urbana: University of Illinois Press, 1986.
Herring, Phillip F., ed. *Joyce's Notes and Early Drafts for "Ulysses."* Charlottesville: University Press of Virginia, 1977.
———, ed. *Joyce's "Ulysses" Notesheets in the British Museum.* Charlottesville: University Press of Virginia, 1972.
———. *Joyce's Uncertainty Principle.* Princeton, N.J.: Princeton University Press, 1987.
Hewitt, Douglas. *English Fiction of the Early Modern Period, 1890–1940.* New York: Longman, 1988.
Hillman, James. *The Myth of Analysis: Three Essays in Archetypal Psychology.* Evanston, Ill.: Northwestern University Press, 1972.
Hoffmeister, Adolf. "Portrait of Joyce." Trans. Norma Rudinsky. In *Portraits of the Artist in Exile: Recollections of James Joyce by Europeans.* Ed. Willard Potts. Seattle: University of Washington Press, 1979. 127–36.
Hopper, Vincent Foster. *Medieval Number Symbolism: Its Sources, Meaning, and Influence on Thought and Expression.* Columbia University Studies in English and Comparative Literature, no. 132. New York: Columbia University Press, 1938.
Hume, David. *A Treatise of Human Nature.* Ed. L. A. Selby-Bigge. Oxford: Clarendon Press, 1888.

James, William. *Essays in Psychical Research*. The Works of William James. Ed. Frederick Burkhardt et al. Cambridge, Mass.: Harvard University Press, 1986.
———. "The Final Impressions of a Psychical Researcher." In *William James on Psychical Research*. Ed. Gardner Murphy and Robert O. Ballou. New York: Viking Press, 1960. 309–25.
———. *The Principles of Psychology*. 1890. New York: Dover, 1950.
Joyce, James. *"Dubliners": Text, Criticism, and Notes*. Ed. Robert Scholes and A. Walton Litz. New York: Viking Press, 1969.
———. *Exiles*. New York: Viking Press, 1951.
———. *Finnegans Wake*. London: Faber and Faber, 1939.
———. *James Joyce Archive*. 63 vols. Ed. Michael Groden et al. New York: Garland, 1978.
———. *Letters of James Joyce*. 3 vols. Ed. Stuart Gilbert (vol. 1) and Richard Ellmann (vols. 2 and 3). New York: Viking Press, 1966.
———. *A Portrait of the Artist as a Young Man*, Ed. R. B. Kershner. Boston: Bedford Books, 1993.
———. *"A Portrait of the Artist as a Young Man": Text, Criticism, and Notes*. Ed. Chester G. Anderson. New York: Viking Press, 1968.
———. *Selected Letters of James Joyce*. Ed. Richard Ellmann. New York: Viking Press, 1975.
———. *Stephen Hero*. Ed. Theodore Spencer. New ed. New York: New Directions, 1963.
———. *"Ulysses": A Critical and Synoptic Edition*. Ed. Hans Walter Gabler et al. New York: Random House, 1986.
Joyce, Stanislaus. *My Brother's Keeper: James Joyce's Early Years*. Ed. Richard Ellmann. New York: Viking Press, 1958.
Jung, Carl Gustav. "On the Psychology of the Unconscious." In *Two Essays on Analytical Psychology. Collected Works*, vol. 7. Trans. R. F. C. Hull. 2nd ed. Princeton, N.J.: Princeton University Press, 1966. 3–119.
———. "The Relations Between the Ego and the Unconscious." In *Two Essays on Analytical Psychology. Collected Works*, vol. 7. Trans. R. F. C. Hull. 2nd ed. Princeton, N.J.: Princeton University Press, 1966. 123–241.
———. "The Soul and Death." In *The Structure and Dynamics of the Psyche. Collected Works*, vol. 8. Trans. R. F. C. Hull. 2nd ed. Princeton, N.J.: Princeton University Press, 1969.
———. *Ulysses: A Monologue*. Trans. W. Stanley Dell. Brooklyn, N.Y.: Haskell House, 1977.
Kain, Richard M. "The Significance of Stephen's Meeting Bloom: A Survey of Interpretations." In *"Ulysses": Fifty Years*. Ed. Thomas F. Staley. Bloomington: Indiana University Press, 1974. 147–60.
Kenner, Hugh. "Lisping in Numbers." In *Historical Fictions: Essays*. San Francisco: North Point Press, 1990. 305–16.
———. "The *Portrait* in Perspective." In *Joyce: A Collection of Critical Essays*. Ed. William M. Chace. Englewood Cliffs, N.J.: Prentice-Hall, 1974. 29–49.

———. "Reflections on the Gabler Era." *James Joyce Quarterly* 26 (Fall 1988): 11–20.
———. *Ulysses*. Rev. ed. Baltimore: Johns Hopkins University Press, 1987.
Kershner, R. B. *Joyce, Bakhtin, and Popular Literature: Chronicles of Disorder.* Chapel Hill: University of North Carolina Press, 1989.
Kimball, Jean. "Freud, Leonardo, and Joyce: The Dimensions of a Childhood Memory." *James Joyce Quarterly* 17 (Winter 1980): 165–82.
Klawitter, Robert. "Henri Bergson and James Joyce's Fictional World." *Comparative Literature Studies* 3 (1966): 429–37.
Kolakowski, Leszek. *Bergson*. Past Masters. New York: Oxford University Press, 1985.
Kristeva, Julia. *Desire in Language: A Semiotic Approach to Literature and Art.* Ed. Leon S. Roudiez. Trans. Thomas Gora, Alice Jardine, and Leon S. Roudiez. New York: Columbia University Press, 1980.
Kumar, Shiv K. *Bergson and the Stream of Consciousness Novel.* New York: New York University Press, 1963.
Kumar, Udaya. *The Joycean Labyrinth: Repetition, Time, and Tradition in "Ulysses."* Oxford: Clarendon Press, 1991.
Lacan, Jacques. "Desire and the Interpretation of Desire in *Hamlet.*" In *Literature and Psychoanalysis: The Question of Reading: Otherwise.* Yale French Studies 55/56. New Haven, Conn.: Yale University, 1977. 11–52.
Lawrence, Karen. *The Odyssey of Style in "Ulysses."* Princeton, N.J.: Princeton University Press, 1981.
Levine, George Lewis. *Darwin and the Novelists: Patterns of Science in Victorian Fiction.* Cambridge, Mass.: Harvard University Press, 1988.
Lewis, Wyndham. *Time and Western Man.* London: Chatto and Windus, 1927.
Liddell, Henry George, and Robert Scott. *An Intermediate Greek-English Lexicon.* Oxford: Clarendon Press, 1889.
Locke, John. *An Essay Concerning Human Understanding.* Ed. A. S. Pringle-Pattison. Oxford: Clarendon Press, 1924.
Lukacher, Ned. *Primal Scenes: Literature, Philosophy, Psychoanalysis.* Ithaca, N.Y.: Cornell University Press, 1986.
MacCabe, Colin. *James Joyce and the Revolution of the Word.* London: Macmillan, 1978.
Maeterlinck, Maurice. *The Blue Bird: A Fairy Tale in Six Acts.* Trans. Alexander Teixeira de Mattos. New York: Dodd, Mead, 1911.
———. *The Unknown Guest.* Trans. Alexander Teixeira de Mattos. New York: Dodd, Mead, 1914.
———. *Wisdom and Destiny.* Trans. Alfred Sutro. New York: Dodd, Mead, 1901.
Maher, Michael. *Psychology.* 2nd ed. New York: Benziger Brothers, [n.d.].
McCarthy, Patrick. *The Riddles of "Finnegans Wake."* Rutherford, N.J.: Fairleigh Dickinson University Press, 1980.
McGee, Patrick. *Paperspace: Style as Ideology in Joyce's "Ulysses."* Lincoln: University of Nebraska Press, 1988.

McHugh, Roland. *Annotations to "Finnegans Wake."* Baltimore: Johns Hopkins University Press, 1980.

———. *The Sigla of "Finnegans Wake."* Austin: University of Texas Press, 1976.

McIntyre, J. Lewis. *Giordano Bruno: Mystic, Martyr.* London: Macmillan, 1903.

Meisel, Perry. *The Myth of the Modern: A Study in British Literature and Criticism After 1850.* New Haven, Conn.: Yale University Press, 1987.

Mercanton, Jacques. "The Hours of James Joyce." Trans. Lloyd C. Parks. In *Portraits of the Artist in Exile: Recollections of James Joyce by Europeans.* Ed. Willard Potts. Seattle: University of Washington Press, 1979. 206–52.

Nietzsche, Friedrich. "On the Uses and Disadvantages of History for Life." In *Untimely Meditations.* Trans. R. J. Hollingdale. Cambridge: Cambridge University Press, 1983. 57–123.

Osteen, Mark. *The Economy of "Ulysses": Making Both Ends Meet.* Syracuse, N.Y.: Syracuse University Press, 1995.

Ovid. *Ovid's Fasti.* Trans. James George Frazer. New York: Putnam, 1931.

Painter, George D. *Marcel Proust: A Biography.* 2 vols. New York: Random House, 1959.

Parrinder, Patrick. *James Joyce.* Cambridge: Cambridge University Press, 1984.

Pecora, Vincent. "'The Dead' and the Generosity of the Word." *PMLA* (March 1986): 233–45.

Piette, Adam. *Remembering and the Sound of Words: Mallarmé, Proust, Joyce, Beckett.* Oxford: Clarendon Press, 1996.

Pilkington, A. E. *Bergson and His Influence: A Reassessment.* Cambridge: Cambridge University Press, 1976.

Plato. *Five Dialogues of Plato Bearing on Poetic Inspiration [Ion, Symposium, Meno, Phaedo, Phaedrus].* New York: E. P. Dutton, 1910.

———. *Phaedo.* Trans. R. S. Bluck. London: Routledge and Kegan Paul, 1955.

———. *Phaedrus.* Vol. 1 of *Plato in Twelve Volumes.* Trans. Harold North Fowler. Loeb Classical Library. Cambridge, Mass.: Harvard University Press, 1914.

———. *Theaetetus.* Trans. Benjamin Jowett. Indianapolis: Bobbs-Merrill, 1949.

Plutarch. *Plutarch's Morals: Theosophical Essays.* Trans. C. W. King. London: G. Bell, 1898.

Potts, Willard, ed. *Portraits of the Artist in Exile: Recollections of James Joyce by Europeans.* Seattle: University of Washington Press, 1979.

Power, Arthur. *Conversations with James Joyce.* New York: Barnes and Noble, 1974.

Proust, Marcel. *Remembrance of Things Past.* Trans. C. K. Scott Moncrieff and Terence Kilmartin. 3 vols. New York: Random House, 1981.

Quillian, William H. *"Hamlet" and the New Poetic: James Joyce and T. S. Eliot.* Ann Arbor, Mich.: UMI Research Press, 1983.

Rickard, John S. "Chiromancy in *Ulysses.*" *James Joyce Quarterly* 33 (Spring 1996): 446–47.

———. "Isis on Sandymount." *James Joyce Quarterly* 20 (Spring 1983): 356–58.

———. "Philotheology in Mecklenburg Street." *James Joyce Quarterly* 23 (Fall 1985): 80–82.

———. "Stephen Dedalus Among School Children: The Schoolroom and the Riddle of Authority in *Ulysses*." *Studies in the Literary Imagination* 30 (Fall 1997): 17–36.

———. "Tradition and Intertextual Memory in James Joyce's *Ulysses*." In *Philosophical Imagination and Cultural Memory: Appropriating Historical Traditions*. Ed. Patricia Cook. Durham, N.C.: Duke University Press, 1993. 195–211.

Riffaterre, Michael. "The Intertextual Unconscious." *Critical Inquiry* 13 (Winter 1987): 371–85.

Riquelme, John Paul. *Teller and Tale in Joyce's Fiction: Oscillating Perspectives*. Baltimore: Johns Hopkins University Press, 1983.

Rose, Danis, and John O'Hanlon, eds. *James Joyce: The Lost Notebook, New Evidence on the Genesis of "Ulysses."* Edinburgh: Split Pea Press, 1989.

Ryan, Judith. *The Vanishing Subject: Early Modern Psychology and Literary Modernism*. Chicago: University of Chicago Press, 1991.

Schutte, William M. *Joyce and Shakespeare: A Study in the Meaning of "Ulysses."* New Haven, Conn.: Yale University Press, 1957.

Schwab, Gabriele. *Subjects Without Selves: Transitional Texts in Modern Fiction*. Cambridge, Mass.: Harvard University Press, 1994.

Schwarz, Daniel. *Reading Joyce's "Ulysses"*. New York: St. Martin's Press, 1987.

Senn, Fritz. "In Classical Idiom: Anthologia Intertextualis." *James Joyce Quarterly* 25 (Fall 1987): 31–48.

———. "In Quest of a *Nisus Formativus Joyceanus*." *Inductive Scrutinies: Focus on Joyce*. Ed. Christine O'Neill. Baltimore: Johns Hopkins University Press. 59–74.

———. "Met Whom What?" *James Joyce Quarterly* 30 (Fall 1992): 109–13.

———. "Nausicaa." In *James Joyce's "Ulysses": Critical Essays*. Ed. Clive Hart and David Hayman. Berkeley: University of California Press, 1974. 277–311.

Shakespeare, William. *The Complete Works of Shakespeare*. Ed. David Bevington. 3rd ed. Glenview, Ill.: Scott, Foresman, 1980.

Shaw, George Bernard. *Back to Methuselah: A Metabiological Pentateuch*. Harmondsworth, Eng.: Penguin, 1939.

———. *Collected Letters, 1911–1925*. Vol. 3 of *Collected Letters*. Ed. Dan H. Laurence. New York: Viking Press, 1985.

Shechner, Mark. *Joyce in Nighttown: A Psychoanalytic Inquiry into "Ulysses"*. Berkeley: University of California Press, 1974.

Silverstein, Norman. "Bruno's Particles of Reminiscence." *James Joyce Quarterly* 2 (Summer 1965): 271–80.

———. "Joyce's 'Circe' Episode: Approaches to *Ulysses* Through a Textual and Interpretative Study of Joyce's Fifteenth Chapter." Ph.D. dissertation, Columbia University, 1960. Ann Arbor, Mich.: UMI Research Press, 1960.

Singer, Dorothea Waley. *Giordano Bruno: His Life and Thought*. New York: Henry Schuman, 1950.

Skelton, Robin. *The Writings of J. M. Synge.* Indianapolis: Bobbs-Merrill, 1971.

Smith, John B. *Imagery and the Mind of Stephen Dedalus: A Computer-Assisted Study of Joyce's "A Portrait of the Artist as a Young Man."* Lewisburg, Pa.: Bucknell University Press, 1980.

Smith, Paul. *Discerning the Subject.* Minneapolis: University of Minnesota Press, 1988.

Solomon, Joseph. *Bergson.* [1912.] Port Washington, N.Y.: Kennikat Press, 1970.

Spoo, Robert. *James Joyce and the Language of History: Dedalus's Nightmare.* New York: Oxford University Press, 1994.

Steppe, Wolfhard, with Hans Walter Gabler. *A Handlist to James Joyce's "Ulysses": A Complete Alphabetical Index to the Critical Reading Text.* New York: Garland, 1986.

Thornton, Weldon. *Allusions in "Ulysses."* Chapel Hill: University of North Carolina Press, 1968.

Tindall, William York. *A Reader's Guide to James Joyce.* New York: Noonday Press, 1959.

Tolomeo, Diane. "The Final Octagon of *Ulysses.*" *James Joyce Quarterly* 10 (Summer 1973): 439–54.

Vico, Giambattista. *The New Science of Giambattista Vico.* Trans. Thomas G. Bergin and Max H. Fisch. Ithaca, N.Y.: Cornell University Press, 1984.

Vries, Ad de. *Dictionary of Symbols and Imagery.* Amsterdam: North-Holland, 1974.

Warner, William Beatty. *Chance and the Text of Experience: Freud, Nietzsche, and Shakespeare's "Hamlet."* Ithaca, N.Y.: Cornell University Press, 1986.

Watt, Stephen. *Joyce, O'Casey, and the Irish Popular Theater.* Syracuse, N.Y.: Syracuse University Press, 1991.

Weir, Lorraine. *Writing Joyce: A Semiotics of the Joyce System.* Bloomington: Indiana University Press, 1989.

Wentworth, Jay A. "Bloom's Self-Therapy in *Ulysses:* Images in Action." *Journal of Mental Imagery* 10, no. 2 (1986): 127–35.

Whitman, Walt. *Complete Poetry and Collected Prose.* New York: Library of America, 1982.

——. "Darwinism—(Then Furthermore)." In *Democratic Vistas and Other Papers.* London: George Routledge and Sons, [1906]. 163–65.

Yates, Frances. *The Art of Memory.* Chicago: University of Chicago Press, 1966.

——. *Giordano Bruno and the Hermetic Tradition.* [1964.] Chicago: University of Chicago Press, 1979.

Yeats, William Butler. "Magic." In *Essays and Introductions.* New York: Collier, 1961. 28–52.

——. *The Poems of W. B. Yeats.* Ed. Richard J. Finneran. New ed. New York: Macmillan, 1983.

Index

Accident. *See* Chance
AE. *See* Russell, George
"Aeolus," 93, 106
Agendath Netaim, 115
Aldington, Richard, 168
Anamnesis, 100–101; 140, 214 n.14
Anderson, Chester, 207 n.3, 209 n.18
Apuleius: *The Golden Ass*, 172–77
Aquinas, Thomas, 8, 24
Argonautica, 74, 78
Aristotle, 9, 24, 27–29, 31, 118; *De Anima*, 25, 28
Art of memory. *See* Memory: "art of"
Atherton, James S., 151, 214 n.15, 215 n.25
Augustine, Saint, 8, 118, 149, 152, 214 n.15; *The City of God*, 152; *Confessions*, 101–2

Ba, 149, 176, 218 n.19, 220 n.5
Barnes, Djuna, 209 n.18
Barthélemy-Madaule, Madeleine, 217 n.16
Barthes, Roland, 206 n.16
Beach, Sylvia, 211 n.5
Beckett, Samuel, 62–63, 211 n.6
Beer, Gillian, 119, 190
Bells. *See* Riddle words
Bennett, John Z., 209 n.20
Bérard, Victor, 79, 80, 152, 218 n.17
Bergson, Henri, 8, 10, 29–34, 60–63, 85, 87–88, 111, 112, 116, 118–19, 129, 132, 133, 135, 191, 208 n.15, 209 n.16, 216 n.6; *Creative Evolution*, 31, 33, 61, 113, 134, 217 n.9
Berkeley, George, 29, 207 n.8
Besant, Annie, 104, 154, 215 n.21; *The Ancient Wisdom*, 106
Black, Martha Fodaski, 217 n.9
Blavatsky, Helena Petrovna, 104, 106, 108, 109, 213 n.6, 215 n.25; *Isis Unveiled*, 105, 176, 177, 217 n.11; *The Key to Theosophy*, 113
Bluck, R. S., 101
Boheemen, Christine van, 179, 220 n.1
Bois, Elie-Joseph, 63
Boone, Joseph A., 205 n.15
Brandes, George, 213 n.4
Breasted, James Henry, 220 n.5
Breuer, Joseph, 48–49
Brivic, Sheldon, 209 n.18
Brooks, Peter, 11–13, 50, 130–31, 205 n.12, 206 n.16
Brown, Dennis, 15, 17
Bruno, Giordano, 8, 10, 118, 143–45, 166; *Ars Memoriae*, 144, 218 n.17; *Cantus Circaeus*, 143–45
Budgen, Frank, 1, 76, 77, 122, 128, 198, 211 n.5; *Further Recollections of James Joyce*, 139; *James Joyce and the Making of "Ulysses,"* 158; *Myselves When Young*, 128
Butler, Samuel, 8, 29, 111, 114, 118, 119, 132–33, 135, 191, 215 n.23, 216 n.6,

Butler, Samuel (cont.)
217 n.7; "The Deadlock in Darwinism," 132; *Unconscious Memory*, 115; *The Way of All Flesh*, 115
Buttigieg, Joseph, 52, 66–71

"Calypso," 80, 90, 154, 184, 194
Campanella, Tommaso, 10; *City of the Sun*, 142
Cannibalism, 130
Casey, Edward S., 9, 23
Certeau, Michel de, 169–70
Chance, 26, 29, 33, 111, 112, 114, 119–23, 127, 128, 130–37, 155, 156, 158, 160–61, 163, 165, 193, 195
Cheng, Vincent, 214 n.7
Childs Murder Case, 147
"Circe," 33, 40, 46, 56, 58, 89, 95, 99–100, 107, 110, 111, 112, 123–24, 126–28, 131, 137–66 passim, 182, 183, 189, 191, 193, 194–96
Cixous, Hélène, 14, 131, 146, 188, 210 nn. 1, 3
Cock. *See* Riddle words
Cockles. *See* Shells
Coincidence, 6, 90–91, 111, 128, 137, 184–85, 197
Collective unconscious, 116
Costello, Peter, 188
Cultural unconscious, 5–6, 11, 12–13, 17, 21, 27, 28, 47, 61, 85, 90, 108, 116, 119, 120, 122, 132, 189, 191, 196–97
Cupid and Psyche, 173–77
"Cyclops," 38, 76–77, 108–9, 116, 213 n.6

Daedalus myth, 19, 37, 74, 168
Dano, Finn, 152
Dante, 219 n.28
Danto, Arthur C., 167
Darwinism, 8, 26–27, 33, 114, 119–21, 132–36, 190, 197, 215 n.27
Davies, H. Neville, 219 n.28
Dennett, Daniel C., 119

Derrida, Jacques, 168–69
Design, 119–21, 129, 135, 178, 197
Destiny, 21, 90, 92, 96–99, 110–14, 123, 128, 129, 131–37, 181, 184, 186, 190–91, 195, 196, 197, 220 n.1
Dettmar, Kevin J. H., 203 n.4
Dickens, Charles, 197
Dio boia, 38, 60, 123, 161, 164
Driesch, Hans, 209 n.16, 216 n.6
Dundes, Alan, 148, 159

Eco, Umberto, 4–5, 7, 171, 189
Élan vital (Bergson), 33, 34, 111, 114, 132–33, 134, 209 n.16, 217 n.16
Eleven. *See* Riddle words
Eliot, T. S., 167, 168, 220 n.1; "The Waste Land," 170
Ellmann, Maud, 15, 17, 20
Ellmann, Richard, 1, 23, 75, 76, 78, 80, 104, 140, 142, 206–7 n.2, 209 n.18, 211 n.5, 212 n.14, 214 n.17, 218 n.21, 221 n.3
Entelechy, 21, 23, 24–29, 33, 47, 90, 96, 112, 118, 122, 123, 129, 132, 136, 181, 191, 209 n.16, 216 n.1
Epiphany, 32, 65, 72, 140
Equanimity, 194, 221 n.3
"Eumaeus," 95, 99, 183–86, 190, 192
Evolution, 8, 13, 26–27, 29, 33, 34, 60, 85, 111, 114–15, 119–22, 132–36, 190–91, 208 n.10, 215 n.27

Fate. *See* Destiny
Ferenczi, Sandor, 135, 212 n.2
Ferrer, Daniel, 127
Forgetting, 9, 38, 53, 76, 81, 89, 182
Fowler, Alastair, 152–53, 219 n.28
Frazer, James, 177
Freud, Sigmund, 8, 10, 11, 35, 36, 47–51, 56–57, 88–89, 118, 131, 196, 209 n.18; "The Aetiology of Hysteria," 49, 51; "Constructions in Analysis," 50, 205 n.12; "Five Lectures on Psycho-Analysis," 67; "From the

History of an Infantile Neurosis," 49-50; "The Mechanism of Hysterical Phenomena," 43; *Moses and Monotheism*, 135, 212 n.2; "Mourning and Melancholia," 41; *A Phylogenetic Fantasy*, 135-36, 212 n.2; *Psychopathology of Everyday Life*, 35, 52-53, 209 n.18; "Remembering, Repeating and Working-Through," 48-49, 130
Friedman, Susan Stanford, 205 n.10
Fromm, Erich, 204 n.7
Froula, Christine, 209-10 n.21

Genette, Gérard, 12, 206 n.16
Gifford, Don, 54, 207 n.8, 210 n.22
Gilbert, Stuart, 188, 217 n.11
Gillespie, Michael Patrick, 172, 207 n.7, 208 n.9, 215 n.21, 217 n.7
Glasheen, Adaline, 80
Goldman, Arnold, 110
Gordon, John, 123, 151
Gose, Elliott B., 144

Habit. *See* Memory: habit as a form of
"Hades," 39, 57, 58, 77, 147, 152
Harkness, Marguerite, 207 n.4
Hart, Clive, 1, 75-76, 77, 80, 218 n.23
Heath, Stephen, 209 n.19, 217 n.14, 218 n.18
Henke, Suzette, 209-10 n.21
Heraclitus, 30, 208 n.15
Herr, Cheryl, 4-7, 12-13, 16, 17, 21, 28, 189, 196, 204 nn. 7, 9
Herring, Phillip, 191-92, 212 n.1
Hillman, James, 141
Hoffmeister, Adolf, 151, 152
Homer: *Iliad, The*, 152, 194; *Odyssey, The*, 13-14, 46-47, 55, 66, 74, 80, 89, 128, 141, 144, 152, 155, 168, 170-71, 175-77, 181, 220 nn. 1, 2
Hopper, Vincent Foster, 219 n.28
Hume, David, 22-24, 25, 29, 31, 76, 207 n.7, 212 n.14

Identity. *See* Subjectivity
Instinct, 5, 13, 21, 47, 111-12, 114-15
Intertextuality. *See* Memory: intertextual
Isis, 173, 175; and Osiris, 176
"Ithaca," 40, 76, 90, 96, 98-99, 121, 185, 186, 190, 192, 194, 221 nn. 3, 4

James, William, 8, 10, 29, 30, 91, 107, 215 n.23
Jameson, Fredric, 5, 204 n.7
Jolas, Maria, 221 n.3
Joyce, James: education and intellectual background, 2, 4, 7-9, 16, 21, 24, 27-28, 118, 120; process of composition, 6, 120, 123, 125-26, 128-29, 146-47, 157, 159, 166, 175; and the Trieste Library, 29, 31, 35, 101, 121, 132, 133, 207 n.7, 208 n.14, 215 nn. 20, 21, 27, 217 n.7, 220 n.3. *See also* Joyce's characters
Works:
—"The Dead," 58, 66-67, 69-71, 87-88, 124, 192
—*Dubliners*, 4, 76, 168, 191-92
—"Eveline," 66, 68-69
—*Exiles*, 125-26
—*Finnegans Wake*, 4, 33, 89, 104, 150, 151, 168, 169, 186, 195, 209 n.19, 211 n.6, 214 n.15, 215 n.25, 218 nn. 23, 24, 220 n.5
—"Ivy Day in the Committee Room," 67
—"A Painful Case," 64-65, 87-88, 192
—"A Portrait of the Artist" (1904), 19, 30, 34
—*A Portrait of the Artist as a Young Man*, 4, 9, 15, 18-20, 21-22, 35, 37, 71-73, 74, 76, 120, 123, 124, 142, 148, 162-64, 168, 209 n.21, 218 n.24
—"The Sisters," 51-52, 55, 66
—*Stephen Hero*, 73, 123, 140, 141-42, 174, 207 n.5, 208 n.10, 214 n.18
—*Ulysses*: burial and exhumation in,

Joyce: *Ulysses* (cont.)
56–58, 148; closure in, 6, 13–14, 46–47, 51, 120–21, 165–66, 170–71, 173, 178–79, 181–98; Darwin in, 121; fox riddle in, 55–57, 145–54, 156–57, 160–61, 188, 210 n.3 (*see also* Riddle words); hallucinations in, 2, 108, 115, 123, 154–65; Homeric parallel in, 13–14, 77, 79, 81, 85–86; Joyce's revisions to, 146–47, 157, 159, 161, 172, 175 (*see also* Joyce, James: process of composition); narrative voices in, 96–97, 105, 108–9; *nostos* of, 46, 66, 141, 181–87, 195; parapraxes in, 53–54; schemas for, 5, 74, 141, 152, 155, 174, 177, 183; subjectivity in, 19–21, 26–27, 32; textual anomalies in, 108–10; as transitional text, 3–6, 17, 21, 119–20, 122, 171. *See also* titles of individual episodes

Joyce, Stanislaus, 169; *My Brother's Keeper*, 104

Joyce's characters:

—Bloom, Ellen (Leopold's mother), 154–55

—Bloom, Leopold: avoidance of unpleasant memories, 34–36, 38–43, 53–55, 57–58, 60, 80, 83, 107, 185; Darwinism and, 121; and difference from other Dubliners, 77–79, 81, 90; dreams of, 98–99; hallucinations of, 154–60; idealization of women, 40, 80–83, 123, 155–60, 172–77, 182, 185–86, 191, 196; isolation in Dublin of, 78; Jewishness of, 38, 77, 115–16, 167; linked to Stephen Dedalus, 13, 112, 113, 127–28, 145, 149, 150, 161–62, 181–85, 190; and Molly, 20, 39–41, 53–54, 80–82, 110, 123, 160, 171–72, 182, 185–86, 190, 191; and *Photo Bits* Nymph, 40, 80–81, 123, 154, 156–60, 165, 191, 196; and Rudy's death, 38–42, 54, 80–83, 96, 123, 147, 149, 154–56, 160, 181, 182, 196; sexual anxieties of, 38–41, 53–55, 80–83, 95, 98, 108, 118, 123, 141, 147, 149, 155–60, 171–72, 174; Shakespeare and, 60, 94–97, 150; subjectivity of, 20, 30; thoughts shared with Stephen Dedalus, 90–91, 94–100, 163–64, 197

—Bloom, Molly, 13, 20, 39–41, 53, 80–83, 98–99, 147, 149, 159, 171–72, 174, 185–87, 190

—Bloom, Rudolph (Leopold's father), 36, 54, 153, 185

—Bloom, Rudy (Leopold's son), 36, 38–41, 42, 46, 92–93, 96, 128, 149, 150, 165, 182

—Boylan, Blazes, 39, 54, 55, 83, 147, 149, 154, 164, 171, 174, 187

—Citizen, The, 38, 116, 196

—Clifford, Martha, 40, 82, 95

—Cohen, Bella, 138, 156–57, 160–61

—Conroy, Gabriel, 66–67, 69–71, 87–88, 192

—Conroy, Gretta, 58, 70–71, 87–88, 125

—Deasy, Mr. Garrett, 45, 94, 112, 163

—Dedalus, May Goulding, 36–38, 41, 42, 46, 95, 111, 128, 163, 192–94

—Dedalus, Simon, 38, 71–72, 95, 192

—Dedalus, Stephen: as artist, 15, 18–20, 37, 57, 73–74, 181; and avoidance of unpleasant memories, 34–38, 42–43, 55–60, 80, 83, 107; Catholicism and, 9, 37–38, 42, 73, 124, 130, 148, 163–64, 167; difference from other Dubliners, 73, 77–79, 90; dreams of, 97–100, 130, 163; hallucinations of, 160–65, 193; and Hamnet Shakespeare, 94, 150; Irishness of, 77, 167–68; isolation in Dublin of, 78; linked to Leopold Bloom, 13, 112, 113, 128, 145, 149, 150, 161–62, 181–85, 190; mother's death, 36–38,

42–43, 55–60, 82, 84–85, 90, 106, 111, 122–23, 130, 141, 145, 148, 150, 153, 161–65, 181, 183, 192–94, 196; and Rudy Bloom, 94, 128, 150; and Shakespeare, 59–60, 93–97, 150; subjectivity of, 18–20, 23, 27, 32, 72, 75; thoughts shared with Leopold Bloom, 90–100, 163–64, 197
—Dignam, Paddy, 41, 56–58, 108–9, 149, 152, 194, 213 n.6
—Dolan, Father, 161–64
—Duffy, Patrick, 64–65, 87–88, 212 n.1
—Higgins, Zoe, 108, 112, 154–56, 160
—Hill, Eveline, 68–69
—Lynch, Vincent, 73, 121, 144–45, 163
—MacDowell, Gerty, 40, 81, 95, 172–77
—"Midwives," 92–94, 103, 164
—M'Intosh, 212 n.1
—Mulligan, Buck, 24, 37, 41, 90, 123, 155, 183
—Penrose, 53–54
—Sinico, Emily, 64–65, 220 n.1
—Virag, Lipoti, 46, 53, 118, 157
Jung, Carl Gustav, 116, 131, 188; "On the Psychology of the Unconscious," 116; "The Soul and Death," 102

Kain, Richard M., 187
Karma, 111, 112–13, 118
Kenner, Hugh, 18, 149, 151, 162, 209–10 n.21, 218 nn. 20, 24
Kershner, R. B., 16, 204 n.9, 207 n.3
Kimball, Jean, 209 n.18
King, Henry: "The Exequy," 153
Klawitter, Robert, 208 n.13
Kock, Paul de, 147
Kolakowski, Leszek, 116
Kristeva, Julia, 205 n.10
Kropotkin, Peter, 135
Kumar, Shiv K., 116, 129, 208 n.13
Kumar, Udaya, 3, 203 nn. 2, 3, 205 n.15, 208 n.13

Lacan, Jacques, 42, 43, 130
Lamarckism, 8, 33, 114–15, 119, 132–36, 190, 212 n.2, 216 n.6
Larbaud, Valéry, 220 n.2
Lawrence, Karen, 20, 75–76, 110, 186, 190, 206 nn. 15, 17, 207 n.6
Leslie, Shane, 220 n.2
"Lestrygonians," 30, 53, 54–55, 78, 82–83, 154, 157, 185
Levine, George, 119, 120, 197
Lewis, Wyndham, 62
Locke, John, 7, 22, 24–25, 31, 45, 88, 100, 207 n.8
"Lotus-Eaters," 30, 54, 76, 81–82, 157, 159, 185, 189
Lukacher, Ned, 49–50

MacCabe, Colin, 169
Maeterlinck, Maurice, 104–5, 111, 112, 113, 116, 137, 191, 214 n.18; *The Unknown Guest*, 105; *Wisdom and Destiny*, 111–12, 221 n.3
Magic, 10, 105, 108, 137–45, 150, 166
Maher, Michael, 24–28, 121, 191, 207 n.7
Mason, Ellsworth, 214 n.17
McCarthy, Patrick, 148
McGee, Patrick, 3, 204 n.8
McHugh, Roland, 215 n.25, 218 n.23
McIntyre, J. Lewis, 144
Meisel, Perry, 179, 220 n.1
Memory: activist models of, 10, 11, 32, 51, 127, 134; Akasic, 105, 106, 127, 183; "art of," 10, 141–45, 166, 217 n.14; habit as a form of, 14, 54, 60–67, 69, 81, 112, 114–15, 132, 182, 183; "hypermnesia," 169; intertextual, 8–9, 11, 37, 167–80; involuntary, 12, 60–61, 63–65, 68–72, 82, 85, 87–88, 97, 100, 110, 116, 124, 127, 128, 137, 138, 140, 146, 155, 162–63, 166; Joyce's, 1–2, 8; "mnemotechnic," 46–47, 54, 76, 96, 118, 124–27, 129,

Memory (cont.)
  131, 137–38, 140, 143, 145, 153, 155–56, 160, 164–66, 181, 191, 192 (see also Memory: textual); nostalgia as a form of, 14, 66–72, 79, 182; passivist models of, 9, 23, 32, 45, 51, 76, 88, 106, 127; place and, 142–43; proleptic, 12–13, 90; racial, 103, 115; shared, 85, 90–100, 107, 108, 110, 129, 145–46, 147, 149, 153, 159, 163–64, 169, 184, 185, 186, 216 n.5; textual, 6, 11, 12, 40, 47, 83, 85, 90, 96, 108, 118–66, 178, 189, 196; triggers, 123, 124–26, 128–29, 136, 145–47, 150, 153, 157–65, 178, 184, 192–95; unconscious, 60, 99, 110, 115, 132, 138; universal, 100–110, 129, 139, 147, 150; unreliability of, 10, 45–46, 182–83; voluntary or hermeneutic, 12, 46, 47, 51, 61, 63–65, 66, 68, 70, 72, 76, 82–86, 87, 97, 110, 118, 142
Memory Theater. See Memory: "art of"
Mercanton, Jacques, 1, 2, 89, 123, 126, 128, 169
Metempsychosis, 101, 103–5, 108–9, 137–38, 214 n.16, 217 n.11
Milton, John: 219 n.29; *Lycidas*, 153
Models of mind, 3–4, 7–8, 21, 45, 90, 92, 99, 107, 110, 195
Modernism, 3, 5, 12, 13, 15–16, 17, 119, 167–68, 170, 179, 196, 197
Moly, 128, 141, 155, 160
Mourning, 41–43, 58–60, 149, 152–53, 165
Myth, 168–78

"Nausicaa," 40, 81, 92, 149, 171–80, 186, 212 n.18
Neo-Lamarckism. See Lamarckism
"Nestor," 45, 55–56, 85, 112, 131, 145, 182
Newman, John Henry, 126

Nietzsche, Friedrich, 69–70
Nisus formativus. See Entelechy
Nostalgia. See Memory: nostalgia as a form of
Numerology, 149, 150–53, 165

O'Donnell, Patrick, 3, 4
Odyssey, The. See Homer
Osteen, Mark, 218 n.24
Ovid, 152–53
"Oxen of the Sun," 46, 81, 83–84, 103, 108–9, 115, 121–23, 126–27, 149, 151, 157, 186, 217 n.14

Painter, George D., 211 nn. 5, 6
Parapraxes, 52–53
Parrinder, Patrick, 203 n.2, 205 n.15
Pecora, Vincent, 70
"Penelope," 39, 151, 186, 195
Piette, Adam, 203 n.2, 206 n.15
Pilkington, A. E., 61–62, 211 n.7
Pius, Antoninus, 221 n.3
Plato, 7, 9, 24, 27, 31, 35, 100; *Meno*, 100–101, 214 n.14; *Phaedo*, 101, 214 n.14; *Phaedrus*, 101, 205 n.13, 211 n.9, 214 n.14; *Theatetus*, 10
Plutarch, 176
Possibility, 65, 88, 190–91, 196, 197, 221 n.4
Potato talisman, 139, 154–55, 160
Predestination. See Destiny
Prolepsis. See Memory: proleptic
"Proteus," 57, 78, 92, 103, 137, 183
Proust, Marcel, 61–64, 72, 82, 85, 87–88, 112, 124, 128–29, 137, 138, 213 n.5
Providence, 128, 216 n.1
Psychoanalysis, 10, 11, 35–36, 47–51, 56, 131, 196

Reichert, Klaus, 203 n.2, 217 n.13
Reincarnation. See Metempsychosis

Repetition, 36, 38, 47, 83, 90, 124, 129–31, 155, 179
Repression, 42, 48–50, 52, 55–56, 58, 60, 89, 115, 127, 130, 138, 145, 154–55, 164, 170
Resistance, 52, 58, 138
Rickard, John S., 215 n.24, 217 n.15, 218 n.19, 219 n.31, 220 n.5
Riddle words, 145–54, 156–57, 160–65, 193–95; bells, 148–49, 164, 194–95; bush, 154, 156; cock, 147–48, 157, 163–64, 195; eleven, 93–94, 146, 149–53, 157, 218 n.24; fox, 57, 146, 148, 156, 160–61, 163, 193–94. *See also* Joyce, James, Works—*Ulysses:* fox riddle in; Memory: triggers
Riffaterre, Michael, 170, 205 n.15
Riquelme, John Paul, 9, 21, 88–89, 186, 195
Russell, George (pseud. AE), 23, 27, 104, 158
Ryan, Judith, 17–18, 206 n.1

Schutte, William, 214 nn. 7, 8, 10
Schwab, Gabriele, 203 n.5
Schwarz, Daniel, 206 n.17
"Scylla and Charybdis," 19, 23, 25, 30, 59, 93, 94, 96–97, 108–9, 112, 113, 136, 148, 191, 213 n.4
Seidman, Robert J., 54, 207 n.8, 210 n.22
Self. *See* Subjectivity
Senn, Fritz, 30, 174, 208 n.12, 214 n.16
Shakespeare, Hamnet, 94–96, 150, 213 n.4
Shakespeare, William, 32, 60, 93–97, 111, 148, 150–51, 178, 213 n.4, 214 n.7; *Hamlet*, 42–43, 58–60, 93–96, 147, 213 nn. 4, 5, 215 n.19
Shaw, George Bernard, 29, 119, 133–34, 135; *Back to Methuselah*, 134; *Man and Superman*, 133

Shechner, Mark, 209 n.18
Shells, 93–94, 213 nn. 5, 6
Silverstein, Norman, 144, 218 n.17
Singer, Dorothea Waley, 145
"Sirens," 77, 79, 147, 148–49, 194
Smith, John B., 219 n.31
Smith, Paul, 16–17, 18
Society for Psychical Research, 91, 107
Solomon, Joseph, 29, 208 n.15
Spencer, Herbert, 135
Spoo, Robert, 122, 148, 210 n.3, 216 n.1, 221 n.4
Stoppard, Tom, 206–7 n.2
Stream of consciousness, 15, 30, 54, 172, 186
Subjectivity, 7, 15–34, 59, 115, 137, 186
Synge, John Millington, 119

"Telemachus," 23, 37, 41, 82, 90, 106, 130, 184
Teleology, 111, 114, 119–21, 131, 132–33, 137, 181, 189–91, 196–97, 216 n.1
Telepathy. *See* Memory: shared
Textual unconscious. *See* Memory: textual
Thackeray, William Makepeace, 54
Theosophy, 8, 104–7, 109, 110, 111, 112–13, 118, 122, 127, 183, 191, 213 n.6
Thornton, Weldon, 55, 103, 111, 160, 184, 207 n.8, 210 n.2, 212 nn. 17 (chap. 2), 3 (chap. 3), 214 n.11
Throwaway, 78, 90, 185
Tindall, William York, 187–88
Tolomeo, Diane, 151

Universal mind, 91–92, 106, 109, 139

Vico, Giambattista, 1
Virgin Mary, 164, 173, 175–77
Vitalism, 136, 209 n.16, 216 n.6
Vries, Ad de, 148

"Wandering Rocks," 57, 74–78, 93–94, 159
Warner, William Beatty, 132
Watt, Stephen, 204 n.9
Weaver, Harriet Shaw, 79
Weir, Lorraine, 203 n.2
Wentworth, Jay A., 131
Whitman, Walt, 113, 215–16 n.27
Winkle, Rip Van, 81, 212 n.17

Yates, Frances, 141–43, 144–45, 217 n.14
Yeats, W. B., 58, 104, 149, 150; "Magic," 105–6, 107, 139

John Rickard is Associate Professor of English at Bucknell University where he teaches modern British and Irish literature. He is the editor of "Irishness and (Post) Modernism" and has published essays on James Joyce and W. B. Yeats.

Library of Congress Cataloging-in-Publication Data
Rickard, John S.
Joyce's book of memory : the mnemotechnic of Ulysses
John S. Rickard.
Includes bibliographical references and index.
ISBN 0-8223-2158-0 (cloth : alk. paper).
— ISBN 0-8223-2170-X (pbk. : alk. paper)
1. Joyce, James, 1882–1941. Ulysses.   2. Psychology in literature.   3. Memory in literature.   I. Title.
PR6019.O9U6874   1999   823'.912—dc21   98-25721   CIP